MILTON STUDIES
XXVIII

MILTON STUDIES
James D. Simmonds, Editor

EDITORIAL BOARD

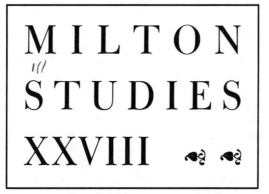

MILTON STUDIES XXVIII

Riven Unities

Authority and Experience, Self and Other in Milton's Poetry

Wendy Furman
Christopher Grose
William Shullenberger

Guest Editors

UNIVERSITY OF PITTSBURGH PRESS
Pittsburgh and London

MILTON STUDIES

is published annually by the University of Pittsburgh Press as a forum for Milton scholarship and criticism. Articles submitted for publication may be biographical; they may interpret some aspect of Milton's writings; or they may define literary, intellectual, or historical contexts—by studying the work of his contemporaries, the traditions which affected his thought and art, contemporary political and religious movements, his influence on other writers, or the history of critical response to his work.

Manuscripts should be upwards of 3,000 words in length and should conform to the old *MLA Style Sheet*. Manuscripts and editorial correspondence should be addressed to Albert C. Labriola, Department of English, Duquesne University, Pittsburgh, Pa., 15282-1703. Manuscripts should be accompanied by a self-addressed envelope and sufficient unattached postage.

Milton Studies does not review books.

Within the United States, *Milton Studies* may be ordered from the University of Pittsburgh Press, Pittsburgh, Pa. 15260.

Library of Congress Catalog Card Number 69–12335

ISBN 0–8229–3718–2

A CIP catalogue record for this book is available from the British Library

US ISSN 0076–8820

Published by the University of Pittsburgh Press, Pittsburgh, Pa. 15260

Copyright © 1992, University of Pittsburgh Press

Manufactured in the United States of America

Printed on acid-free paper

Eurospan, London

CONTENTS

PREFACE   vii

BARBARA K.
   LEWALSKI   Milton: Divine Revelation and the
                     Poetics of Experience   3

GEORGIA B.
   CHRISTOPHER   Subject and Macrosubject in *L'Allegro*
                     and *Il Penseroso*   23

DAVID LOEWENSTEIN   "Fair Offspring Nurs't in Princely
                     Lore": On the Question of Milton's
                     Early Radicalism   37

STEPHEN M. BUHLER   Kingly States: The Politics in *Paradise
                     Lost*   49

MICHAEL C.
   SCHOENFELDT   "Among Unequals What Society?":
                     Strategic Courtesy and Christian
                     Humility in *Paradise Lost*   69

ILONA BELL   Milton's Dialogue with Petrarch   91

WENDY FURMAN   "Consider first, that Great / Or Bright
                     infers not Excellence": Mapping the
                     Feminine in Mary Groom's Miltonic
                     Cosmos   121

WILLIAM
   SHULLENBERGER   Sorting the Seeds: The Regeneration of
                     Love in *Paradise Lost*   163

WILLIAM E. ENGEL   The Experience of Death and
                     Difference in *Paradise Lost*   185

JOHN STEADMAN   Efficient Causality and Catastrophe in
                     Samson Agonistes   211

PREFACE

RIVEN UNITIES is a collection of unusual scope, both in the variety of its methodologies and in the breadth of its coverage. Here the reader will encounter a broad spectrum of conversations with works ranging from the early lyric and dramatic pieces to *Samson Agonistes* (while focusing, not surprisingly, on *Paradise Lost*), as Milton takes on all comers—from Aristotle to Petrarch; from Freud to Jacques Derrida; from Castiglione to *Paradise Lost*'s first female illustrator, Mary Groom. But, whatever their epistemological roots and assumptions, all the conversations here are true, even intimate, conversations with the Miltonic text. Indeed, what has impressed the editors of this book—from the time preliminary versions of five of these papers were delivered at the Spring 1989 Southwest Regional Conference of the Renaissance Conference of Southern California—is the sense that the most compelling topics in current Milton studies are precisely those of primary importance to the poet himself. These topics are unified ultimately by the central problem, taken on here broadly by Barbara Lewalski and then more specifically in the essays that follow, of how to reconcile every kind of authority—whether textual, religious, political, or domestic—with one's own complex and irreducible experience; how to fashion a self and how to mediate between that self and the other—whether that other be God; political and social hierarchies; one's "best image and dearer half"; or the ultimate "other," death. Four of the papers here address social and political issues; five deal specifically, and in a variety of ways, with the problem of gender; five ponder with Milton the fragility of the self—whether in the face of the fluidity of the subject's identity, or in the face of the self's dissolution when "a man becommeth no man." In various ways most address the epic's persistent suggestion that even in prelapsarian Eden, matters like domestic relations, gender, all the evidences of hierarchy—indeed including corporeality itself—are fluid and quite possibly temporary (Milton's more disquieting word is "mutable"), and that all such titles and structures which serve "for distinction" will finally yield to a better polity in which "God shall be All in All" (*PL* III, 341).

Especially prominent in the essays here is the treatment of the first marriage and the place of Eve—and indeed of "the feminine"—in *Paradise*

Lost. These studies, whatever their individual focus, make it easier to remember the embryo of the idea of *Paradise Lost,* conceived as early as 1644, when Milton could still envision a future for a whole nation "fraught with an universall insight into things" (YP II, p. 406). Eve's retirement in Book VIII (and elsewhere) has recently become almost as popular a scholarly site as the episode at her mirror-lake. The *Of Education* may reassure us that she undertakes it for good reason. Like a number of other early works, Milton's letter to Samuel Hartlib entertains a complex valuation of retirement, for wisdom's sake as well as the attractions of escape—an adjustment to periods of "extreame need" (YP II, p. 364), when no better recourse is at hand. Eve's reluctance to attend Adam's "wary" questioning of Raphael recalls *Of Education*'s ambivalent presentation of some young gentlemen who will "retire themselves knowing no better"—the wisest course, Milton adds, given the circumstances. Moreover, those who retire in this fashion happen to be those "of a more delicious and airie spirit," close relatives of the poets Milton had discussed in just these terms two years earlier in *The Reason of Church Government* (YP II, p. 376; I, p. 817).

Throughout *Of Education*, indeed, the cultivation of "delight"—seen here in a number of other contexts—is a key agenda item in any attempt to repair the ruins of our first parents. Open the word out into its constituent elements and you have something like "Simple, sensuous, and passionate"—one of several antithetic formulations for what Milton the educator calls "the most intellective abstractions of Logick & metaphysicks" (YP II, p. 374). The importance of "delight," along with similar terms anticipating Samson's "intimate impulse," is clear from the way they are used in the intricacies of Milton's partitioning and sequencing. The word helps us negotiate the transitions in Milton's curriculum—from the self to the ever wider society beyond the self; from the immediate environs of an ordered earth to the "grounds of law and justice"; and on to the remoter outposts like "theology" and "tragedy." And in its guise as "poetry," *delight* seems to prompt the appearance—often set forward here—of a radically different scale of valuation, at the notoriously tricky threshold of "subsequent or indeed rather precedent."

If *Of Education* gives us some of the earliest tracks of Eve, it also puts us in touch with Adam's tendency to "studious thoughts abstruse," and his occasional deficiencies as a teacher: his forgetfulness that the Almighty is somehow One, or that the primal "mind or fancy"—Adam does remember its gender in Book VIII—is naturally "apt to rove." And from the opening request for the Muse's special knowing (a knowing closer to Paul's prayer for the Ephesians that they might "know the love of Christ, which passeth knowledge" [iii, 17–19] than to "studious thoughts," abstruse or otherwise) to Eve's arresting final "I know" (XII, 610), *Paradise Lost* enacts its own conflicted search for a longed-for and absent feminine center—the kind of quest with which Milton had originally (in 1637) associated his own vocational intention: "to seek beauty throughout all the shapes and forms of things" (YP I, p. 326). *Of Education* makes a useful center for other recurrent themes in the pages that follow. We are reminded that for Milton an important precondition for successful policy in the discursive realm was the recognition of experience "in this body"; that the body Satan chose to inhabit for the purpose of temptation featured the apt proleptic detail of a riven tongue; and that the mutual or "unanimous" discourse of our first parents was also the way Milton formulated the young scholar's "judicious conversing among pure authors" (*PL* X, 518; see YP II, pp. 368–73). As it happens, the phrase—along with its accompanying promise of delight—is a not inappropriate description of the original occasion for half of these essays: the meeting of the RCSC, held on April 7–8, 1989, in the almost Edenic splendor (temperatures above 100 degrees notwithstanding) of the Henry E. Huntington Library. Thanks are due to the Huntington staff, who annually host the RCSC's Southwest Regional Conference, and who have graciously consented to the Huntington's becoming the RCSC's permanent home.

An enormous debt of gratitude is also owed to those involved in the production of this volume. First, the editors wish to thank the members of the RCSC Editorial Advisory Board, who approved the initial project; helped in the initial selection of essays for inclusion in the volume; and lent financial support at every stage in the process. The EAB has been ably and energetically chaired by Professor Ricardo Quinones of Claremont McKenna College. The other members are Professor Anne J. Cruz, University of California, Irvine; Professor Eunice Howe, University of Southern California; Professor John Steadman, the Huntington Library; Professor Stanley Stewart, University of California, Riverside; and Professor Virginia Tufte, University of Southern California. Thanks are also due to Whittier College for providing a fellowship fund especially for the preliminary editing and computer typing of the volume. Cecily Bilodeau and Rebecca Totaro, Milton students and enthusiasts both, shared the fellowship (in both senses), and spent countless hours in preparing the manuscript—as did Pam Hengst, Whittier College English department secretary, once Cecily and Rebecca left campus for the summer. The work of all three has been invaluable, their care and patience exemplary. Many thanks must go to Robert Olsabeck, operations assistant of Whittier College's Computing Services, who bore with every difficulty and assisted at every point in the manuscript's production—"in the close" going so far as to devote a Saturday evening to its printing. Finally, of course, our gratitude extends most of all to the contributors in this volume, whose thoughtful work, endless patience through revision, and cooperation with regard to deadlines were an inspiration and delight.

Wendy Furman

Christopher Grose

William Shullenberger

MILTON STUDIES
XXVIII

MILTON: DIVINE REVELATION AND THE POETICS OF EXPERIENCE

Barbara K. Lewalski

THE WORD "EXPERIENCE" echoes throughout Milton's poetry, with its antonyms, synonyms, and related tropes—notably, taste. In *Il Penseroso*, the panorama of sights, sounds, and activities, literary and actual, which comprise the life of the studious melancholic speaker may in old age make him a prophet: "Till old experience do attain / To something like Prophetic strain" (173–74).[1] In *Paradise Lost* Satan regards his marshaled troops in Hell with "experienc't eye" (I, 568); and Eve lies down beside her pool in Eden "with unexperienc't thought" (IV, 457). Abdiel insists that the angels are "by experience taught" to know God's benevolence and providence (V, 826); and Adam uses the same phrase about the lessons of self-knowledge he has derived from the vicarious experience of Raphael's narrations (VIII, 190). After his forces are defeated and cast into hell, Satan hopes to draw lessons of hope and resolve from the "experience of this great event" (I, 118). Eve, after eating the forbidden fruit, praises first the tree and then experience as her "best guide," and she offers the fruit to Adam on that basis: "On my experience, *Adam*, freely taste" (IX, 988). In *Paradise Regained* Satan continually offers his own worldly goods and kingdoms—"Best school of best experience"—to remedy what he terms Christ's "unexperienc't" state (III, 238–40). And as the tragedy of *Samson Agonistes* ends, the chorus claims to have gained a "new acquist / Of true experience from this great event" (1755–56), that is, from the manifestation of God's ways with Israel's would-be liberator, Samson.

That "experience" is a prominent concern in Milton's poetry is hardly surprising, given the centrality accorded the term in Milton's poetics. The key text is the famous passage on poetics in Milton's *Apology,* in which he observes that the epic poet cannot "sing high praises of heroick men, or famous Cities, unless he have in himselfe the experience and the practice of all that which is praise-worthy" (YP I, p. 890).[2] But what is this experience? this praxis? And what is its status in relation to the authority of divine revelation? That issue is posed in highly suggestive terms in the preface to Book II of Milton's *Reason of Church Government,* in which Milton first ascribes the creation of the true poem to illumination by "that eternal Spirit who can enrich with all utterance and knowledge, and sends out his Seraphim with the hallow'd fire of his Altar to teach and purify the lips of whom he pleases"—making revelation itself an Isaiah-like experience. He then immediately links this kind of experience with another kind—arduous education and extensive experience of life: "To this must be added industrious and select reading, steddy observation, insight into all seemly and generous arts and affaires" (YP I, pp. 820–21).

"Experience" is hardly a new term in Milton criticism, but Miltonists (like Christopher Hill and Robert Fallon) have chiefly focused on Milton's own life experience as reflected in his works, or else (like Stanley Fish) on the reader's experience in responding to Milton's texts.[3] I want to approach this issue from a different and relatively neglected perspective, exploring the ways in which Milton's great poems thematize the encounter of divine revelation and human experience. To my mind, the few Miltonists who have considered this matter (notably, Kathleen Swaim and Georgia Christopher) have tended to define the role of experience in Milton's theology and poetics rather too narrowly and too negatively.[4] My questions, posed with special reference to *Paradise Lost,* are: In connection with the authoritative Word of God, what counts as experience and how does it teach? And how does this matter for our ongoing engagement with Milton's epic?

We can probe such questions by looking closely at the hermeneutic problems dramatized in the epic as several characters undertake to "read" a divine text with some reference to the claims of experience (however understood) and on the basis of that reading proceed to make crucial, self-defining life choices. The action of Milton's epic turns on four texts of revelation, all of which pose problems of interpretation and response. Those texts are: God's proclamation declaring his Son King of the angels; his language defining human marriage; his prohibition to Adam and Eve against eating the fruit of the Tree of Knowledge of Good and Evil; and his judicial decree and promise that the seed of the woman will crush the serpent's head.

But first we need to recall how divine revelation is treated in the Miltonic texts, and what meanings attach to the concept of experience in Milton's culture. For English Protestantism, the dominant ideological code of the era, divine revelation was of course the ultimate authority, and was usually identified with the Scriptures. As his theological treatise, *De Doctrina Christiana,* indicates, Milton shares several hermeneutic principles with Protestants generally, and specifically with his English Puritan contemporaries: the divine inspiration of the Bible; its sole sufficiency as an arbiter of faith; its complete clarity even to the unlearned in all matters pertaining to salvation; the right and responsibility of every Christian to read and interpret scripture for himself or herself, as taught by the Spirit.[5] But while those precepts supplied grounds for the Puritan challenge to the Laudian church and the monarchy, for most Puritans their radical potential was tamed by the interpretative authority over the biblical text claimed and exercised by ministers and civil magistrates.[6] However, as Christopher Hill has shown, that radical potential erupted in the sects— Quakers, Familists, Ranters, Muggletonians, Fifth Monarchists, Seekers, and others—whose claims to individual prophecy were often characterized by enthusiasm, antinomian practices, millenarian fervor, and civil anarchy.[7]

Milton took neither of these directions, largely because of the way in which he came to read the texts of divine revelation. By the time he wrote *The Doctrine and Discipline of Divorce* (1643), Milton had concluded (in direct opposition to his position in *The Reason of Church Government* of 1642) that biblical interpretation must appeal beyond the letter of the scripture text. He seems to have moved decisively to this new ground as he weighed his own painful experience in marriage against the apparent categorical prohibitions of divorce in Matthew v, 31–32, and xix, 3–12. *The Doctrine and Discipline of Divorce* opens with resounding denunciations of "crabbed textuists" (YP II, p. 233), of interpreters who rest "in the meere element of the Text" (p. 236), and of unthinking adherents to "long custom and the letter of the Text" (p. 240). It decries the "oppression" arising from "the strictnes of a literall interpreting" (p. 242) and concludes that "there is scarse any one saying in the Gospel, but must be read with limitations and distinctions, to be rightly understood" (p. 338). With such formulation, this treatise begins to develop the two overarching hermeneutic principles that governed Milton's scriptural interpretation throughout his later prose and poetry.

The first such principle of interpretation was a radical concept of Christian liberty, according to which the entire Mosaic Law—the Decalogue as well as the ceremonial law—is abrogated as a law for Christians. From this concept Milton extrapolated standards for testing such apparently enslaving biblical texts as those prohibiting divorce or requiring submission to monarchs. The promotion of human freedom is one such standard, since Milton supposed the Christian religion to be in its very essence "our free, elective, and rational worship" (YP VII, p. 260). Another measure is charity and human good, allowing Milton to declare categorically that "who so preferrs either Matrimony, or other Ordinance before the good of man and the plain exigence of Charity . . . he is no better then a Pharise, and understands not the Gospel" (YP II, p. 233). This cluster of ideas permits Milton in prose tracts and poems to read the scriptures as a thoroughly radical, utopian text, the primary guarantor of and model for human liberty—personal, intellectual, political, and poetic. Yet as his *Christian Doctrine* makes clear, none of this sanctions antinomian licentiousness, because the works of faith which flow from the internal law of God inscribed on the heart comprise a higher moral standard: "It is not a less perfect life that is required from Christians but, in fact, a more perfect life than was required from those who were under the law" (YP VI, p. 535).[8] According to Miltonic Christian liberty, then, the final appeal in interpreting a scripture text is always to the Christian individual's experience of the law in the heart. Yet the standard of measure is a life that freely but manifestly conforms to widely recognized moral principles.

Milton's second major interpretative principle is also radical—the primacy of the indwelling Spirit of God over the external scripture in authorizing faith and revealing truth. It is extrapolated from the biblical promise that all the Lord's people will be prophets: "We have, particularly under the gospel, a double scripture. There is the external scripture of the written word, and the internal scripture of the Holy Spirit . . . . The preeminent and supreme authority, however, is the authority of the Spirit, which is internal, and the individual possession of each man" (YP VI, p. 587). This principle necessitates toleration and openness to emergent truth. But Milton clearly does not expect the internal prophetic Spirit to manifest itself in enthusiastic testimony. Instead, he appeals constantly to reasoned argument, textual evidence, and common human experience as normative guides to interpret the divine revelation conveyed by scripture and the Spirit. Indeed, his preface to *De Doctrina Christiana* formally offers his own experience and practice as a model to others for their interpretative efforts:

I made up my mind to puzzle out a religious creed for myself by my own exertions, and to acquaint myself with it thoroughly. In this the only authority I accepted was God's self-revelation, and accordingly I read and pondered the Holy Scriptures themselves with all possible diligence. . . .

In religion as in other things, I discerned, God offers all his rewards not to those who are thoughtless and credulous, but to those who labor constantly and seek tirelessly after truth. . . . [A]ssuredly I do not urge or enforce anything upon my own authority. On the contrary, I advise every reader, and set him an example by doing the same myself, to withhold his consent from those opinions about which he does not feel fully convinced, until the evidence of the Bible convinces him and induces his reason to assent and to believe. (YP VI, pp. 118–22)

Again, right understanding arises in the final analysis from the Spirit's illumination; but that inner experience is founded on, and finds its only grounds for persuading others in, such normative measures as reason, evidence, diligence, and tireless labor. Milton's stance toward divine revelation can be seen as a remarkable personal amalgam of Renaissance and Reformation concepts, as well as of several core ideas of Western culture which were taking on something of their modern meaning in the seventeenth century: individual liberty, rationalism, empiricism, pluralism, internalized moral discipline.

What, we may now ask, is the status of "experience" in Milton's culture and in his own prose tracts? If we think back to that earlier (though hardly definitive) poetic spokesperson for the claims of experience in relation to authority, the Wife of Bath, we see that for her the term carries a specific, limited meaning—personal, life experiences—and that its lessons are applied to a single, albeit for her all-important, topic: "Experience, though noon auctoritee / Were in this world, is right ynough for me / To speke of wo that is in mariage."9 Milton's characters, I shall argue, invoke experience as a more complex, multivalent term, calling variously upon the full spectrum of meanings it could carry in the mid-seventeenth century. In humanist rhetorical discourse, as Barbara Shapiro notes, the term still referred to experience codified in various kinds of texts and available as example: notably, the experience of a people rendered in history and cultural tradition; the experience of others conveyed through testimony; and even the experience of fictional characters (an Aeneas or an Odysseus) provided through literary representation.10 The term could also refer—as in Montaigne's famous essay "On Experience"—to psychological experience formulated through introspection—the careful observation and analysis of one's own nature, temperament, habits.11 It could refer as well to sense experience methodically observed, collected, and tested by experiment, as in the emergent empiricism of Bacon and others associated with the new science and new philosophy.

The term had special resonance and importance for English Puritans, who inherited and further elaborated the Reformation dictum that saving faith is not formal but experiential, less a matter of the intellect than of the will and the heart. In Calvin's words, the "chief hinge" of faith involves "experiencing . . . in ourselves" God's promises and goodness for us.12 Puritan theologians like William Perkins focused on the conversion experience and the panoply of emotions, sensations, and psychological states that attend its various phases; that experience was powerfully dramatized in Bunyan's autobiography, *Grace Abounding to the Chief of Sinners* (1666), as various scripture texts engage with Bunyan physically, calling him, shaking him, beating him, pursuing him down the street, loading him with chains, casting him into dark dungeons.[13] Puritan preachers like Richard Sibbes often dwelled on life experiences—spiritual trials and temptations, God's providences, graces, afflictions, and threatenings—as a second scripture, the proving ground of the Word.[14] Puritan radicals like William Dell and George Fox appealed constantly to the inner spiritual experience of the Spirit's illumination and activity in the saints.[15] Codifying all this, Puritan manuals of meditation like that of Isaac Ambrose (1650) urged meditation on such experiences as will demonstrate how the doctrines, threatenings, and promises of scripture "are daily verified in others, and in my own selfe," and on such remembered "tastes" of God's goodness as can help us turn to him in new situations "as a tryed friend." Ambrose warns, however, that the lessons of experience are easily misread unless Christians use the scriptures as a "construing book to the book of God's Providences," interpreting all God's works "out of his Words."[16]

Milton's concern, early to late, with the uses and the problematics of experience owes something to this pervasive Puritan emphasis, but in his usage the term draws upon the full range of seventeenth-century meanings. In his *Art of Logic* Milton follows Aristotle in describing experience as one of the four "helpers" to reason, in that it judges the "common agreement" of particular instances and so provides the principles of any field of knowledge (YP VIII, pp. 213–14). In *Of Education* he concentrates on the experiences of others, variously conveyed. He would have his pupils learn some things from testimony—what he calls the "helpful experiences" of hunters, foulers, fishermen, shepherds, gardeners, architects, engineers, mariners, anatomists—as well as from direct observation in their travels throughout England and abroad (YP II, pp. 393–94, 412–14). But that tract especially emphasizes the experience afforded by history and cultural tradition: languages, we recall, are to be studied because "every nation affords not experience and tradition enough for all kinde of learning" (YP II, p. 369). Developing this range of meaning, Milton's polemical tracts supporting the revolution often marshall historical experience, past and present, inviting his audience to make "seasonable use of gravest autorities, experiences, examples," as *The Ready and Easy Way* puts it (YP VII, p. 448). Yet his tracts also inveigh constantly against the bondage of custom, recognizing in it a codification of past experience and misleading testimony that inhibits needful change.[17]

A major counterpoise to the dead hand of custom is immediate, personal experience of several kinds, read as an interpretative commentary on God's word. In his preface to Book II of *The Reason of Church Government*, Milton explained his turn from poetry to polemics as a response to a divine call sounded for him in the events of 1639–42, portending an opportunity to reform church and state (YP I, pp. 803–06). Milton's divorce tracts appeal continually and poignantly to psychological and common social experience, to what "lamented experience daily teaches" about the desperate unhappiness of union with an intellectually unfit wife, or about the matrimonial pitfalls awaiting chaste young men who must choose their helpmates in very restrictive social circumstances (YP II, pp. 312, 249–50). Often he emphasizes moral and intellectual experience. "The experience of a good conscience" (YP I, p. 935) is defined in several tracts as the ground of the moral life; and *Areopagitica* memorably extols the experience of active engagement with evil and falsehood as the only means for the warfaring Christian or his society to grow in virtue and truth: "I cannot praise a fugitive and cloister'd vertue, unexercis'd & unbreath'd, that never sallies out and sees her adversary, but slinks out of the race, where that immortal garland is to be run for, not without dust and heat" (YP II, p. 515). Finally, there is inner spiritual experience—illumination by the Spirit of God— always the final authority in interpreting divine revelation and dramatized as such in *Paradise Regained.*

The range and complexity of experience in Milton's usage means that he does not, like Isaac Ambrose, simply appeal from experience to scripture as the final arbiter of interpretation. Indeed he often does very nearly the reverse, exploring the importance of experience in its many senses to a right understanding of divine revelation. His major poems all focus upon characters making choices grounded upon better or worse interpretations of God's decrees—of divine revelation—and invoking the category of experience to probe the ambiguities and deeper meanings of such decrees and the life choices they may dictate. The characters in Milton's poems advance in understanding through a complex exchange in which text comments on experience and experience upon text—or we might say, in which theory and praxis comment on and illuminate each other.

In *Paradise Lost* I mean to focus on four pivotal texts of revelation which are set forth as divine decrees requiring interpretation and response in terms of experience and all that it may mean. The first decree, God's proclamation of his Son as king of the angels, is staged as a solemn, sudden, awe-inspiring pronouncement delivered on a day of joyous festival, replete with song, dance, parades, feasting, courtly ceremonies, and pastoral delights:

> Hear all ye Angels, Progeny of Light,
> Thrones, Dominations, Princedoms, Virtues, Powers,
> Hear my Decree, which unrevok'd shall stand.

This day I have begot whom I declare
My only Son, and on this holy Hill
Him have anointed, whom ye now behold
At my right hand; your Head I him appoint;
And by my Self have sworn to him shall bow
All knees in Heav'n, and shall confess him Lord:
Under his great Vice-gerent Reign abide
United as one individual Soul
For ever happy: him who disobeys
Mee disobeys, breaks union, and that day
Cast out from God and blessed vision, falls
Into utter darkness, deep ingulft, his place
Ordain'd without redemption, without end.   (V, 600–15)

The literal text is clear enough, but its deeper meaning and implications are quite ambiguous: the angels do not yet know why the Son is thus suddenly elevated, or what his elevation will really mean for their lives and their society. These issues are at the heart of the tense debate between Satan and Abdiel exploring the basis of political societies and choices, a debate unique in literary treatments of the war in heaven.

Satan assumes that the Son's elevation must bring with it the angels' demotion—and most notably his own. His first speech (V, 772–802) develops from Aristotelian principles a reasoned argument that monarchy violates the essential liberty and equality of heaven: since all its inhabitants are substantially equal—in freedom if not in nature—and are perfectly good without law, they ought by right "to govern not to serve." Here, misapplied, are time-honored republican arguments concerning the rights of a free citizenry, which were also Milton's own arguments about the bases of human government and political liberty in *The Tenure of Kings and Magistrates*.[18] Abdiel first corrects Satan's political theory in the light of heaven's special circumstances (V, 809–48), disposing of the false premise of substantial equality by pointing to the immeasurable divide between Creator and creature. But this does not speak to the dark suspicion that motivates Satan's challenge, the assumption that the Son's elevation must inevitably degrade the angels. To counter this fear, Abdiel appeals to the angels' past experience of God's beneficence (portrayed through the poem's vivid descriptions of the joys and festivities of heaven), and on that basis reinterprets the new proclamation as a kind of "incarnation" honoring the angels:

Yet by experience taught we know how good,
And of our good, and of our dignity
How provident he is, how far from thought

To make us less, bent rather to exalt
Our happy state under one Head more near
United.

. . . .

                              nor by his Reign obscur'd,
But more illustrious made, since he the Head
One of our number thus reduc't becomes,
His Laws our Laws, all honor to him done
Returns our own.   (V, 826–31, 41–45)

Satan responds by claiming self-creation, basing this claim on a wholly specious appeal to experience:

                              who saw
When this creation was? remember'st thou
Thy making, while the Maker gave thee being?
We know no time when we were not as now;
Know none before us, self-begot, self-rais'd
By our own quick'ning power.   (V, 856–61)

Here as often elsewhere Satan is a thorough-going empiricist, who demands proof by sense experience as the only basis for knowledge. But the absence of experience can conclude nothing, especially in this case, since none of us can remember the originary moment—whatever the angelic equivalent may be to the meeting of sperm and egg or (in the poem's myth) the shaping of a human being from the dust. "For who himself beginning knew?" Adam later asks (VIII, 251). Still less can this inevitable ignorance be a basis to disavow all derivation and to devise an originary story of self-creation. This debate draws a stark contrast between Satan's empiricism turned to folly and monomania and Abdiel's appropriate use of his society's common historical experience of God's ways to interpret this new decree.

The second text comprises God's words instituting and defining human marriage. We do not hear these words directly in the poem, but only as they are recalled and reported by Eve and Adam in their autobiographical narratives. According to both reports, God indicates that Adam was created first and that Eve is (in some unspecified sense) his image, but in neither of these accounts does God proclaim gender hierarchy. The several commentators on God's words—Eve, Adam, Raphael, the Son of God at the Judgment, the bard—offer different interpretations of them, arising from their own diverse perspectives and experience.

Eve tells how a divine voice rescued her from fixation at the mirror stage—"pin'd with vain desire" for her own image reflected in the water—and led her to a substantial and responsive object of love. That voice does not tell Eve that she was made for Adam, but comes close to suggesting that Adam was intended to meet *her* needs, to bring *her* delight, and to make possible the multiplication of *her* image (substantial as opposed to shadowy) in her children:

> hee
> Whose image thou art, him thou shalt *enjoy*
> Inseparably thine, to him shalt bear
> Multitudes like *thyself*, and thence be call'd
> *Mother of human Race*.   (IV, 471–75; emphasis mine)

Eve then glosses those words, Adam's wooing, and her own eventual yielding in marriage in the light of her subsequent experience: "and from that time see / How beauty is excell'd by manly grace / And wisdom, which alone is truly fair" (489–91). Eve's delight in Adam leads her to "see" a physical hierarchy—manly grace over female beauty—though her many glowing tributes to Adam's superiority are less a matter of ideology than the idealizing raptures of first love. Yet Eve's valuation of wisdom as "alone . . . truly fair"—superior, that is, to both female beauty and manly grace—intimates that she locates wisdom not only in Adam but also in the divine words and in her own wise choices and words, just recounted. Eve's glorification of wisdom, and the unfixed meaning of that abstract term (later personified in the poem as female, VII, 10) make some space for future experience to modify Eve's view of gender hierarchy.

Adam's dialogue with Raphael produces a direct conflict between ideology and experience, in terms illuminated by James Turner's recent study, *One Flesh*.[19] Adam reports a dialogue with God in which he initiated a request for an "equal" mate: "Among unequals what society / Can sort, what harmony or true delight? / Which must be mutual" (VIII, 383–85). After testing Adam's understanding of himself, God informs him that such a partner—made in God's image as the brutes were not—was always part of the divine plan, and that she will be exactly what Adam needs and wants: "What next I bring shall please thee, be assur'd, / Thy likeness, thy fit help, thy other self, / Thy wish, exactly to thy heart's desire" (VIII, 449–51). Adam testifies ecstatically to his delight in Eve, but also to the troubling discrepancy between the orthodox notion of gender hierarchy he has worked out for himself, and his experience of Eve's beauty, reason, nobility of mind and character, and indeed wisdom, which quite contradicts it:

> For well I understand in the prime end
> Of Nature her th'inferior, in the mind

> And inward Faculties, which most excel,
> In outward also her resembling less
> His Image who made both
> . . . .
>   yet when I approach
> Her loveliness, so absolute she seems
> And in herself complete, so well to know
> Her own, that what she wills to do or say
> Seems wisest, virtuousest, discreetest, best;
> . . . .
> Authority and Reason on her wait,
> As one intended first, not after made
> Occasionally; and to consummate all
> Greatness of mind and nobleness thir seat
> Build in her loveliest.   (VIII, 540–58)

Raphael's comments on all this strongly reinforce gender hierarchy, and his apparently strict Neoplatonic advice about ascending to heavenly love seems to deprecate human sexuality and passion. We might read this scene as a foundation text for Eve Sedgwick's paradigm—with the woman as an object of negotiation and definition by two men who establish their sense of themselves, and their relationship with each other, through her.[20] But Adam resists Raphael's reading of human marriage, posing a question about the sex life of angels which seems intended to discover what experiential basis Raphael has for his opinion. Raphael's answer underscores the vast difference in condition and experience between angelic love— characterized as it is by free and variable choice of sex as well as total mixing in love embraces—and human love, characterized by enduring sexual difference; monogamous, companionate marriage; and procreation. These large differences call into some question the value of Raphael's unmeditated advice for Adam, requiring him to adjust them thoughtfully to his own circumstances and experience.[21] Milton's poem highlights Adam's quandary over the conflict of ideology and experience in reading the Genesis marriage text, registering in such scenes mid-seventeenth-century conflicts over women's nature and over familial patterns.[22] And while the poem generally supports gender hierarchy, it problematizes both the divine and the angelic testimony on this issue, and also thematizes how human experience continually calls that ideology into question.

God's third decree, the prohibition against eating the fruit of the Tree of Knowledge of Good and Evil, is first stated formally by Eve when she is led unawares to that tree by Satan embodied in the serpent. Her paraphrase indicates that she understands its literal meaning perfectly and that she knows it to be a direct command of God, distinct from the Law of Reason which governs all other prelapsarian behavior:

> But of this Tree we may not taste nor touch;
> God so commanded, and left that Command
> Sole Daughter of his voice; the rest, we live
> Law to ourselves, our Reason is our Law.
> . . . .
> God hath said, Ye shall not eat
> Thereof, nor shall ye touch it, lest ye die.   (IX, 651–63)

But Satan's challenge to the text of prohibition goes beyond the literal meaning, raising the fundamental issue of what this prohibition means for human life. What is the significance of the name "Tree of Knowledge of Good and Evil"? Why did God forbid it? Does it bring access to special knowledge or special powers? And if so, is it finally reasonable to obey such a prohibition? Once these questions are raised Eve cannot ignore them—nor should she, given what we have seen of Milton's insistence in tract after tract that God's laws are always to be interpreted in the light of charity, human liberty, and human good, and that if they are beyond reason they will nonetheless accord with it. The decree of prohibition also asks for interpretation in the light of experience, rightly construed.

Satan's temptation is grounded upon false testimony of personal experience—the supposed serpent's autobiographical narrative describing how he gained speech and reason by eating apples from the forbidden tree. Eve might, the Satanic serpent argues, reasonably expect from the same act a proportional elevation in the scale of being: "That ye should be as Gods, since I as Man, / Internal Man, is but proportion meet, / I of brute human, yee of human Gods" (IX, 710–12). If God is just and means Eve well he will not punish her for seeking such advancement (as he has not punished the serpent); therefore the death threatened in the text must in fact mean transportation to higher status. Or, if God does envy the advancement of humankind, his prohibition does not deserve to be obeyed.

While Eve has no means to know that the serpent's experience is fabricated, clearly she should not allow secondhand testimony—always problematic in Milton's analyses—to supplant her own story. In this situation she is called upon to construe a divine text in the light of her own experience of God's ways, to interpret its as yet unknown implications by what she does know, drawing upon the rich fund of personal experience she has already gained. This experience includes not only the virtual experience of evil provided by her dream, but also the vicarious imaginative experience provided by Raphael's narratives of the temptation of the angels and Abdiel's moral heroism; of the battle in heaven and its fearsome consequences for the rebels; and of the wondrous processes of creation, through which all beings are infused with and participate in God's vitality, goodness, and prolific creativity (Books V–VII).[23] Especially does her experience include the joy and sweetness of her life in Eden and with Adam, which have heretofore formed the constant burden of her speech and song. For Eve, and for Adam later, the best defense would be to construe the as yet unknown implications of a divine decree by such previous experience, reprising Abdiel, whose story they have heard: "Yet by experience taught we know how good, / And of our good, and of our dignity / How provident he is" (V, 826–28). Instead, Eve allows the serpent's fabricated experience to blot out her own, and to supply terms for interpreting the text of prohibition as injury—as a withholding from humans of the knowledge signified by the tree's name.

Fallen Eve turns radical empiricist when she apostrophizes the tree itself as the source of all knowledge and her experience of it through experiment as the only access to wisdom: "Experience, next to thee I owe, / Best guide; not following thee, I had remain'd / In ignorance, thou op'n'st Wisdom's way, / And giv'st access, though secret she retire" (IX, 807–10). But, ironically, Eve's experiment was based on a faulty hypothesis grounded on the serpent's false testimony. And the divinizing effects she thinks she observes in herself—"op'n'd eyes" and "growing up to Godhead"—are an illusion. As the serpent's story to Eve provides a case of false testimony about personal experience, hers to Adam provides a case of deluded testimony: "On my experience, *Adam,* freely taste" (IX, 988). Adam does so, not because he credits Eve's testimony but because in his despair he (like Eve earlier) cannot bring his own experience of God's goodness to bear upon the seemingly impossible choice posed by his strictly literal reading of the situation. He cannot, that is to say, imagine divine forgiveness of a repentant Eve, or rise to the true Christian heroism of offering to bear her punishment. Unable to hold fast to their experience of God, Adam and Eve soon find that the true meaning of the text of prohibition is expounded to them as experiential knowledge of evil in all its psychological and spiritual forms: lust, anger, guilt, shame, fear, jealousy, hatred, discord, despair, spiritual death: "our Eyes / Op'n'd we find indeed, and find we know / Both Good and Evil, Good lost and Evil got" (IX, 1070–72).

The fourth divine decree is the so-called *protevangelium,* the messianic promise of redemption, which the metaphorical terms of the divine judgment on the serpent (Genesis iii, 15) were thought to signify. In Mil-

ton's epic this text is the focus of interpretative attention from its first
ambiguous pronouncement by the Son when he judges Adam, Eve, and the
serpent: "Between Thee and the Woman I will put / Enmity, and between
thine and her Seed; / Her Seed shall bruise thy head, thou bruise his heel"
(X, 179–81). Satan, reporting his success with Adam and Eve to his cohort
in hell, interprets this text literally, as a matter of bruises, heels and heads:

> that which to mee belongs,
> Is enmity, which he will put between
> Mee and Mankind; I am to bruise his heel;
> His Seed, when is not set, shall bruise my head:
> A World who would not purchase with a bruise,
> Or much more grievous pain?   (X, 496–501)

Adam and Eve, however, cannot begin to consider what this text means
for them, or indeed even remember it, until Eve's repentance breaks
through the cycle of angry recriminations to restore love and harmony
between them. After this restorative experience Adam recalls the text,
but understands only that it promises some future good which they should
not relinquish by following Eve's first proposal of suicide or childlessness.

This text also requires the exegesis of experience—in Adam's case
historical and psychological experience, as he strives to interpret scenes
and stories of human history from the Fall to the Apocalypse.[24] This prophetic history, mediated to Adam by the angelic messenger Michael in
visions and narratives, teaches him to read history emblematically, as a
series of episodes displaying again and again the ravages and proliferation
of the evil he has unleashed upon the world. It teaches him also to read
history typologically, as a movement "From shadowy Types to Truth" (XII,
303), in which the meaning of the messianic promise becomes ever clearer
as the new covenant is progressively revealed.[25]

But this history is not simply presented: it must be proved on Adam's
pulses. He takes an active role in interpreting the prophetic scenes and
narratives, learning through a strenuous dialogic process of faulty formulation and correction, just what sin and death are to mean in human experience, and just what crushing the serpent must entail in Messiah's passion
and death. In doing so, Adam identifies so closely with his progeny, whose
story this is, that he himself seems to feel their wickedness, their misery
and pain, and their eventual triumph. At last he understands the messianic promise as redemption history, which in the teeth of sin and death
confirms God's goodness:

> O goodness infinite, goodness immense!
> That all this good of evil shall produce,

> And evil turn to good; more wonderful
> Than that which by creation first brought forth
> Light out of darkness!   (XII, 469–73)

This joyful experience of divine goodness leads Adam to adopt Abdiel's perspective on God's ways and enables him to apply the text of promise to himself, finding in Christ a pattern for his own life choices and acknowledging him "my Redeemer ever blest" (XII, 573).

For Eve also, understanding and acceptance of the text of promise must be founded on experience—in her case an inner spiritual experience mediated through dream. Eve was made to sleep during Adam's encounter with history and must await Adam's subsequent report of it to her. Yet through prophetic dreams she experiences directly what is fundamental in that history—its adumbration of divine goodness—and is thereby enabled to claim her own central agency in bringing the messianic promise into history:

> Whence thou return'st, and whither went'st, I know;
> For God is also in sleep, and Dreams advise,
> Which he hath sent propitious, some great good
> Presaging
>   . . . .
> This further consolation yet secure
> I carry hence; though all by mee is lost,
> Such favor I unworthy am voutsaf'd
> By mee the Promis'd Seed shall all restore.   (XII, 610–23)

The Miltonic bard must also engage directly with biblical revelation—all of it—in writing his great epic, and he traces the anxieties of that engagement in the proems to Books I, III, and VII. But in the proem to Book IX he voices a new confidence, based in part on the experience he alludes to, of making reasoned, judicious, well-considered choices regarding heroic subject and literary mode: "Since first this Subject for Heroic Song / Pleas'd me long choosing, and beginning late" (IX, 25–6). It is also based on divine illumination perceived as long-continued, dreamlike imaginative experiences (like Eve's dream, perhaps?)[26] in which the Heavenly Muse "deigns / Her nightly visitation unimplor'd, / And dictates to me slumb'ring, or inspires / Easy my unpremeditated Verse" (IX, 21–24). The epic bard's formal poetics reprises the terms Milton so continually invokes in describing all engagements with divine revelation: on the one hand, the authority and truth of divine revelation, and on the other, the need for diligent thought and the widest and most profound experience—including the experience of divine illumination—to understand it rightly.[27]

From *Paradise Lost*, what might we conclude about the meaning and the role of experience in Milton's representation of reading divine revelation, making life choices, and making poetry? For one thing, that the problems of reading experience cannot be solved by a simple appeal to the revealed word of God—for that revealed word also requires an appeal to experience to clarify its meaning. For another, that "experience" is a very complex field comprised of many elements—history, testimony, day-by-day occurrences, sense experience, psychological states, inner spiritual experience, and more. For yet another, that the testimony of others is especially problematic, and must always be weighed against other factors, especially the claims of personal experience. Finally, that there is special danger in relying upon a single dimension of experience—whether it be history, or testimony, or sense experience, or possibly delusory inner illumination (as in Eve's Satan-inspired dream in Book IV)—without the balance and confirmation provided by the other dimensions. But though Milton highlights all these hermeneutical difficulties, he does not allow his characters, his readers, or himself any appeal to undecidability, or to theological or cultural determinism, as an excuse for wrong readings and wrong choices. Rather, in prose and poetry he calls for the constant exercise of judgment, based on hard reasoning and a delicate weighing of evidence and claims, as well as for the constant effort to see new problems against a broad range of knowledge and experience, of all kinds. *Paradise Lost* portrays the need for that sort of rigorous intellectual regimen to meet the perplexing challenges and choices life continually presents, as well in heaven as on earth, as well before as after the Fall.

Throughout his poetry and prose, Milton makes a formidable claim for the responsible private conscience as the ultimate measure of truth and goodness. The best formulation is that of Jesus in *Paradise Regained*, in regard to the formal tradition of learning conveyed by books:

> who reads
> Incessantly, and to his reading brings not
> A spirit and judgment equal or superior
> (And what he brings, what needs he elsewhere seek)
> Uncertain and unsettl'd still remains,
> Deep verst in books and shallow in himself.   (IV, 321–27)

At the same time, Milton's prose tracts and poems show writer and characters continually explaining their private conscientious views in public arenas, in the idioms of public discourse.[28] They thereby show themselves accountable to, though not finally subjected to, public norms, steering an uneasy but salutary passage between the Scylla of authoritarianism (or

Foucauldian containment) on the one hand, and the Charybdis of antinomianism (or moral anarchy) on the other.

The fact that *Paradise Lost* is an epic theodicy and therefore thematizes issues of the goodness and justice of God's ways, prompts the further question, How does the Miltonic emphasis on experience bear upon these issues? It does so by undertaking to prove on the pulses of characters, bard, and readers the proposition that experience will finally affirm God's goodness—which is to say, the goodness of the human condition. We can hardly help finding that perception quixotic, though perhaps also rather wonderful, in a poet who himself experienced the agony of blindness throughout his most creative years, as well as the utter defeat of the political cause to which he gave twenty years of his life.

We might also ask, how does the Miltonic emphasis on experience matter for our continuing engagement with this poem? I am suggesting that it is important for contemporary readers to recognize the central and highly complex role *Paradise Lost* accords to human experience in glossing the authoritative divine texts that ground the action. If we do so we may feel less need to explode the Miltonic text, or to focus only on its margins or gaps, or to subvert its central values in order to resist its sometimes repugnant formulations regarding gender hierarchy and other matters. Instead, we may find that by thematizing the role of experience as he does, Milton himself makes a space for revision in his poem's ideology, to meet the experience of future readers.

Harvard University

NOTES

1. *John Milton: Complete Poems and Major Prose*, ed. Merritt Y. Hughes (Indianapolis, 1957). References to Milton's poetry are to this edition.

2. *Complete Prose Works of John Milton*, 8 vols., ed. Don M. Wolfe et al. (New Haven, 1953–82). References to Milton's prose are to this edition, and subsequent volume and page references will appear in the text as YP.

3. Christopher Hill, *Milton and the English Revolution* (London, 1977); Hill, *The Experience of Defeat: Milton and Some Contemporaries* (New York, 1984); Robert T. Fallon, *Captain or Colonel: The Soldier in Milton's Life and Art* (Columbia, Mo., 1984); Stanley Fish, *Surprised by Sin: The Reader in Paradise Lost* (New York, 1967).

4. Kathleen M. Swaim, *Before and After the Fall: Contrasting Modes in Paradise Lost* (Amherst, 1986); Georgia B. Christopher, *Milton and the Science of the Saints* (Princeton, 1982).

5. Some important studies of Milton's hermeneutic principles include Maurice

Kelley's Introduction to YP VI; Kelley, *This Great Argument: A study of Milton's "De Doctrina Christiana" as a Gloss Upon Paradise Lost* (Princeton, 1941); James H. Sims, *The Bible in Milton's Epics* (Gainesville, 1962); Hugh MacCallum, "Milton and the Figurative Interpretation of the Bible," *UTQ* 31 (1962), 397–415; John R. Knott, Jr., *The Sword of the Spirit: Puritan Responses to the Bible* (Chicago, 1971), pp. 106–130; Mary Ann Radzinowicz, *Toward Samson Agonistes* (Princeton, 1978), pp. 173–349; Dennis Danielson, *Milton's Good God: A Study in Literary Theodicy* (Cambridge, 1982).

6. For useful discussion of Puritan attitudes and concepts see William H. Haller, *The Rise of Puritanism* (New York, 1938); and John F. New, *Anglican and Puritan* (Stanford, 1964).

7. Christopher Hill, *The World Turned Upside Down: Radical Ideas During the English Revolution* (London, 1972); Hill, *Milton and the English Revolution*.

8. For a balanced discussion of this issue see Joan S. Bennett, "Liberty Under the Law," in *Milton Studies* XII, ed. James D. Simmonds (Pittsburgh, 1978), pp. 141–63; Bennett, *Reviving Liberty: Radical Christian Humanism in Milton's Great Poems* (Cambridge, 1989).

9. "The Prologue of the Wyves Tale of Bathe," 1–3, *The Poetical Works of Chaucer*, ed. F. N. Robinson (Boston, 1933), p. 91.

10. Barbara Shapiro, *Probability and Certainty in Seventeenth-Century England: A Study of the Relationships Between Natural Science, Religion, History, Law, and Literature* (Princeton, 1983).

11. Michel de Montaigne, *Essais*, trans. John Florio (London, 1603).

12. John Calvin, *Institutes of the Christian Religion*, III.2.15–16, ed. John T. McNeill, 2 vols. (Philadelphia, 1967), I, 561.

13. William Perkins, *A Golden Chaine: or, The Description of Theologie*, in *Workes*, 3 vols. (London, 1612–13), I, pp. 78–80; Perkins, *A Treatise Tending Unto a Declaration, Whether a Man be in the Estate of Damnation, or in the Estate of Grace*, ibid., I, pp. 364–74; John Bunyan, *Grace Abounding to the Chief of Sinners*, ed. G. B. Harrison (New York, 1976). See discussion in Lewalski, *Protestant Poetics and the Seventeenth-Century Religious Lyric* (Princeton, 1979), pp. 20–25.

14. Richard Sibbes, *The Soules Conflict with it Selfe* (London, 1635).

15. William Dell, *The Tryal of Spirits both in Teachers and Hearers* (London, 1653); George Fox, *Journal*, ed. Rufus M. Jones (London, 1948), 1–40.

16. Isaac Ambrose, *Prima, Media, and Ultima: The First, Middle, and Last Things* (London, 1659), pp. 164–89. See Lewalski, *Protestant Poetics*, pp. 158–62.

17. *Doctrine and Discipline of Divorce*, YP II, pp. 222–24; *Tetrachordon*, YP II, p. 578; *The Tenure of Kings and Magistrates*, YP III, pp. 190–97; *Eikonoklastes*, YP III, pp. 337–40.

18. Cf. *Tenure*, YP III, pp. 198–203. See discussion of Satanic misuses of classical republican argument in Lewalski, *Paradise Lost and the Rhetoric of Literary Forms* (Princeton, 1985), pp. 94–95, 156–59.

19. James Turner, *One Flesh: Paradisal Marriage and Sexual Relations in the Age of Milton* (Oxford, 1987).

20. Eve Kosofsky Sedgwick, *Between Men: English Literature and Male Homosocial Desire* (New York, 1985).

21. The differences are noted in Marshall Grossman, *"Authors to Themselves": Milton and the Revelation of History* (Cambridge, 1987), pp. 118–25.

22. See discussion in Turner, *One Flesh*, pp. 106–23; Linda Woodbridge, *Women and the English Renaissance: Literature and the Nature of Womankind, 1540–1620* (Urbana,

1986); Lawrence Stone, *The Family, Sex and Marriage in England, 1500–1800* (New York, 1977). I take issue here with Mary Nyquist's impressive argument in "The Genesis of Gendered Subjectivity in the Divorce Tracts and in *Paradise Lost*," *Re-Memembering Milton: Essays on the Texts and Traditions* (New York, 1987), pp. 99–127, claiming that Eve's and Adam's creation stories display their entire conformation to the norms of gender hierarchy in the era of emergent capitalism.

23. See Lewalski, "Innocence and Experience in Milton's Eden," *New Essays on Paradise Lost*, ed. Thomas Kranidas (Berkeley and Los Angeles, 1969), pp. 86–117.

24. For accounts of the place of history in Paradise Lost see, e.g., C. A. Patrides, *The Grand Design of God: The Literary Form of the Christian View of History* (London and Toronto, 1972); Achsah Guibbory, *The Map of Time: Seventeenth-Century English Literature and Ideas of Pattern in History* (Urbana, 1989), pp. 169–211; David Loewenstein, *Milton and the Drama of History: Historical Vision, Iconoclasm, and the Literary Imagination* (Cambridge, Mass., 1990), pp. 92–125. Grossman, *"Authors to Themselves:" Milton and the Revelation of History*.

25. See discussion in Lewalski, *Paradise Lost and the Rhetoric of Literary Forms*, pp. 254–79; Lewalski, "Structure and the Symbolism of Vision in Michael's Prophecy, *Paradise Lost* XI–XII," *PQ* 42 (1963), 25–35.

26. The parallels between Eve's imagination and art, and the poet's own, are traced suggestively in Diane McColley, "Eve and the Arts of Eden," *Milton and the Idea of Woman*, ed. Julia Walker (Urbana, 1988), pp. 100–19.

27. Studies offering a different account of Milton's claims to a poetics of prophecy include William Kerrigan, *The Prophetic Milton* (Charlottesville, 1974); Joseph Wittreich, *Visionary Poetics: Milton's Tradition and His Legacy* (San Marino, 1979); John Guillory, *Poetic Authority: Spenser, Milton, and Literary History* (New York, 1984).

28. I argue this issue in regard to *Samson Agonistes* in "Milton's *Samson* and the 'New Acquist of True [Political] Experience,' " in *Milton Studies XXIV*, ed. James D. Simmonds (Pittsburgh, 1988), pp. 233–51.

SUBJECT AND MACROSUBJECT IN
L'ALLEGRO AND IL PENSEROSO

Georgia B. Christopher

> The word "I" is to be understood only in the sense of a non-committal
> *formal indicator,* indicating something which may perhaps reveal
> itself as its "opposite" in some particular context of Being.
>
> —*Heidegger*

SUBJECTIVITY, Catherine Belsey declares, became a major theme
for Milton in the 1640s,[1] but criticism over the last decade has shown
that even in the early 1630s Milton was focusing upon the workings—or
antics—of the poetic subject. Thomas Greene has observed that in the
companion poems, *L'Allegro* and *Il Penseroso*, Milton deals with consciousness, presenting "serial acts of perception";[2] Christopher Grose has
described the quality of that consciousness in all its nuance;[3] and Dana
Brand has argued that the poems represent two different speakers, one
flighty and unfixed, the other a stable and secure self.[4] It would be tempting to argue that the poems represent separate stages in the seventeenth-
century struggle to forge the modern self-constructed subject.[5] I shall
argue, however, that Milton's companion poems present a strong and
unified subject, which we can locate at a midpoint in the evolution of the
modern subject. By subject, I will refer to the "speaker," the kind of self
he presents, and the operations of consciousness he performs. In contrast
to the late medieval *subject,* which is the ground for transcendent forces
to play upon, Milton's subject is defined by his own mental moves and
acts of perception. And he is strongly unified, although he plays up and
down the ontological scales from near absolute being to frivolous fiction.
Above all, this subject is not static; its unity depends upon the fact that it
is riven, that a current, as it were, plays between the poles of a moving
paradox.

   In *L'Allegro* and *Il Penseroso*, Milton does not figure the poetic
subject, or speaker, by means of the familiar tropes of devotional poetry—
the beseiged city, the enclosed garden, and the inner room of the heart—
that appear so frequently in Donne, Herbert, and Vaughan.[6] In their

poetry a mise en scene from morality plays or medieval romances has been reduced to miniature scale and interiorized, but the trope is nevertheless one of actual space and on occasion may entertain metaphysical visitors. For Milton, however, subjectivity in *L'Allegro* and *Il Penseroso* occupies an oneiric space between a magus and his apparitions. Milton figures the poetic subject as much by rhetorical maneuver as by sensuous image, and in the process elides the grammatical subject "I," virtually eliminating the authorial function. The subjectivity thus presented is extraordinarily mobile, temporally inflected, and qualitatively rich.

In the opening speech of *L'Allegro*, Milton establishes the poetic subject as a mock magus like Prospero, who has power to conjure up and dismiss apparitions. We watch the subject evoke himself in the process of invoking another being. He begins by pronouncing an elaborate formula for dismissing an unwanted apparition:

> Hence loathed Melancholy
>   Of Cerberus and blackest midnight born,
> In *Stygian* Cave forlorn
>   'Mongst horrid shapes, and shrieks, and sights unholy,
> Find out some uncouth cell,
>   Where brooding darkness spreads his jealous wings,
> And the night-Raven sings;
>   There under *Ebon* shades, and low-brow'd rocks,
> As ragged as thy Locks,
>   In dark *Cimmerian* desert ever dwell.　　　　　　　　(1–10)[7]

This elaborate speech is reducible to "Go to hell, Melancholy!"[8] but the fact that it belongs to the category of undergraduate "Quips and Cranks" should not obscure the connection established between magus and apparition, which is to say, between a poetic subject and his fictions. The mock conjuration continues, if with a somewhat less grandiose tone, as the subject conjures up the desired apparition in the place of Melancholy. Mirth, however, does not actually appear to sight, and the speaker seems to vanish as if he has conjured himself away in the process of calling up a parade of appearances. The first person goes underground, leaving a trail of locutions with no grammatical subject at all.

Milton was not the last young poet to be enamored of lists of dangling participles. The following is one among many that appear without benefit of a grammatical subject in *L'Allegro:* "Sometime walking not unseen / By Hedgerow Elms, on Hillocks green" (57–58). The persona remains largely out of sight throughout most of the poem, with only an occasional possessive pronoun to remind us of his existence.[9] The poem is propelled swiftly, if somewhat jerkily, by linguistic "shifters"—designations for time or place, or syntactical unit. (*Or,* the index word for an alternative, is a favorite.) Nevertheless, something of a narrative is intimated by a series of rhetorical notations—dangling participles, ablative absolutes, infinitives, and other sentence scraps, often entailing several dependent clauses. The subject thus should be understood as the ground of multiple, fleeting appearances and as such is infinitely more complex and more mysterious than a mere "authorial function."

L'Allegro comprises a veritable cinematic montage that seems to run on its own. Herbert Phelan has worked out a useful analogy between the poem's rhetorical and syntactical vagaries and cinematic techniques such as the voice-over, the quick cut, the panning shot, and the dissolve.[10] The cinematic metaphor is particularly useful in showing how the discontinuities of matter and syntax in *L'Allegro* point, not to the lack of a subject or its flimsiness, but to its power. The variety of literary materials and the quick changes of rhetorical construction in Milton's montage do not indicate that the subject is unfixed or unstable. We recognize the images, scraps of language, and literary allusions as all having been selected by a single consciousness, just as when visiting a family museum we immediately recognize that the paintings have all been chosen by a single eye, rather than by a committee bent on filling gaps in a taxonomy.[11] Paradoxically, in film—as in *L'Allegro*—disjunctions are perceived only because there is a continuity, a regular flow of items—which is to say, because there is a unified subject. Continuity, as film theorist Jean-Louis Baudry has argued, is the very principle of the "subject."[12]

Baudry points out that a cinemagoer is placed in the position of the subject, a particular kind of subject. He is like a dreamer located in the dark, where his body is placed in an inert position. As in the case of a dream, film images (both sight and sound) seem to appear spontaneously, yet they have a clear associative rationale. The moviegoer holds a position analogous to the movie projector; in other words, he assumes the place of the selecting and projecting eye, while the fact of projection is suppressed. Yet the film-going "subject," for all his passivity, is extremely powerful. Like the dreamer, he overrides the constraints of time and space. A panning shot can allow the cinemagoer to see things from a moving point of view that is physically impossible. In short, the position of the moviegoer is very like that of an almighty, infantile ego who, "in an almost hallucinatory manner," believes in the omnipotence of thought (Baudry, pp. 30, 34) and magically produces objects of desire.

The montage in *L'Allegro* similarly displays a very strong and expansive subject who is unified in his compelling drive for gratification. As in film, the fact that the subject's projecting apparatus is at work is suppressed for most of the poem. What seems to unify the subject here is not the grammatical manifestation, "I," but eros. To be sure, the eroticism of the poem is of the delicate variety reminiscent of the "cleanly wantonness" in Herrick's *Hesperides:* one scenario offered for the generation of Mirth is that she issues from the delicate "playing" of *Zephyr* with *Aurora*, "As he met her once a-Maying" and "fill'd her with a daughter fair" (19–20, 23). The naming of Mirth's attendants—"wanton Wiles, Nods, and Becks, and Wreathed Smiles" (27–28)—yields an operative definition of Mirth that includes the joy and solace that Allison and Nicholas enjoyed in Chaucer's famous tale. This is not to say that there is a rigid allegorical identification of Mirth with things sexual. *L'Allegro* comprises such a category only in the sense that the items presented cohere like a set of Wittgensteinian family resemblances. For example, the verbal play of the opening "conjuration" has nothing particularly erotic about it, but does relate to the love play of Mirth's progenitors (14–25) in its excess of energy and animal spirits.

The motif of sexual submission appears early in the poem and remains its purported goal. The pastoral frame, introduced by line 40, foregrounds desire; for the immediate model furnished by Marlowe in "The Passionate Shepherd to his Love"—"Come live with me and be my love / And we will all those pleasures prove"—assumes a connection between the sensuous and the sensual, in its proposed exchange of ivy and birdsong for sexual submission. The dominance of optical images in Milton's poem is appropriate to the erotic quest of *L'Allegro:* it is "on Beds of Violets blue" (21) that Mirth is born, and by the end of the poem the subject languishes by the riverside longing for what Hymen (in a saffron robe) will bring.

At this point the subject in *L'Allegro* executes a curious circular maneuver. At the beginning of the poem, he sets himself up as the wooer, the seducer: "But come thou Goddess fair and free" (11) . . . "Haste thee nymph" (25). Images of masculine dominance and assertion then crowd the beginning section of the poem—a cock strutting before his Dames, a ploughman, a mower. The impression of masculine dominance, however, soon gives way to something more passive—"stories told" (100), chivalric romances, the daydreams of pastoral poets (129–30), and Shakespeare's comedies on the boards. All of these literary genres dealing in amorous themes belong to the spectrum of family resemblances of Mirth, in that both eroticism and fiction involve the creation and manipulation of illusion.

Furthermore, literary genres all have in common the presentation of illusion before an immobile and passive audience. These presentations, like film, disregard the limits of human eyesight, bodily position, and orderly progression in time. Thus *L'Allegro*, in the terms Baudry has suggested, begins to thematize its own operations to the extent that it mimes the infantile and almighty subject. Of course the poetic subject here is not infantile, though he shares with the child the power to conjure up presences. The child, the moviegoer, and Milton's subject alike are powerless yet extraordinarily powerful: they conjure up or recreate an alternative reality at will.

From the images of daytime masculine dominance, the poem arrives by line 135 at a bedtime stasis that looks suspiciously pre-oedipal—a longing for a cradlelike existence:

> Lap me in soft Lydian Airs . . .
> Such as the meeting soul may pierce
> In notes, with many a winding bout
> Of linked sweetness long drawn out.   (136–140)

A wish for the lullaby and the breast seems to be conflated with desire for a mature sexual object. The subject has just been dreaming of the masque of Hymen (125), and he wants a "sweet oblivion." Just so, Lacan insists upon the subject's "profoundest desire to be 'One' again";[13] and as Christopher Grose puts it, he wishes to "extend delight into an indefinite future" (p. 191). In a series of dreamlike fusions, the poet seems to conflate the desired love object with an esthetic substitute: he would at least be "Married to immortal verse" (137). It is just at this point that the poem returns to the pastoral paradigm introduced near the beginning.

The First Person reemerges, having arrived at a decisive evaluation of the sensuous and sensual pleasures offered: "These delights if thou canst give / Mirth, with thee I mean to live" (151–52). The subject has turned into the love object—a coy beloved responding to the blandishments of a seducer[14] who promises the power of poetry (magic appearances)—a poetry that may protect him against the reality of "eating Cares." He wants nothing less than a poetic power so exorbitant that it will win the girl, even if she be Eurydice in hell. He wants "Such strains as would have won the ear / Of *Pluto*, to have quite set free / His half-regain'd *Eurydice*" (148–50). The subject would only commit himself to Mirth *if* poetry could grant him magic power over actual cases.

What are we to make of this curious maneuver in which the wooer turns himself into the love object? Is this simply more evidence that narcissism and Renaissance love poetry share a common paradigm?[15] We might term the speaker's playing out the active and passive positions "the

Teiresias maneuver," except that gender confusion is not really the issue. Nor is this simply a display of Keatsian "negative capability," though Milton will treat Eve's love song and Adam's soliloquy of despair with equal sensitivity in *Paradise Lost*. Rather, the switch in subject positions figures an intrasubjective condition: the subject is ex-centric to himself. According to Lacan, there is an irreducible narcissistic component in man (or child) that makes him see himself in the Other without being aware that what he contemplates as his self *is* the Other (Wilden, p. 172). What Greene sees as the ontological queasiness of a speaker who plays with attitudes and positions but commits himself to none (p. 174), is simply the structure of human subjectivity: an alienation that inevitably comes with human language and self-consciousness.

Turning to *Il Penseroso*, one finds the subject in this poem to be more articulate and visible than before, the first person being very much in evidence throughout. Eros this time is directed, not toward carnal knowledge, but toward divine knowledge and/or natural philosophy. In this poem, the subject seems to execute another kind of Teiresias maneuver: that of exchanging eyes for (in)sight. In a way that prefigures the contingencies underlying Milton's epic, *Il Penseroso* presents the subject as a splendid isolate with a diminished visual field, who sets himself apart in dark or semidark enclosed spaces—a glade, a cloister, a fire-lit room, a hermitage, a cell. As in Rembrandt's paintings, the spectrum has been reduced, but the result is an increase both in power and in nuance. As the number of objects in the visual field diminishes, those remaining acquire great intensity. *Il Penseroso* is by no means devoid of light, but what light remains serves to define and privilege the dark: Day is "kerchief't in a comely cloud," and the subject bids "glowing Embers . . . / [to] teach light to counterfeit a gloom" (79–80).

The reduction in the number and color of objects also automatically gives more force to the aural images in the poem: "the far-off *Curfew* sound" (74); the Bellman's calling of the watch (83–84); the "Sweet Bird" (61); and the "pealing Organ" (161). The fact that aural rather than optical imagery dominates this poem lends it a certain ontological weight, since the visual image is a copy (that is, an inferior reproduction) while an aural image is a repetition that does not require translation into another sensory channel (Baudry, p. 47). Thus presence is intimately linked to sound, as the evangelical tradition in which Milton was reared understood when it valued hearing over seeing. Milton would go on to construct the heaven of *Paradise Lost* mainly from utterance and without any grand visual symbol like Dante's multifoliate rose.

What the subject of *Il Penseroso* has lost in terms of daylight images and engagement with the world, however, is compensated by an epistemological bonus: access to great invisible reaches of knowledge. The celebrated tower passage (86–121), which seems to be a version of "the stronghold of wisdom" described in *Prolusions* VII, treats an experience of intellectual mastery. First, there is an encyclopedic grasp of the disciplines of philosophy and natural philosophy:

> Or let my Lamp at midnight hour
> Be seen in some high lonely Tow'r,
> Where I may oft outwatch the *Bear,*
> With thrice great *Hermes,* or unsphere
> The spirit of *Plato* to unfold
> What Worlds, or what vast Regions hold
> The immortal mind that hath forsook
> Her mansion in this fleshly nook:
> And of those *Daemons* that are found
> In fire, air, flood, or underground,
> Whose power hath a true consent
> With Planet or with Element.   (85–96)

Then the Tower experience sweeps together all history and literature, beginning with Aeschylus: "Sometime let Gorgeous Tragedy / In Scepter'd Pall come sweeping by" (97–98). The subject, we notice, is now at a great distance from the objects of knowledge—both spatially (the stars and the herbs to which they correspond) and temporally (the history of Thebes and the destruction of Troy). The literature that attracts this subject most is "The story of *Cambuscan* bold" (110), with its magical ring and horse made of brass. No doubt this Romance holds a climactic place in the tower sequence because its meaning is veiled rather than near at hand, requiring the reader to become a seer, a Teiresias—to penetrate the obvious and visible surface, first into the realm of the concrete referents of the text, and then into the realm of the Platonic Intelligibles.

  In the tower passage Milton treats an experience that Shakespeare never dealt with: the exaltation of studying after midnight when everything is likely to seem more profound. As in *Prolusions* VII, when Milton confesses that the delights "of secret study and learning . . . easily surpass all others,"[16] the poet in *Il Penseroso* conjures up the moment when one seems to have got at the truth of things in one grand sweeping insight, to have "unsphere[d] / The spirit of *Plato*" (88–89). This meeting of great disembodied minds is a secular and academic version of the Beatific Vision. Its provenance is medieval, but it adumbrates the Cartesian and Lockean understanding that the essence of the subject is mind. Here the student subject has joined the "vast Regions hold[ing] / The immortal mind that hath forsook / Her mansion in this fleshly nook" (90–92).

Il Penseroso thus offers an ascetic algebra in which sight and insight, ordinary human fulfillment and extraordinary achievement, operate within a balanced equation: the potency of the tower experience seems to be bought at the price of suppressing earthy and earthly objects of desire and directing desire toward a transcendent realm. The psychic "plot" of *Il Penseroso*, one might say, is that of sublimation. It would be going too far to suggest that the subject of this poem has made a Faustian pact exchanging gratified human love for extraordinary intellectual and spiritual power, but he does prefigure the "Teresias" of *Paradise Lost*, whose loss of sight gains compensation in heavenly vision. At the end of *Il Penseroso*, the subject projects a time when, after foregoing or suppressing the world of *L'Allegro*, he will attain "something like Prophetic strain" (174). He vows: "These pleasures *Melancholy* give, / And I with thee will choose to live" (175–76). It is possible to read an implicit *if* in the above lines and to conjure up again the coy beloved responding to a seducer's proposition like the one that appeared at the end of *L'Allegro*. But the *if* has disappeared, and the subject seems rather to be a votary making a petition and swearing lifelong devotion.

A look at the generic shape of the poem, in any case, suggests that this final couplet should be read as a performative speech, as a declaration of commitment. Indeed a commitment seems already in the process of formation by the middle of the poem with a series of imperatives:

> Or *let* my Lamp at midnight hour
> . . . .
> Sometime *let* Gorgeous Tragedy
> . . . .
> Goddess *bring* [me]
> To arched walks of twilight groves,
> . . . .
> *Hide* me from Day's garish eye,
> . . . .
> And *let* some strange mysterious dream
> . . . .
> But *let* my due feet never fail
> To walk the studious Cloister's pale
> (85, 97, 132–33, 141, 147, 155–56; emphasis mine)

These imperatives are profoundly ambiguous. On the one hand, they may be read as imperial commands, signifying (like the tower itself) the power of a subject who can magically summon up objects of study and contemplation. On the other hand, these repeated *Let's* may be read as prayer—as supplication to Lady Melancholy. Stella Revard has established that the nearest generic models for Milton's companion poems are the Greek hymns and odes, which invoke and describe a deity, make supplication, and offer praise.[17] Melancholy thus stands in the place of a pagan deity like Urania, but has a more than *pro forma* religious role; for she seems to function like Dante's veiled Beatrice as an intermediary figure who dispenses blessing. If we keep in mind the liturgical character of the poem, the final couplet appears less like the reply of a reluctant shepherd and more like a solemn, mutual covenant: "These pleasures *Melancholy* give, / And I with thee will choose to live" (175–76).

The ambiguous litany of *Let's* defines the subject of *Il Penseroso* as paradoxically weak and needy despite all his power, just as the subject of *L'Allegro* is unified but given to disjointed perceptions. Finally, the subjects in these poems seem very much alike, as Dr. Johnson noticed when he said that *L'Allegro* and *Il Penseroso* were not sufficiently distinguished.[18] Thus we cannot speak of a *debat* between a medieval soul and a protomodern constructed self. The poems, however, do contain evidence that a struggle to forge a modern subject is under way: namely that within each poem a discrepancy exists between representational modes—the emblematic versus the perceptual. The telling discrepancy is that between the emblematic deity invoked at the beginning of each poem and the perceptual images, notations, longings, and memories that follow in montage. In each case, the presiding Lady belongs to an earlier style of representation.

Lady Melancholy, for example, is an emblematic figure and comes with a previously assigned meaning, whereas the items in montage take their meaning from separate acts of attention by a particular subject. Lady Melancholy, whose provenance stretches back through Spenser to Dante's Earthly Paradise, comes preread, as it were. She might as well be the character Contemplation in a morality play, the kind of figure who would lead Everyman to jilt Wanton and Liberty in order to insure a good death. In the elaboration of this emblem, pious and classical signifiers alike belong to a well established lexicon of emblematic meanings. Lady Melancholy is dressed like a nun in "Wisdom's hue" (16), and she is a child of the Golden Age, her father being Saturn. Her gestures—upturned face with "looks commercing with the skies" and her subsequent downward gaze (39, 44)—belong to the iconography of morality plays and mythographical compendia.

As a signifier, however, Lady Melancholy is somewhat more complex than her counterpart in a morality play. She exhibits both the behavior of an exemplary worshipper and the essential mystery of the divine. Her posture is that of a devotee deep in meditation and prayer; but like the God in *Paradise Lost*, who appears "dark with excessive bright," her "Saintly visage is too bright / To hit the Sense of human sight" (13–14), and so her face must be overlaid with black to accommodate "our weaker view" (15). Like Dante's veiled Beatrice, who serves as a Christ-bearing figure in the Corpus Christi parade that appears at the end of the *Purgatorio*, Lady Melancholy is a divinity-bearing figure, whose pious and numinous attributes stand as a type—not of beatific—but of academic "ecstasies" (165), for which the subject petitions.

In sharp contrast to emblematic Melancholy are the distinctly perceptual items that follow in montage. The two representational categories, however, are not always sharply distinguished. Phelan has shrewdly observed how the poem modulates between a mythic, allegorical moon, *Cynthia* (who in line 60 might at first be read as belonging to the retinue of Melancholy), and a "real" moon that appears "o'er th' accustom'd Oak" (67; Phelan, p. 6). Though we can scarcely admit any "real" moons into the text, we can say that images seem to play up and down the scales, from near absolute being to fanciful fiction, creating considerable "ontological uncertainty."[19] The sighting of the moon, for instance, seems to introduce a specific act of perception taking place at the very moment, especially because no literary precedent has been found for the following lines:

> I walk unseen
> On the dry smooth-shaven Green,
> To behold the wand'ring Moon,
> Riding near her highest noon,
> Like *one* that has been led astray.   (65–69)

The moment is interesting because the paradoxes of the subject come into open play here: he is an "unseen" figure on a well-lighted ground; the first person ("I") quickly turns into a distanced "one," and we watch the subject going into eclipse, becoming decentered, as if his domain were somehow located *between* light and dark.

In *L'Allegro* as well there are numerous moments that suggest that an immediate act of perception is taking place, even when the object of perception is designated by a highly conventional label—the Ploughman, the Milkmaid, or "Spicy Nut-brown Ale." Other items in the montages flaunt their literary and fictive status: Corydon and Phillis, Morpheus and Hymen. As both poems use roughly the same mix of signifying ingredients, one cannot set *L'Allegro* and *Il Penseroso* against each other in some sort of *debate* between the medieval soul and the modern subject. They both seem to belong to "a single embracing mind" (Greene, p. 172). The two poems, though discontinuous and distinctively different, display the operations of a single consciousness in the same way as do the various items in *L'Allegro*'s montage. The macrosubject generates them all.

If we then assume a macrosubject as the ground of the two poems, the tension between types of signifying practice will locate *both* poems at an intermediate stage in the development of the modern subject—somewhere between the emblematics of the morality plays and the illusionistic perspective of the Restoration stage. Insofar as Milton's emblems hark back to medieval practice, they stand for that part of the subject's identity which is inherited in a neat cultural package. Mirth and Melancholy stand like saints who confer identity upon their namesakes and limn a destiny for their devotees. The inherited identity, however, is modified by the expository montage that enacts (rather than stands for) the modern subject's construction of itself. The choices and acts of attention are highly particularized and characterize an individualistic subject that looks even beyond the Restoration to the subjective epics of the Romantic poets.

If we admit to a macrosubject generating both *L'Allegro* and *Il Penseroso*, then the serial placement of the poems invites us to examine the diachronic life of the macrosubject within the linear course of the twin poems. The synchronic character of the macrosubject is readily recognizable, just as the individual configuration of President Nixon's features is recognizable even in his baby pictures. History, of course, modifies identity, and the development of Milton's macrosubject, though subtle, is important. A diurnal pattern propels the poems and links them in a developmental sequence: the first begins at dawn and concludes with the dark of night, while the second begins in twilight and climaxes with an epiphanic morning.

In the first poem desire is treated as cleanly wantonness and the subject's love-longing hallowed by a vision of Hymen, but when we come to *Il Penseroso*, we find that a note of transgression has been introduced. Lady Melancholy is likened to Cassiopeia whose beauty *offended* the Nereid (19–21), and Lady Melancholy is herself a product of the incestuous union between Vesta and Saturn. The explanation that incest was not then felt a "stain," only calls attention to the fact of pollution. There is also more than a hint of trespass about entering the realm of the pure Intelligible or "unsphering" Plato. The introduction of pain heightens the self-consciousness of the subject in *Il Penseroso*, shoring up the illusion that what is being presented is an actual moment of perception. While *L'Allegro* ends with its subject lounging by a riverside in a veritable daze of pastoral desire, the subject of *Il Penseroso* identifies with the wandering moon "like one that had been led astray" (69) and yearns for the nightingale, long associated with the pain and betrayal of love, to sing "her sweetest, saddest plight" (57). The macrosubject, it would seem, has moved from the position of the yearning lover in the first poem to that of a man who has lost his love or been betrayed.

The reality of loss seems to have moved *Il Penseroso* from a psychic paradigm of narcissism to one of sublimation. That is to say, the subject of *Il Penseroso* has matured in that, thwarted in his original amorous quest, he turns his desires toward a grander object with implied benefits to society, if not civilization. Instead of carnal knowledge, this subject reaches for total and complete knowledge, a grand "vision," which for Milton means entering the two-story universe of Platonic Intelligibles. His activity is now more deliberate; the objects of his desire are conceptual and verbal. If the inclusion of transcendent regions in *Il Penseroso* seems to look backward in time, we need to remember that in turning from Lady Mirth to Mistress Melancholy, the macrosubject is not choosing between cosmic good and evil, as in a morality play, for neither Lady is really evil. What separates them is less a great ontological divide than a metaphysical class distinction. The first poem deals with many separate acts of attention, that is to say, with sensory choice. The second poem deals with choice as commitment spanning an entire life.

Finally, the poems put the reader in a position analogous to that of the macrosubject, who generates the disjunctive sequences of mirth and melancholy—placing the reader in the shoes of a magus able to summon up unlikely and mutually exclusive appearances. The reader, much like a moviegoer or a dreaming subject, experiences temporarily the hallucinatory power analogous to that of an infantile subject who would, impossibly, be everything, without having to make choices. At the same time the macrosubject, by the sequential placement of the two poems, has defined a developmental pattern that gives the reader fictive experiences of *both* infantile power *and* of limitations transmuted by adult choice. Hence the reader, like the dreamer and the macrosubject, has it both ways: he has the pleasure of indiscriminate desire *and* the gratification of defining himself by discrimination and choice. Milton's macrosubject is the greatest magician of all, presenting a riven unity that plays between both/and *and* either/or.

Emory University

NOTES

1. Catherine Belsey, *John Milton: Language, Gender, Power* (Oxford, 1988), p. 85.
2. Thomas E. Greene, "The Meeting Soul in Milton's Companion Poems," *ELR* 14 (Spring, 1984), 168.

3. Christopher Grose, "The Lydian Airs of *L'Allegro* and *Il Penseroso*," *JEGP* 83 (April 1984).

4. Dana Brand, "Self-Construction and Self-Dissolution in *L'Allegro* and *Il Penseroso*," *MQ* 15 (1981), 118–19.

5. See Catherine Belsey, *The Subject of Tragedy* (London, 1983), pp. 118–19, for an account of the making of the modern subject during the Renaissance.

6. See Barbara K. Lewalski, *Protestant Poetics and the Seventeenth-Century Religious Lyric* (Princeton, 1979), ch. 6.

7. *John Milton: Complete Poems and Major Prose*, ed. Merritt Y. Hughes (Indianapolis, 1957). References to Milton's poetry are to this edition.

8. The corresponding dismissal of a specter in *Il Penseroso* carries the minimal joke of calling Mirth a bastard (cf. line 2).

9. *me* (38, 36); *my* (46); *mine* (46); and us (117).

10. Herbert J. Phelan, "What is the Persona Doing in *L'Allegro* and *Il Penseroso?*" in *Milton Studies XXII*, ed. James D. Simmonds (Pittsburgh, 1985), pp. 3–20.

11. For example, the Chrysler Museum in Norfolk, Virginia, or the Phillips Collection in Washington, D.C. during its early days.

12. Jean-Louis Baudry, "Ideological Effects of the Basic Cinematographic Apparatus," in *Apparatus*, ed. T. H. Kyng Cha (New York, 1980), p. 34.

13. Anthony Wilden "Lacan and the Discourse of the Other," in *The Language of the Self*, trans. Anthony Wilden (Baltimore, 1968), p. 191.

14. Greene (p. 171) has also noted the change in subject position of the speaker, but discusses it in connection with the conditional element in the last half of the respective poems.

15. See Wilden, "Lacan and the Discourse of the Other," p. 165.

16. "So at last, Gentlemen, when the cycle of universal knowledge has been completed, still the spirit will be restless in our dark imprisonment here, and it will rove about until the bounds of creation itself no longer limit the divine magnificence of its quest. Then most happenings and events about us will become obvious so quickly that almost nothing can happen without warning or by accident to a man who is in possession of the stronghold of wisdom. Truly he will seem to have the stars under his control and dominion, land and sea at his command, and the winds and storms submissive to his will. Mother nature herself has surrendered to him. It is as if some god had abdicated the government of the world and committed its justice, laws, and administration to him as ruler" (*Prolusions* VII, Hughes, p. 625).

17. Stella P. Revard, "*L'Allegro* and *Il Penseroso*: Classical Tradition and Renaissance Mythography," *PMLA* 101 (1986), 338.

18. Samuel Johnson, *Lives of English the Poets*, ed. George Birkbeck Hill (Oxford, 1905), vol. 1, p. 66.

19. Greene notes that the poems modulate quickly between several levels of reality (p. 174), but does not discuss representational modes as such.

"FAIR OFFSPRING NURS'T IN PRINCELY LORE": ON THE QUESTION OF MILTON'S EARLY RADICALISM

David Loewenstein

I N 1649 MILTON, the revolutionary apologist for Parliament, returned to one of his early poetic themes, placing it in a polemical context
we associate with his later political radicalism. Inspired at times with apocalyptic zeal, he proceeded in *Eikonoklastes* to demolish the "Stage-work"
(YP III, p. 530) of the highly popular piece of royalist propaganda, *Eikon
Basilike*, a work, he scornfully observed, "drawn out to the full measure of a
Masking Scene" (p. 342). As he developed his polemical attack aimed at
shattering the icon of the Stuart player-king, the revolutionary writer chose
to present Charles not as a suffering and patient martyr (as the royalist book
had done), but as a Comus-Circe figure, who enchants and intoxicates the
people with "the *Circaean* cup of servitude," "spic'd and temperd to thir
bane" (pp. 488, 582)—turning them into "a credulous and hapless herd" (p.
601), "arrant beasts," and "clamouring & fighting brutes" (p. 581). Be-
witched by the king's charms, the populace resembles Comus's deformed
"rout of Monsters, headed like the sundry sorts of wild Beasts" that accompany him in Milton's early entertainment. Like Comus, the king appears in
Milton's polemic as a consummate rhetorician and master of theatrical arts:
he uses "glozing words and illusions" (p. 582)—again specifically recalling
the figure of Milton's Ludlow masque, who "cheat[s] the eye with blear
illusion" (*Comus* 155) and who pleases the ear with "well-plac'd words of
glozing courtesy" (161).

Milton's reappropriation of his own earlier work in the revolutionary
context of 1649 would indeed seem to link his early poetry with his later
political radicalism. His aristocratic entertainment, whose political occasion and themes might seem at first so unlike those of his polemical tract,
does in one sense anticipate his revolutionary outlook and fears: the
masque's vision of a people overcome by intemperate luxury and revelry,
and made remiss by the skillful politics of illusion and theatricality, would
be confirmed in that "graceless age" (YP III, p. 348) fifteen years later,
when the spectacle and rhetoric of the king's book managed to have such a

powerful and enticing effect on Milton's countrymen. The revolutionary writer, moreover, would respond to the dissipating social effects of the king's bewitching arts and powers with a vehement passion resembling Lady Alice's "flame of sacred vehemence" (795), which threatens to shatter "into heaps" Comus's "magic structures rear'd so high" (798–99).

But however compelling we might find this explicit connection between Milton's prerevolutionary work and his revolutionary writing, the relation between his early poetry and his subsequent radicalism remains more problematic than my brief example might suggest. Exactly how radical or revolutionary, after all, were the political implications of Milton's early poems? To what extent do the young Milton's writings look forward to the revolutionary career? Since the publication of Christopher Hill's *Milton and the English Revolution* in 1977, scholars have begun to show more interest in rediscovering the radical political implications of Milton's poetry. This trend is in one sense highly encouraging: Milton's writings have too often been de-historicized, and their political and ideological values ignored by commentators more interested in explaining their purely literary or formal qualities than in examining how aesthetic and historical concerns may intersect.[1] In recent years, some of the most exciting revisionary work has focused on Milton's poems of the prerevolutionary period.[2] The critical tendency has been to stress the more radical, subversive implications of Milton's early writings—to extend, in effect, Hill's argument for Milton's radicalism by finding evidence for its development even in the poems of the 1620s and early 1630s. Such revisionary and challenging criticism has begun to give us a young Milton who, well before writing *Lycidas*, seems consistent in his political radicalism and revolutionary outlook. Michael Wilding, for example, urges us to "rediscover the radicalism of Milton's earlier years" and entitles his discussion "Milton's Early Radicalism," while Terry Eagleton has recently proclaimed that "*Comus* is in its own way a radical blast against the Establishment."[3]

My aim here is to reexamine the controversial issue of Milton's early radicalism by commenting on selected aesthetic and political themes of the Nativity ode and *Comus*, and then to suggest a number of comparisons and connections with the revolutionary prose works. My discussion of Milton's early writings makes no attempt to be comprehensive (or, for that matter, to examine closely all the recent discussions of the poet's early politics); but it does argue for a view of the young Milton that sees him as less consistently radical in his politics than a number of stimulating studies have suggested.[4]

While the claims for Milton's early radicalism are often highly provocative, they will need to be refined as we attempt to provide a more

nuanced account of the ways—sometimes contradictory—that Milton politicized the aesthetic in his prerevolutionary writings.[5] Aligning Milton's
poems with routine orthodoxy can of course often diminish their achievement, as can the opposite tendency to detach them, along with Milton's
aesthetics in general, from sociopolitical values and contexts. Still, a view
that transforms the young Milton into a radical, who from the beginning
consistently blasts the establishment, also presents the danger of creating
a monolithic, schematic account of his early career—one that can too
easily flatten out or overlook contradictory and heterogeneous impulses in
the writings. Milton's political stance in the prerevolutionary poetry does
at times anticipate his revolutionary polemics; but his political impulses
during this period are also less consistent and sometimes more contradictory than recent defenders of his early radicalism have been urging.[6] An
aristocratic entertainment like *Comus* reveals the young Milton in some
ways ambivalent in his social commitments, registering in his work certain
unresolved tensions: engaged by the world of aristocratic culture while
also suspicious of it, he projects a vision of a reformed aristocracy that
would itself find further expression in his revolutionary writings.

   If we are looking for evidence of Milton's emerging political radicalism, we might begin with his Nativity poem of 1629, that "humble ode"
(24) which inaugurates in such a bold way Milton's voice of apocalyptic
prophecy. Written by a highly precocious poet as an annunciation of his
prophetic career, the future-oriented poem already highlights an apocalyptic vision of history and purification: thus at the Last Judgment

> The aged Earth aghast
> With terror of that blast,
>   Shall from the surface to the center shake,
> When at the world's last session,
> The dreadful Judge in middle Air shall spread his throne.   (160–64)

These apocalyptic lines precede the final long section dramatizing the
banishing of pagan idols and the reformation of religion, which ensues
with Christ's entry into history. Wilding, who uses Milton's tracts of the
1640s to illuminate political meanings in the early poems, reminds us that
such apocalyptic visions in Milton's revolutionary years had "radical Utopian political implications," and he links Milton's early prophetic poem
with the fiery apocalyptic vision concluding *Of Reformation Touching
Church-Discipline In England* (1641), Milton's first antiprelatical tract.[7]
Yet proving that Milton's early apocalyptic vision in the Nativity ode
implies a revolutionary component and reveals his emerging political radicalism is not quite so simple. Can we indeed interpret the development of

Milton's early politics retrospectively—that is, from the perspective of the revolutionary writings of the tumultuous 1640s?

Though they were put to political uses, Protestant apocalyptic visions and beliefs were by no means always revolutionary in their political import; on the contrary, they could be perfectly conservative and orthodox. John Foxe's immensely popular *Acts and Monuments*, after all, was an apocalyptic work that, with its ideal of a new Constantine, essentially buttressed Elizabethan orthodoxy, supporting the reformed Church of England and the Anglican challenge to the popish Antichrist.[8] It envisions no millennium in which a period of dramatic transformation of the social order occurs—quite unlike Milton's apocalyptic tracts, in which he passionately writes of "these reforming times" when God's "Kingdome is now at hand" (YP I, pp. 722, 707). It is true that two years before Milton's ode, Joseph Mede, Fellow of Milton's Cambridge College, published his *Clavis Apocalyptica*, the elaborate commentary on the Book of Revelation that would later provoke much revolutionary fervor. But it was not until the early 1640s, when it was translated into English by the order of the Long Parliament, that its potential for promoting radical millennial ideas became most apparent.[9] There is, in fact, little evidence to suggest that Milton would have registered its radical implications in his poetry of the late 1620s—as he would in his controversial prose works of the early 1640s, when the shattering crisis of political and ecclesiastical authority encouraged more revolutionary interpretations of apocalyptic visions.

We need, I believe, to explore further connections between Milton's poetry and revolutionary works, and to challenge the tendency to isolate the poetic from the political in Milton's writings. But as we do so, we also need to be wary of projecting, in too consistent a fashion, his later radicalism back into his earlier poetry—a tendency that a radical polemic like *Eikonoklastes*, with its political use of the Circe-Comus myth, might itself encourage—confronting instead the more heterogeneous, contradictory directions of this young writer's literary career.

In its presentation of the cosmic sweep of history, the Nativity ode registers dazzling multiple time-shifts that look back to the Creation and ahead to the Apocalypse. Yet while the young Milton is particularly innovative in dramatizing the relation of his prophetic vision to the Incarnation and the sacred spectacle of history, he has still to radicalize apocalyptic themes as he would do in his heated polemics of the 1640s—or in *Lycidas*, for that matter. Indeed, the Nativity ode's prophetic vision draws frequently upon the language and figures of spectacular court masques, suggesting Milton's fascination with the sophisticated mechanics of that aristocratic Jacobean and Caroline art form he would master and reform five years later. The poem inaugurating Milton's sacred literary vocation is full of masquelike scenes placed in an elaborate prophetic and typological framework: for example, the allegorical "meek-ey'd Peace / . . . softly sliding / Down through the turning sphere" and dividing the clouds (46–50); or the throned virtues "With radiant feet the tissued clouds down steering" as "Heav'n as at some festival" opens "wide the Gates of her high Palace Hall" (141–48). Inigo Jones's masque machinery, of course, included revolving globes, opening shutters, and descending clouds[10]—all to help "Time . . . run back, and fetch the age of gold" (135). Perfectly familiar with this most distinctive form of aristocratic Stuart culture, the young Milton registers no profound uneasiness with its ideological implications—unlike the vehement Lady of *Comus,* or the revolutionary writer in his 1649 polemic against the theatrical representation of Stuart court culture and power. In the concluding scene of the poem, where Milton displays "the Courtly Stable" of Christ (237–44), the poet has indeed refocused the perspective and energies of the Stuart masque normally reserved for the earthly king: here, in the poem's final resplendent tableau, the universe's gaze is centered on the kenotic Christ as king. But if the young poet in the Nativity ode reforms the royal perspective of the court masque, he does so by drawing extensively upon its features in order to dramatize the poem's sacred spectacle.

Indeed, in its self-conscious anticipation of a great literary future, the Nativity ode would seem to promise—from the pen of its ambitious young author—masquelike productions placed in a prophetic framework, just as surely as it portends revolutionary apocalyptic writings. There is little need, in any case, to see the ode as a text with politically radical implications, a work whose spectacular vision of apocalypse would inevitably lead the young prophetic poet on to the revolutionary millennialism of the 1640s. Even the poem's lengthy section dramatizing the banishing of pagan idols—a section that seems to anticipate the apocalyptic writer who, in his prose polemics and *Samson Agonistes,* purifies religion by virulently casting down "Idolatrous Rites" (*SA* 1378)—begins as an intensely elegiac passage, highlighting the "loud lament" and "weeping" of the fleeing nymphs (183). The young Protestant poet's response to that great moment of historical deliverance is far from unequivocal: Milton simultaneously breaks the idolatrous spell of paganism and mourns its loss.

The revolutionary polemicist carefully placed his prophetic ode at the beginning of the *Poems* of 1645—a volume, however, containing not only *Lycidas,* with its voice of apocalypse and prophecy foretelling "by occasion," like one of his impassioned polemics, "the ruin of our corrupted

Clergy" in the revolutionary years, but also an extremely diverse variety of other panegyrics. *Lycidas* appears in a volume that includes such assorted and sundry tributes as an entertainment honoring the Countess Dowager of Derby, long associated with the world of courtly culture and masquing; early Latin elegies commemorating prominent Anglican bishops; and a Jonsonian-style epitaph on a Roman Catholic marchioness whose husband, the Marquis of Winchester, proved to be a particularly ardent royalist—resisting the siege to his stronghold by Parliament's forces during the two years immediately preceding the publication of Milton's *Poems*.[11] We should be careful, in other words, of plotting Milton's prerevolutionary career—with its heterogeneous political and artistic tendencies—in too uniform or coherent a fashion. The controversialist who chose to publish his diverse juvenilia in a revolutionary era may well have sought, as Thomas Corns has recently suggested, to declare not so much his radical identity as his respectability and cultural authority.[12] In any case, this gesture of artful self-presentation did not prevent Milton from producing a volume that, if it anticipated aspects of his later revolutionary Puritan attitudes, simultaneously registered certain contradictory political tendencies or impulses of his youthful career. It revealed layers of past attitudes—social and aesthetic—which we should avoid neatly reconciling into a too-schematic view of Milton's prerevolutionary writings and poetic development.

Indeed, as we assess the heterogeneous impulses of his early works, we perhaps need to show something of a Foucauldian willingness to describe dissensions, irregularities, and contradictions within a text or series of writings (what the Milton of *Areopagitica* might call their "dissimilitudes"), rather than feel compelled to discover a principle of cohesion and unity informing them—in this particular case, Milton's early radicalism.[13] In cultural and political terms, moreover, Milton's diverse collection presents a young writer who, at various times, aligned himself with both conservative and potentially more radical elements of the Stuart world. This is a world we sometimes too neatly divide into such opposing camps as Puritanism and court culture, godliness and entertainment, the court and the country, and so on.[14] The varied literary productions of Milton's early career themselves indicate the problem of using cultural and aesthetic forms to measure and gauge political divisions between such groups as Puritans and Cavaliers in the age of Charles I.[15] In addition, it can be misleading to determine the consistency and direction of an individual's social views, especially during the prerevolutionary years, on the basis of hindsight and later historical developments. Reminding us that "Everyone was a royalist before 1642," one historian has recently warned that "When writing about the 1620s and 1630s . . . it is highly misleading to describe someone as 'a future parliamentarian' or 'future royalist,' referring to their activities in the later Civil War. . . . One of the mistakes of analyzing historical development is to assume the events proceed evenly along an unbroken line."[16] The same point might well be made about Milton's literary productions and career, particularly his development in the prerevolutionary days: as the varied 1645 volume suggests, his early political and ideological commitments hardly seem to have developed "evenly along an unbroken line."

Comus could itself be construed as a hybrid of potentially incompatible elements. A masque written to celebrate an important aristocratic occasion, this is also a theatrical work dramatizing—like Milton's political tracts or one of "those Dramatick constitutions" (YP I, p. 814) he was considering in the early 1640s—the political dangers of extravagant luxury, idolatry, dissolute revelry and debauchery, and the need for social reform.[17] It is apparent enough that *Comus* is no ordinary court masque, focusing its visual perspective on the Stuart king both as principal spectator and as object of a wondrous apotheosis.[18] Milton has boldly reformed the courtly entertainment by highlighting the Egerton children's difficulty in overcoming the threatening forces of evil; by having the masquers engage directly with the antimasque; by giving a young aristocratic woman, Lady Alice Egerton, the power of vehement arguments; and by using a public occasion to dramatize personal ideals—especially chastity and (more strongly in the 1637 version) the high mystery of virginity. Yet despite its boldly experimental features, *Comus* need not be construed as a consistently radical attempt to subvert aristocratic social values and aesthetics—by highlighting text over spectacle or by having the representative of royal authority, the new Lord President of Wales, play no part in the action's resolution.

There are ways in which the dynamics of Milton's aristocratic work suggest ambivalent or conflicting impulses in his earlier social and aesthetic sensibility. For one thing, its highly sophisticated blending of art and life, "Hall" and "Bow'r" (45), fiction and occasion, suggests the young Milton's ongoing fascination with the world of aristocratic culture and the theatrical dynamics of its most distinctive aesthetic form. Indeed, while *Comus* constantly points to the dangers and seductiveness of illusion and extravagant revelry, it falls far short of expressing a strong or consistent antitheatrical impulse in Milton's early politicized work, as Norbrook seems to suggest.[19] On the contrary, even as he reforms the genre in striking ways, the masque's numerous metatheatrical moments convey Milton's sense of pride and bravura as the writer of a brilliant theatrical entertainment at an important aristocratic occasion. These self-conscious theatrical moments (like those in Jonson's masques) are Milton's way of signaling to his courtly audience his own skill and virtuosity in having mastered the dramatic conventions of this aristocratic form perfected by Jonson—particularly its sophisticated art of dramatic pretence. Thus, for example, the Lady's complaint about night's "dark lantern"—which closes "up the Stars / That nature hung in Heav'n" (197–98) when she appears all alone in the dark, mazelike wood—conceals beneath its metaphor a self-conscious reference to the actual lighting mechanism of court entertainments; and a few lines later, she again calls attention to the illusion of the masque's art when she wonders out loud whether she has just seen "a sable cloud / Turn forth her silver lining on the night" (221–22).

An even more pronounced sense of artistic bravura lies behind Lady Alice's response to Comus who, in the "fair pretence" of pastoral disguise (160), offers to conduct her from the dark forest to a safe cottage. She praises his

> honest offer'd courtesy,
> Which oft is sooner found in lowly sheds
> With smoky rafters, than in tap'stry Halls
> And Courts of Princes, where it first was nam'd,
> And yet is most pretended.   (323–27)

Milton here not only dramatizes Lady Alice's danger in the face of perverted pastoral innocence: he also teases his courtly audience, sitting in the "tap'stry" hall of Ludlow Castle watching his aristocratic entertainment. The wittiness of this metatheatrical passage and its context—which subvert the simple polarization of court and country—depends precisely on a shared understanding between poet and his aristocratic audience of the dynamics of masquing itself, orchestrated so brilliantly by the young Milton, where the boundaries between fiction and social reality blur. The author of *Comus* is in many ways perfectly at home in the sophisticated world of aristocratic culture and art—daring to flaunt its dramatic rules, while experimenting with the conventions of its principal genre.[20]

The more iconoclastic passages aimed at the politics of revelry and Cavalier intemperance, however, suggest the young Milton's ambivalent impulses—between his aesthetic pleasure and accomplishment in writing for a significant royal occasion and his suspicion (more evident here than in his ode) of the aristocratic values associated with the world of masquing, luxury, and excess. The Lady's sharp critique of "lewdly-pamper'd Luxury" which "Now heaps upon some few with vast excess" (770–71) does indeed call into question the aristocratic extravagance and ostentation embodied by spectacular court entertainments. That is, after all, the mode of Cavalier life and art the sensual Comus himself promotes, when he urges the Lady not to hoard her beauty but to display it "In courts, at feasts, and high solemnities" (746)—precisely what she is doing at that very moment in the masque.

While it is certainly innovative for Milton to give an aristocratic young woman this forceful speech of social criticism, however, hers is by no means a unique complaint in seventeenth-century court masques. By Milton's time, in fact, it was something of a *topos.* Thus, for example, the puritanical Plutus of Jonson's *Love Restored,* performed at court in 1612, had attacked the conspicuous waste of aristocratic entertainments, when he called them "superfluous excesses," "vanities in these high places," and "the ruin of states," which should be replaced by "more frugal pastimes."[21] The Lady's iconoclastic argument against luxury nonetheless reveals an uneasiness in the young Milton's own social and aesthetic impulses, as his early work celebrates aristocratic ideals and culture, while challenging the extravagant social assumptions which sustain them. The revolutionary writer would later speak with the iconoclastic and fearless voice of the Lady when he scorns the extravagance, theatricalism, and luxury of the Stuart court—"a dissolute and haughtie court," a place, as he puts in *The Readie and Easie Way* (YP VII, p. 425), "of vast expence and luxurie, masks and revels, to the debaushing of our prime gentry both male and female." Similarly, toward the end of the *Second Defense of the English People,* he warns the elite politicians of Cromwell's Protectorate about the dangers of feigning virtue and piety as they slip "into royalist luxury and folly" (*"in regium luxum atque socordiam"*).[22]

Yet we should not overlook what is potentially the most radical idea in the Lady's vehement speech: her critique of luxury among the rich and privileged, and her call for the redispensing of wealth so that "Nature's full blessings would be well dispens't / In unsuperfluous even proportion," giving "a moderate and beseeming share" to "every just man that now pines with want" (768–73). This is a reformist vision that, if it were actually put into practice throughout England, might anticipate the radical egalitarian vision of a group like the Diggers, who in the revolutionary years imagined making "the Earth . . . a common Treasury for all to live comfortably upon."[23] Such a vision was based on a system of social and economic equality among the people, as opposed to a political system supported by "kingly power" that protects the privileges and riches of "some few." Yet the Lady's potentially radical vision and critique, however forcefully and passionately conveyed here, is in fact promoted specifically neither in the Ludlow masque (where the Lady also shows disdain for the

behavior of "the loose unletter'd Hinds" [174]), nor in Milton's subsequent revolutionary polemics—where, even as he attacks forms of kingly
power, the controversialist often shows great disdain for the politics of
"the Common sort" (*Eikonoklastes,* YP III, p. 339).[24]

The revolutionary Milton believed instead that political authority and
power should be placed in the hands of a "mild Aristocracy of elective
Dukes," as he put it in his first polemical tract (YP I, p. 575)—a meritorious aristocracy, but a political elite nonetheless. Though performed for a
royalist occasion and well before Milton's revolutionary writings, *Comus*
is itself about the education of that aristocracy—those "fair offspring nurs't
in Princely lore" (34)—who will govern a reformed and purified nation (a
theme highlighted by the restorative Sabrina's association with mythic
British history [824–32, 922–23]), as they resist the debilitating powers of
Circean arts. In that sense Milton's early aristocratic work, without yet
being a consistent expression of his radical politics, looks ahead to that
mixture of aristocratic and reformist political vision that will inform his
revolutionary writings. In the middle of his *Apology for Smectymnuus*
(1642), for example, the polemicist would praise the members of Parliament as "being either of ancient and high Nobility or at least of knowne
and well reputed ancestry . . . a great advantage towards vertue one way"
in the same breath that he would deplore a life of "welth, ease, and
flattery" with its "temptation of riches, high birth, and that usuall bringing
up"—all of which is "too remisse" and "as much a hindrance another way"
(YP I, p. 923). This anxiety about the politics of "high Nobility," with all its
temptations, is already present and fully articulated in Milton's masque.
Moreover, while his early social criticism would find further expression in
his controversial polemics, his aristocratic ideals of power, governance,
and authority would also carry over into the revolutionary writings. And
this, I think, complicates a view of the young Milton consistently radical
in his social and political impulses, and on a steady course toward revolutionary engagement.

Indeed, it complicates our image of the older, politically-engaged
Milton as well. For as Milton became more fervently committed to revolutionary ideals, he also kept, though in a modified form, some of the more
aristocratic social allegiances registered in his early writings. Wilding has
recently complained about the "image of the elitist Milton."[25] Yet neither
Comus nor the most radical of Milton's polemics—where Milton virulently
attacks the theatricality and extravagance of Stuart court culture, while
simultaneously spurning the aesthetic and political sentiments of "the
blockish vulgar" and the "Image-doting rabble" (YP III, pp. 339, 601)—will
support a view of an apocalyptic revolutionary who does not also possess

deeply felt elitist ideals. We need to explore further the politics of Milton's early writings, including the controversial issue of his early radicalism. Yet as we do so, we need also to confront certain dissimilitudes within Milton's political ideals—those incongruous, sometimes contradictory social impulses—registered not only in the poems of his youth, but also in the passionate and engaged writings of his revolutionary years.

University of Wisconsin

NOTES

All references to Milton's poetry are taken from *John Milton: Complete Poems and Major Prose*, ed. Merritt Y. Hughes (Indianapolis, 1957); references to Milton's prose are taken from the *Complete Prose Works of John Milton*, 8 vols., ed. Don M. Wolfe et al. (New Haven, 1953–82), and references will appear in the text as YP followed by volume and page number.

1. On the intersection of formal and historical concerns in new historical studies in the Renaissance, see Louis A. Montrose, "Professing the Renaissance: The Poetics and Politics of Culture," in *The New Historicism*, ed. H. Aram Veeser (New York, 1989), p. 17.

2. See, for example David Norbrook, *Poetry and Politics in the English Renaissance* (London, 1984), pp. 235–85; Leah S. Marcus, *The Politics of Mirth: Jonson, Herrick, Milton, Marvell, and the Defense of Old Holiday Pastimes* (Chicago, 1986), ch. 6; Michael Wilding, *Dragons Teeth: Literature in the English Revolution* (Oxford, 1987), esp. ch. 2. Marcus expands her impressive contextual argument about *Comus* as an anti-Laudian masque in "The Earl of Bridgewater's Legal Life: Toward a Political Reading of *Comus*," *MQ* 21 (1987), 13–23. She observes that "there is an elemental radicalism about the work, despite the state occasion for which it was composed" (14).

3. Wilding, *Dragons Teeth*, p. 27; Terry Eagleton, "Preface" to Catherine Belsey, *John Milton: Language, Genre, Power* (Oxford, 1988), p. viii.

4. Since writing the original version of this paper (delivered at the Southwest Regional Conference of the Renaissance Conference of Southern California, in April 1989), I have seen Annabel Patterson's astute essay, " 'Forc'd Fingers': Milton's Early Poems and Ideological Constraint," in *"The Muses Common-weale": Poetry and Politics in the Seventeenth Century* (New York, 1988), pp. 9–22. Patterson detects internal stress and ideological contradiction in the early poems, including *L'Allegro*, which she analyzes in terms of the way Milton aestheticizes the ideology of work and recreation. Though we begin with different texts and often focus on different details, we reach similar conclusions about "conflicts in Milton himself" (12).

5. Among the most impressive accounts to date are Norbrook's in *Poetry and Politics in the English Renaissance* and Patterson's recent essay cited in note 4.

6. Wilding in fact acknowledges that the 1645 volume "may have expressed contradictions within Milton's own political thinking" (p. 9; cf. p. 3); but his discussion of Milton's early career downplays contradictions in order to highlight the consistency of the poet's emerging radicalism.

7. Cf. Norbrook, pp. 17, 283.

8. William Lamont, *Godly Rule: Politics and Religion, 1603– 1660* (London, 1969), pp. 33, 35, 48.

9. See Joseph Mede, *The Key of the Revelation*, trans. Richard More (London, 1643).

10. See Stephen Orgel and Roy Strong, *Inigo Jones: The Theatre of the Stuart Court*, 2 vols. (Berkeley and Los Angeles, 1973).

11. He resisted the siege of his stronghold, Basing House, from August 1643 to 16 October 1645; see William Riley Parker, *Milton: A Biography* (Oxford, 1968), 2:768.

12. Thomas N. Corns, "Milton's Quest for Respectability," *MLR* 77 (1982), 769–79; and "Ideology in the *Poemata* (1645)," in *Milton Studies* XIX, ed. James A. Freeman and Anthony Low (Pittsburgh, 1984), pp. 195–203. See also John K. Hale, "Milton's Self-Presentation in *Poems . . . 1645*," *MQ* 25 (1991, 37–48).

13. See Michel Foucault, *The Archeology of Knowledge*, trans. A. M. Sheridan Smith (New York, 1972), pp. 149–56; cf. pp. 160, 169.

14. See Conrad Russell, *The Crisis of Parliaments: English History, 1509–1660* (London, 1971), p. 178; and Derek Hirst, *Authority and Conflict: England, 1603–1658* (London, 1986), pp. 163–64.

15. The performance of masques was even revived during Cromwell's Protectorate; James Shirley's *Cupid and Death* (1653) is one example. See David Norbrook, "The Reformation of the Masque," in *The Court Masque*, ed. David Lindley (Manchester, 1984), p. 106, on masques in the 1650s.

16. Barry Coward, "Was there an English Revolution in the Middle of the Seventeenth Century?" in *Politics and People in Revolutionary England: Essays in Honour of Ivan Roots*, ed. Colin Jones, Maylin Newitt, and Stephen Roberts (Oxford, 1986), p. 16.

17. The masque's "idealistically reformist spirit" has been explored at length in Cedric C. Brown, *Milton's Aristocratic Entertainments* (Cambridge, 1985), p. 2 and *passim*.

18. See, in addition to the studies mentioned in note 2, David Norbrook, "The Reformation of the Masque"; and Maryann Cale McGuire, *Milton's Puritan Masque* (Athens, Ga. 1983), on *Comus* as an example of reformed recreation.

19. See Norbrook, *Poetry and Politics in the English Renaissance*, p. 258, who makes a comparison with the "consciously anti-theatrical" *Samson Agonistes*.

20. Here and elsewhere in this essay I have expanded a number of points made in my review of Brown's *Aristocratic Entertainments*, in *Seventeenth-Century News* 44 (1986), 33–34.

21. Stephen Orgel, ed., *The Complete Masques* (New Haven, 1969), p. 192; see also Orgel's note to this passage on p. 483. Cf. Brown, who suggests that the Lady's critique is "unique in the masque of the period" (*Milton's Aristocratic Entertainments*, p. 92).

22. *The Works of John Milton*, 18 vols., ed. Frank Allen Patterson et al. (New York, 1931–38), vol. VIII, pp. 242–44.

23. Gerrard Winstanley, *The Works of Gerrard Winstanley*, ed. George H. Sabine (New York, 1941), p. 253; cf. pp. 305, 419, 573.

24. Nevertheless, it may be worth mentioning that, in his marginalia on William Browne's *Britannia's Pastorals* (1613–16), Milton does at one point note that the "Poor labour to feed the luxury of the rich" (*The Works of John Milton*, vol. XVIII, p. 339).

25. Wilding, *Dragons Teeth*, p. 20. Yet even Hill acknowledges this dimension of Milton's writings, noting that Milton never resolved a number of "his tensions"—including the tension between "radicalism and elitism" (*Milton and the English Revolution* [1977; rpt. Harmondsworth, 1979], p. 464).

KINGLY STATES:
THE POLITICS IN *PARADISE LOST*

Stephen M. Buhler

S EVERAL RECENT STUDIES have affirmed yet once more the
political messages and significances in *Paradise Lost*. This reaffirmation enables us to see closer connections not only between the productions of Milton's left and right hands, but also between his religious
thought and political theories. Milton's conviction that no one could "wish
to dominate and remain a Christian" (YP IV, p. 379)[1] is clear in many of his
prose works, but it finds its most dramatic expression in the different
versions of dominion which respond to the Son's version of kingship in
Paradise Lost. Fallen approaches to rule ignore the crucial importance of
service in any authority, an importance Milton developed from scripture,
promoted in the tracts, and considers at length in his epic reworking of
scriptural accounts of sacred history.

In her examination of "The Politics of *Paradise Lost*," Mary Ann
Radzinowicz rightly stresses the role of merit both in Milton's political
thought and in his poetic account of the divine kingdom.[2] Throughout his
works, Milton argues that meritocracy is the form of government most in
accord with divine precept and with natural law. One of Milton's earliest
applications of this belief can be found in *Tetrachordon*, where he considers the possibility that a wife might "exceed her husband in prudence and
dexterity"; in such cases, Milton argues, the husband should "contentedly
yeeld" to her decisions, since "a superior and more naturall law" dictates
"that the wiser should govern the lesse wise" (YP II, p. 589). In a similar
vein, the *Second Defence* of a decade later contains the assertion that
there is "nothing in human society more pleasing to God, or more agree-
able to reason, nothing in the state more just, nothing more expedient,
than the rule of the man most fit to rule" (YP IV, pp. 671–72).

It is not surprising, then, that the Son's kingship is a matter of "Merit
more than Birthright" (*PL* III, 309).[3] But the basis of this merit—how
Messiah "earns" his throne, how his authority is justified by Milton—
deserves closer examination: his meritoriousness, his goodness, is made
clear in his loving service of fallen humankind. Satan's reaction to the

49

Son's rule, in contrast, is a rejection of precisely such service; when Satan justifies his rebellion by insisting that angels were "ordain'd to govern, not to serve" (V, 802), he makes what is clearly presented as a false distinction throughout *Paradise Lost*. For the Son, and for all true rulers, governing and serving are one and the same.

The exaltation of the Son in Book III, in fact, makes this identity explicit: the Son will become man, will suffer and die, in order "to save / A world from utter loss" (III, 307–08). Willing self-sacrifice is the cornerstone of the Son's monarchy; it is through the Passion, the Father tells him, that Messiah has been

> Found worthiest to be so by being Good,
> Far more than Great or High; because in thee
> Love hath abounded more than Glory abounds,
> Therefore thy Humiliation shall exalt
> With thee thy Manhood also to this Throne.   (III, 310–14)

It is the "Humiliation"—the humbling oneself, the self-sacrifice, the service—which constitutes not only the authority of this throne but all true authority.[4] The confused, jarring resonances which the term *service* can carry are present in Milton's usage throughout *Paradise Lost*, but the model of governance which is consistently celebrated by Milton incorporates the "humiliating" as well as the ennobling aspects of the Son's ministry, his serving others.

Milton considers human government to have at least the potential to follow the Son's example here; in *The Readie and Easie Way* he asserts that one can find no "government [which] coms neerer to this precept of Christ, then a free Commonwealth; wherin they who are greatest, are perpetual servants and drudges to the public at thir own cost and charges, [and] neglect thir own affairs" (YP VII, p. 425). Here, the "greatest" have their greatness confirmed in their disregard for personal gain and glory, in their dedication to self-sacrifice, in their willingness to take on the duties and the drudgeries of service.

In *The Readie and Easie Way*, Milton cites Luke, chapter xxii, in support of this idea, as he does in the first *Defence* (YP IV, p. 378). In the earlier work, though, he finds and uses an additional source from scripture, Matthew, chapter xx, for his view of the Son's reign and all legitimate governance:

Jesus called them unto him, and said, "Ye know that the princes of the Gentiles exercise dominion over them, and they that are great exercise authority upon them. But it shall not be so among you: but whosoever will be great among you, let him be your minister; And whosoever will be chief among you, let him be your servant: Even as the Son of man came not to be ministered unto, but to minister, and to give his life a ransom for many." (Matt. xx, 25–28)[5]

This message comes in immediate response to an outbreak of jealousy and resentment among the apostles over a question of status: who would sit at Christ's right and left hands when he established his kingdom? The Lord's reply makes it clear that such concern with rank, and with the conventional trappings and workings of power, is meaningless in his kingdom: to exercise authority as Christ does requires that one follow his example of service and perhaps that one "drink of the cup" (22) of his Passion and sacrifice.

In *Paradise Lost*, Milton suggests that angels may need instruction as much as apostles do. When, in Book VI, the faithful Abdiel confronts Satan on the field of battle, the two combatants ceremoniously accuse each other of political ignorance; in so doing, they reveal the limits of their respective understandings. Before he delivers the first blow of the battle on the plains of heaven, Abdiel rebuts Satan's characterization of the fight as being waged between "Servility"—God's way—and "freedom"—the way followed by Satan's synod:

> Unjustly thou deprav'st it with the name
> Of *Servitude* to serve whom God ordains,
> Or Nature; God and Nature bid the same,
> When he who rules is worthiest, and excels
> Them whom he governs. This is servitude,
> To serve th' unwise, or him who hath rebell'd
> Against his worthier. (VI, 174–80)

Abdiel then announces his intention of sending the Adversary off to "Reign . . . in Hell," choosing himself, as he has at the conclusion of the preceding book, to "serve / In Heav'n God ever blest" (VI, 183–184).

We will return to the distinction between *service* and *servitude* drawn by Abdiel, whose name, of course, means "servant of God." First, though, we should consider the immediate effects of the utterances and actions which are based upon—perhaps motivated by—that distinction. In our experience of the poem, Abdiel's resolve to serve steals a considerable portion of Satan's thunder, since it reveals that one of Satan's most resonant rallying cries is simply a formulaic reversal—or "depraving"—of this speech of Abdiel's. Satan, though, survives the blow that is delivered following the speech: Abdiel's "noble stroke" drives him back "ten paces huge" and down upon one knee, but Satan rebounds from this rather literal setback and from all other mischances in his battle with the angels. Only the intervention of the Son finally prompts Satan and his "timorous flock" to hurl themselves "Down from the verge of Heav'n" (VI, 857, 865).

Satan's temporary recoveries and Abdiel's being denied the victory take place, to an extent, because even the faithful angels have not fully understood the nature of divine rule and its relation to service. Abdiel, along with others of God's faithful remnant, has at this point but a limited understanding of service and rule. In his solitary debate against Satan, Abdiel shows that his awareness of heavenly politics does extend to a recognition of the role of merit in the Son's kingship. When first surrounded by the rebellious angels, he contends that the Son is "by right endu'd / With Regal Sceptre" and "rightful King" (V, 815–816, 818). Here, he implies that the Son deserves to reign, even though the term *right*, at least in fallen history, only infrequently equals *desert*; just before the battle, Abdiel clarifies his position by proclaiming the Son as "worthiest." What calls his comprehension into question is the fact that the reign of the Messiah and his meriting of that sceptre are predicated on a version of the behavior Abdiel dismisses as "*Servitude*": serving the unwise, the rebellious—in a manner which is very different from that which Abdiel rightly refuses—will in fact be the Son's special concern and calling in the Incarnation. There is a different kind of service, an unforeseen dimension to "minist'ring," which will be enacted for the benefit of fallen humankind in all its folly and rebelliousness. Christ "made himself of no reputation, and took upon him the form of a servant," as Paul instructs the Philippians; "he humbled himself" and was exalted in and through that humbling, that humiliation (Phil. ii, 7–9).[6]

So Abdiel does not have the complete answer to Satan's willful rejection of the Son's rule or to his decision to be the first of those who ignore the Father's warning that "him who disobeys / Mee disobeys, breaks union" (*PL* V, 611–12). The obedience which Satan rejects, and which Abdiel cannot fully justify, is adherence to the great commandment the Son delivers in the Gospel of John before embodying it himself: "That ye love one another, as I have loved you. Greater love hath no man than this, that a man lay down his life for his friends" (John xv, 12–13). That self-sacrifice is enacted, in *Paradise Lost,* in the offer which leads to the Son's exaltation, and reenacted in the Passion described in Michael's proto-evangelical account. The instructive power of the Son's offer is seen in Raphael's exchanges with Adam and Eve. Raphael's insight here suggests that after admiration at the Son's self-sacrifice (which had "seiz'd / All Heav'n, what this might mean" [III, 271–72]) comes understanding and consciously chosen attempts at emulation of heaven's king:

> Myself and all th' Angelic Host that stand
> In sight of God enthron'd, our happy state

> Hold, as you yours, while our obedience holds;
> On other surety none; freely we serve,
> Because we freely love, as in our will
> To love or not; in this we stand or fall.   (V, 535–40)

The question of angelic fallibility and limitation might lead us to suspect Raphael's account of things, since not a few angels do indeed fall and the others are initially incapable of articulating why and how one may keep from falling. Raphael, though, *has* learned to articulate how one need not fall: after having been educated himself by the Son's example, loving service provides both the prompting and the message in Raphael's embassy to Eden.

Milton himself marked the lesson well: in his *Commonplace Book*, two of the pages headed "*Rex*" provide evidence demonstrating how inextricably linked kingship and service were in his mind (YP I, pp. 439, 474–75). The first of these entries, page 182, includes a reference to some verses Francesco Berni added in his revision of Matteo Maria Boiardo's *Orlando Innamorato*:

> *Un Re, se vuole il suo debito fare,*
> *Non è Re veramente, ma fattore*
> *Del popolo, che gli è dato a governare,*
> *Per ben del qual l'ha fatto Dio Signore*
> *E non perchè l'attenda a scorticare;*
> *Anzi bisogna che sia servidore*
> *D'ogniuno.*

[A King, if he wishes to do as he should, is truly not a King, but a steward of the people who are given him to govern, for the good of that which the Lord God has made, and not for its exploitation. Rather, it is necessary that he be the servant of all.][7]

After giving the canto and stanza numbers (VII, 3) from Book I, Milton quotes the first two lines verbatim, and concludes with "*del popolo*"; he also adds an "&c." to note the relevance of the remaining lines in the stanza. Berni suggests that the role of the steward-king is divinely sanctioned not only by asserting the ruler's responsibility for preserving the good in God's creation, but also by means of the echo between *fattore* ("steward") and *qual l'ha fatto Dio Signore* ("that which the Lord God has made").[8] Christ's example and injunction are, perhaps, more clearly invoked in the allusion to the *servidore / D'ogniuno* ("the servant of all").

Page 195 in the *Commonplace Book* also refers to the role of service in rule. Milton there summarizes Saint Augustine's conclusion to *De civitate dei* 19.14: "*Si in principatu politico aliqua est servitus*," writes

Milton, "*magis proprie servus est qui praeest, quam qui subest.*" Although the paraphrase's main point ("the ruler, rather than the subject, is more properly a servant") is faithful to the spirit of the original, Augustine's own words have additional application to Milton's works:

Sed in domo iusti viventis ex fide et adhuc ab illa caelesti civitate peregrinantis etiam qui imperant serviunt eis quibus videntur imperare. Neque enim dominandi cupiditate imperant, sed officio consulendi, nec principandi superbia, sed providendi misericordia.

[But in the home of the just man who lives by faith and who is still a pilgrim in exile from the celestial city, even those who give commands serve those whom they seem to command. For they command not through lust for rule but through dutiful concern for others, not with pride in exercising princely rule but with mercy in providing for others.][9]

Milton cites the same passage in the *Defence* (YP IV, p. 419), following Augustine's text much more closely.[10] In addition to this direct reference, Milton's statement earlier in the *Defence* about the enmity between Christianity and the desire for dominance may well be indebted to Augustine's account of the just man not seeking to dominate. Certainly the just man's motives of dutiful concern and merciful providing for others are, in *Paradise Lost*, shown to be derived from Christ's example and presented as hallmarks of his reign.

But such motives and such an *imitatio Christi* are admittedly rare in human history and governance. When Milton does present more familiar patterns of kingship in *Paradise Lost*, Satan rather than the Son is the person and the model involved: regal trappings, ornate pomp, courtly servility, and the illusory glories of conquest have their origins, according to Milton, in the satanic sensibility. Both Christopher Hill and Stevie Davies have noted at length the political significance of Satan's being presented as the one whose state is kingly in the work, and what follows here will necessarily parallel many of their observations.[11] I will focus more specifically, though, on how Satan's actions have, as their basis, his misreading of the meaning and nature of the Son's kingship and therefore of all "true autority" (*PL* IV, 295). From this misapprehension stem both the Primal Sin and the monarchial patterns all too familiar throughout the history of fallen humankind. Rather than follow the true model of kingship provided by the Messiah, human kings have usually followed Satan's lead in confusing tyranny with authority, and in founding monarchial practice upon diabolic principles.

Satan's mistaken response to the Father's speech in Book V has been studied in exegetical terms by Georgia Christopher, who notes that Milton "treats the primal sin as a literary lapse, a misconstruction of a divine text."[12] The text involved is Psalm 2, in which the Lord proclaims his anointed to be his own begotten son. The importance of Satan's misreading is, however, not only literary but political, since the Psalms can provide—especially in the Protestant tradition—lessons in the principles of governance. Psalm 2 opens with stern warnings to the kings and rulers of the earth, and concludes with an account of what will result if they do not "Kiss the Son" and embrace his rule. Any political significances found in the psalm could be further grounded in the Protestant reemphasis on the literal meaning of Scripture, which underscored what were seen as the historical realities David confronted and commemorated in sacred song.

John Calvin's commentaries time and again move from the historical dimension to the christological to the contemporary and political, with the boundaries between these categories virtually disappearing. Discussing Psalm 2, Calvin first establishes a very real political crisis, as we see in Arthur Golding's translation:

We know how many conspired against David, and endeavored to let [i.e., to prevent, hinder] him that he should not reign. . . . not only a small band, but whole nations with their kings conspire[d] against him. . . . Moreover it is uncertain whether he spake only of inward enemies, or whether he extend his complaint to foreigners also. Certainly in as much as enemies rose up against him on all sides . . . I willingly admit that he meaneth them both. [13]

Calvin goes on to apply this situation to Jesus, observing that, "as they had erst done against David," first the Jews and then the Gentiles "began to rage against Christ"; a "like madness" is seen in contemporary circumstances, since "through the default and malice of men . . . the world begin[s] to buskle [i.e., be in commotion] as soon as a throne is a setting up for Christ."[14] As the last excerpt implies and as Calvin's own life and work make explicit, calls for a reformed Church were often linked with a call for reformed government. The Psalms were frequently invoked in this dual project, not only in Calvin's time but during the Puritan Revolution in England.

Calvin weaves together a portrait of the ideal Christian ruler with threads from different psalmic texts. In his commentary on Psalm 110, Calvin notes that the "sacred majesty wherein David excelled" was that "of being the image of God's only begotten son,"[15] and the accuracy of this image in David is proclaimed in the second psalm. By virtue of this Christlike majesty, the psalmist is the medium by which Christ, in Psalm 28,

prescribeth a law to earthly kings by his own example, that they should be so addicted to the public profit, that they should not desire safety [Calvin's French reads *prospérité* here] but for their subjects' sakes. But how far they are from this effect, it booteth not to tell. For being blinded with pride, they despise the rest of the world as much, as though their gloriousness and royalty ought to exempt them from the common state of mankind. And yet it is no marvel that mankind is so proudly and spitefully trodden under foot: considering that for the most part, they take scorn to bear the yoke of Christ.[16]

There is a deft ambiguity here, which can also be found in Calvin's French and Latin versions of the passage: it may be all humankind that "for the most part" scorns the Christian life and therefore deserves subjection, as Milton says in *Paradise Lost*, "to violent Lords" (XII, 93); it may be, as the context would suggest, kings who generally eschew following Christ's example. Whichever group is Calvin's primary target, the Psalms provide not only the materials and the occasions for political commentary, but also a criterion for judging true authority: acting for the good of the people, as did Christ and his type, David.

Such use of the Psalms for political comment and guidance was often extended by the English Puritans, perhaps nowhere as compellingly as in Oliver Cromwell's address to the newly convened Nominated (also known as "Barebones") Parliament. Delivered on 4 July 1653, the speech is filled with psalmic echoes and allusions, drawn especially from Psalm 110; Cromwell clearly saw both David's political realities and his messianic prophecies as being repeated and refulfilled in the events of that summer. As Christopher Hill has observed, the Lord General "regarded the meeting of this assembly as the high point of the Revolution, the moment at which all its contradictions would be resolved."[17] This optimism, often expressed with near-apocalyptic fervor, is found in Cromwell's exhortation to the new members: "Truly you are called by God to rule with Him, and for Him."[18] Further confirmation of Cromwell's hopes for a cessation of internal strife and a turning back of all foreign threats—repeating the crisis and the deliverance described in Psalm 2—might have come from the summer's naval successes against the Dutch; these victories occasioned a call from Parliament that August for a day of "Publique Thanksgiving" to God for the "victory lately vouchsafed to their Fleet at Sea."[19]

Given these contexts, Milton's own verse translation of the psalm from which the investiture speech in *Paradise Lost* is taken lends itself to a highly contemporary and political reading. Michael Fixler has persuasively argued that the 1653 translations of Psalms 1–8 are both celebrations and vindications of "th'assembly of just men" proclaimed in the first psalm and fulfilled, once again, by history in the Parliament which Cromwell had just convened.[20] Milton's version of Psalm 2 is dated 8 August 1653, and his only interpolation, a parenthetical "(though ye rebel)," is, perhaps, less a warning to those within England and without who "Lay deep plots" against the Lord's anointed (Hughes 162) than a touch of biblically sanctioned, derisive satisfaction.

In *Paradise Lost*, Abdiel goes so far as to associate the golden sceptre of the Son's rule with the rod of iron which the anointed one uses, in Psalm 2, to chastise those who plot against him: "That Golden Sceptre which thou didst reject," he warns Satan, "Is now an Iron Rod to bruise and break / Thy disobedience" (*PL* V, 886–88). Beelzebub echoes this distinction and identity during his oration in Pandaemonium,[21] and Milton had used the figure in *Of Reformation* to warn those of the Laudian party who reject "the zealous, and meek censure of the Church" (YP I, p. 605). What inspires such wrath in all these cases is the notion of rule which Milton associates with Satan and the satanic response to the Son's own rule. Satan, in Milton's depiction, has had to develop his own model for authority in order to respond as he does—both as a reader of the divine text and as a rebel against God's anointed.

The interconnections between the exegetical and the political realms can be seen not only in Satan's response but also in the response of readers of the poem who have sympathized with Satan. When William Empson—now sorely missed—characterized Milton's God as "in any case, an authoritarian character,"[22] he provided what may be the clearest exposition we have of what Satan's attitudes actually are toward God, the divine speech, and the Son's rule. When the Father reveals the Son's "vicegerent reign" to the angels, Satan views the event as a power play; such a *fait accompli* is, in Empson's words, "just what one would expect from an usurping angel" (p. 103) rather than from a just and loving deity. As Satan later wonders, in response to the voice from heaven which is heard at Christ's baptism in *Paradise Regained*, "what will he not do to advance his Son?" (I, 88). Empson is, I think, very close to the mark here, since Satan's own rebellion, his actually becoming an "usurping angel," comes as a direct result of the way he interprets the politics of the Father's speech.

While this speech is the occasion for the resultant rebellion, Satan focuses his attentions and energies less on the speaker and more on the subject of the pronouncement, on the object of the speech-act. Satan becomes almost entirely concerned with the Son, and with what he sees as the precedents and policies implicit in the Son's investiture. To Satan, the Son is an usurper; he has been allowed to appropriate a great deal of the angelic order and degree.[23] Satan concludes that such appropriation of office is a given in the political order of things, and thinking himself impaired by this maneuver sets out to reply in kind. The impact of this example on human history is made clearest in the depiction of one of Satan's kingly imitators, Nimrod. In Book XII, Michael foretells how Nimrod "Will arrogate Dominion undeserv'd / Over his brethren" (*PL* XII, 27–28). The satanic origin of Nimrod's policies is suggested in Michael's comment on his name: "from Rebellion [he] shall derive his name, / Though of Rebellion others he accuse" (XII, 36–37). The parallels with Satan's own revolt and with his accusations against Abdiel are unmistakable. Adam bitterly denounces his descendant as an "Usurper" whose "Authority usurpt" unworthily encroaches upon the rights of man and the kingdom of God.

Satan's understanding of his own threatened office, we learn, is based not so much upon action or responsibility as upon title and prestige. As Satan addresses the angels who are to revolt with him, he first invokes their "magnific Titles" and expresses his concern that such offices may be "merely titular" in light of the Son's newly announced status. He assumes that power derives from the title, as we see in his strongest argument against paying "Knee-tribute" to the Son: such "prostration vile" would be an "abuse / Of those Imperial Titles which assert" the angels' authority (V, 782, 800–01). The other fallen angels follow Satan's misreading of the divine state and their own rank, seeing power as something which must be seized and titles as conferring, rather than reflecting, power and responsibility. Beelzebub, too, addresses the fallen angels as "Thrones and Imperial Powers," as "Ethereal Virtues," and urges them to retain "these Titles now" and to refrain from "changing style" (II, 310–12). The style— that is, the name, the title—takes precedent over the reality of their being no longer ethereal virtues, but princes of hell. This last touch may be, among other things, Milton's critique of the "Platonic politics" of the court masque, in which rulers and courtiers portray ethereal virtues, imaginatively embodying them.[24] Milton dismisses such "performance" of virtue, and such identification with it, as purely and perhaps irredeemably nominal.

Concern with the name, not the meaning (to reverse the terms of the Invocation in Book VII), was often ascribed to the Stuart monarchy and its apologists. This accusation was, of course, not entirely unjust; as many have observed, King James, his successor, and their supporters were keenly interested in the titles and forms of royalty—especially upon "the stile of *Gods.*"[25] James himself expresses the notion both in verse and in prose; the phrase appears in the introductory sonnet to *Basilikon Doron*, and its justification can be found in the king's speech to Parliament on 21 March 1609: "Kings are not onely God's Lieutenants upon earth, and sit upon God's throne, but even by God himself they are called Gods."[26]

Calvin had also noted this nominal equation, which is based upon the Lord's addressing "the mighty" in Psalm 82 as "gods" and "children of the most High"; on occasion he even expands on the equivalence, but only in the interest of asserting monarchial power over that of the papacy, and only with the most severe reservations.[27] James, however, feels no such constraint and goes on to compare the authority of earthly kings and the heavenly king in ways which increasing numbers of English citizens thought unequivocally blasphemous. Focusing upon the royal "resemblance of Divine power upon earth," James instructs Parliament in these terms:

[I]f you will consider the Attributes to God, you shall see how they agree in the person of a King. God hath power to create, or destroy, make, or unmake at his pleasure, to give life, or send death, to judge all, and to be judged nor accomptable to none: To raise low things, and to make high things low at his pleasure, and to God are both soule and body due. And the like power have Kings.[28]

The sentiment is similarly expressed more than a generation later in a line from Dryden's *Tyrannic Love:* "Monarchs are the Gods vicegerents."[29] Any notion of service, or even of public welfare or *prospérité*, is notably absent from these accounts, and opponents to the Stuart court would profitably concentrate on this absence. By contrast, even those supporters of Parliament who granted some measure of divine vicegerency to monarchs still perceived strict limitations to monarchial title and claims. Henry Parker, in his *Observations* of 1642, expresses the belief that if we "weigh names and things together," we may "admit that God sheds here *some* rays of majesty upon his vicegerents on earth" (emphasis mine).[30] Parker warns, though, that it would be a mistake to conclude that God "does this out of particular love to Princes themselves, and not to communities of men." If kings "are sanctified with some of God's royaltie . . . it is not for themselves, it is for an extrinsical end, and that is the prosperitie of God's people, and that end is more sacred than the meanes."[31] While conceding the utility (and even the divine instrumentality) of royal titles and degrees, Parker implies that the Stuarts and their followers and apologists have placed an undue emphasis on such titles in and for themselves.

Milton's own sentiments may be deduced from his relegating overconcern with "styles" to the fallen angels and their tyrannical imitators. In Book XI, Michael observes that the first warrior-kings, the giants of Genesis vi, seek "to be styl'd great Conquerors, / Patrons of Mankind, Gods, and Sons of God," despite the fact that they are "rightlier call'd . . . Plagues of men" (*PL* XI, 695–97).[32] In *The Tenure of Kings and Magis-*

trates, Milton had drawn sharp distinctions between noble titles and performances; rulers are to be called by the people "Not to be thir Lords and Masters (though afterward those names in som places were giv'n voluntarily to such as had bin authors of inestimable good to the people) but to be thir Deputies and Commissioners" (YP III, p. 199). For Milton, such titles reward those who have already served the people, and oblige others to engage in true service.

In the satanic perspective, however, kingship depends not so much upon the service provided by the ruler as upon the homage offered by the ruled. Early in Book I, Satan disdains "To bow and sue for grace / With suppliant knee, and deify his power" (*PL* I, 111–12).[33] His use of the verb strongly implies that the heavenly king is made divine *through* such ceremonies; certainly earthly rulers from ancient times to the seventeenth century had endeavored to legitimize their claims to divinity—or their share thereto—by means of display and carefully orchestrated homage. In *The Readie and Easie Way,* Milton focuses on the hollowness of such ceremonious claims: a king "pageant[s] himself up and down in progress among the perpetual bowings and cringings of an abject people, on either side deifying and adoring him *for nothing don that can deserve it*" (YP VII, p. 426; emphasis mine). Perhaps as anxious over their own deserts as they are certain of the "deifying" power of homage, Satan and his followers place strong importance on ceremony and pomp, even though they decry both. Like Satan, Mammon announces his preference for "Hard liberty before the easy yoke / Of servile Pomp" (*PL* II, 256–57), but such distaste is forgotten once Satan successfully guides the council from his "Throne of Royal state" to an ultimate confirmation of his supremacy. When he does so, homage, divinity, and rule are linked: the fallen angels, in tribute to Satan, "bend / With awful reverence prone; and as a God / Extol him" (477–79).

Even in heaven, Satan has shown evidence of his crucial misunderstanding of the difference between service and servility; Gabriel later accuses him of having outwardly "fawn'd, and cring'd, and servilely ador'd / Heav'n's awful Monarch" (IV, 959–60), while inwardly plotting rebellion. This confusion of service and servility, with its concomitant privileging of external form over internal substance, continues when Satan tempts Eve to seek after divinity and rule, to be "A Goddess among Gods," and "Empress of this fair World" (IX, 547, 568): in his opening salutation, Satan "bow'd / His turret Crest, and sleek enamell'd Neck, / Fawning, and lick'd the ground whereon she trod" (IX, 524–26). Milton already, in *The Tenure of Kings and Magistrates,* had associated such idolatrous and duplicitous behavior with the corruption to be found in the Stuart court, where "bad men, as being all naturally servile . . . have been alwayes readiest with the falsifi'd names of *Loyalty*, and *Obedience*, to colour over thir base compliances" (YP III, pp. 190–91).

Indeed, the style—including the manner—of earthly monarchists struck many Puritan thinkers, Milton included, as idolatrous seeking after false gods. In *The Readie and Easie Way*, Milton refers to kingship as "heathenish government" and as *"gentilish* imitation" (YP VII, pp. 424, 429); in Book III of *Paradise Lost* he draws a subtler, but still unmistakable, parallel between fallen monarchy and idolatry. The warrior-kings of Genesis are here the first figures in the series of idolators who are consigned to the Paradise of Fools: having attempted to rival heaven's king, as had Satan, with "many a vain exploit" during their lifetimes, they remain unaware of their folly. They are followed by Nimrod and his crew, who are full of unrepentant hopes of seizing the godlike heights, who "still with vain design / New *Babels* . . . would build" (III, 467–68).

The account of how the fallen angels adopted the various guises of pagan demigods suggests further parallels between many human versions of monarchy and what Milton presents as their diabolic originals. In Book I of *Paradise Lost*, we are told that the gentiles were led astray by the fallen angels into practicing "gay Religions full of Pomp and Gold," and setting up "various Idols through the Heathen World" for the gentiles "to adore for Deities" (I, 372–75). There is, of course, an obvious hint here that Roman Catholicism and the Laudian form of Protestantism associated with the Stuart court are contemporary instances of "Religions full of Pomp and Gold." Milton also links these fallen angels to an insistent concern with the "stile of Gods" as the word *Names* recurs throughout this passage: "Though of thir Names . . . Be no memorial" (361–62); "Nor had they yet . . . Got them new Names" (364–65); "known to men by various Names, / And various Idols" (374–75); "thir Names then known" (376). There is also a more overt extension of such religious idolatry into the political sphere: "First *Moloch*, horrid King" (392), whose name means "king," begins the procession of false gods,[34] and several instances of Israelite apostasy—falling into false worship—are linked to the folly of kings. Solomon ("that uxorious King" [444]) contributed to idolatry by building a temple to Moloch (399–405). In similar fashion, Ahaz ("King" and "sottish Conqueror" [471–72]) paid homage to one of the gods of Syria, and Jeroboam ("the Rebel King" [484]) worshipped the Egyptian deities, the gods who presided over Israel's slavery. There are, in all these epithets, obvious applications to the Stuart kings as Milton saw them.

Finally, as the fallen angels first hold court in Pandaemonium, they are described as "great Seraphic Lords" who "In close recess and secret conclave sat"; we witness the convening of "A thousand Demi-Gods" in something rather less than open parliamentary session (I, 794–96). The political import of this vision for Milton may be suggested by a passage in *The Readie and Easie Way*, which sharply contrasts parliamentary rulers with their monarchial counterparts. Members of Parliament "are not elevated above thir brethren; [they] live soberly in thir families, walk the streets as other men, may be spoken to freely, familiarly, friendly, without adoration. Wheras a king must be ador'd like a Demigod, with a dissolute and haughtie court about him" (YP VII, p. 425).

Some of Milton's vehemence in linking kings and courtiers with demigods may indeed be a reaction against his own earlier dabblings in a poetics which accords with "Platonic politics," since the published fragments of *Arcades* show him surprisingly at home with the formulas he would later charge with idolatry. The Genius of the Wood comes very close to "deifying" Alice Spencer, the Countess Dowager of Derby, in these lines:

> Whate'er the skill of lesser gods can show,
> I will assay, her worth to celebrate,
> And so attend ye toward her glittering state;
> Where ye may all that are of noble stem
> Approach, and kiss her sacred vesture's hem. (78–83)

Quite a shift in attitude is marked by the progression from the Genius's "lesser Gods" to the narrator's and the polemicist's "Demi-Gods," and later to Samson's bitter self-portrait as "a petty God / [Who] walk'd about admir'd of all" (*SA* 529–30).

Like the humane and accessible member of council, and unlike the overceremonious and removed prince (or proud Samson) who affects divinity, are Adam and Eve, the unfallen rulers who enjoy "Dominion giv'n / Over all other Creatures" (*PL* IV, 430–31). In Book V, Milton observes that Adam can confer and receive "honor due" very simply, since

> himself was all his state,
> More solemn than the tedious pomp that waits
> On Princes . . . [with] thir rich Retinue long
> Of Horses led, and Grooms besmear'd with Gold. (353–56)

There is clear disapproval in the way in which "other Creatures" take precedence over man in this kind of procession, as well as a deft polemic touch in capturing the defilement at work in wearing even the most gorgeous of liveries. There is also a rather rueful note in the subsequent line, which acknowledges the perennial allure of such pomp and spectacle: the sight "Dazzles the crowd, and sets them all agape." In Milton's telling, our first parents were the first to switch allegiance to the satanic— the courtly—version of authority, and their susceptibility to its allure persists in their offspring.[35]

Perhaps the greatest danger lies in preferring show to substance, in making hypocrisy not just possible but inevitable, in considering (as in Parker's formulation) the means of governance to be more sacred than the ends. After all, Satan does appear, at times, to conform with aspects of the messianic model for rule—a reign based upon self-sacrifice. He does take on the "hazard more" of journeying to the newly created world. Milton's narrator makes explicit the partial, if abortive, virtue involved in Satan's volunteering: "for the general safety he despis'd / His own" (*PL* II, 481– 82). Along with the clear irony here—"general safety" is by no means the purpose of this expedition—Milton may also be conceding (or exploiting) the undeniable appeal a note of self-sacrifice has, even in considering a fallen monarch. We may well see here a reference to the last days of Charles, whose example "bad men" could use to "boast / Thir specious deeds on earth, which glory excites, / Or close ambition varnisht o'er with zeal" (483–85).

That Satan's deeds are specious—that his hazarding cannot be equated with the meritorious kind typified by the good shepherd who "giveth his life for the sheep"—can be found in the ultimate aims of the sacrifice. In opposition to the renewal sought by the Son, Satan and his legions seek "with Hell fire / To waste [God's] whole Creation, or possess / All as [their] own" (364–66); Satan goes so far as to assure Death, near the end of Book II, that on Earth, after the Fall, he "shall be fed and fill'd / Immeasurably, all things shall be [his] prey" (843–44). Indeed, all of Satan's proposals concerning earth—as they are offered to the council in hell, to Sin and Death, and to Chaos, as well—smack of imperial expansionism and hegemony. After the Fall, Satan is greeted by Sin as "Monarch" (X, 375); his victory speech follows in the same vein, proclaiming that he has "made one Realm / Hell and this World, one Realm" (391–92), as he extends "Th' Infernal Empire" (389). More immediately, Satan's aims and ends involve the corruption of Adam and Eve: vainglory, deceit, distrust, enmity, and despair are among the first fruits of Satan's hazarding and conquest, and they result from Adam's and Eve's emulation of Satan's self-serving sacrifice. Eve insists to Adam that "for thee / Chiefly I sought" godhead in eating the fruit (IX, 877–78); Adam decides to hazard death himself rather than risk living without her (908, 959); but their apparent regard for each other soon evaporates in mutual recrimination.

Throughout *The Readie and Easie Way* Milton ascribes corrupting effects to the monarchial patterns followed by humankind. He argues that England has found "kingship by long experience a government unnecessarie, burdensom and dangerous" (YP VII, p. 409); he further warns against any admiration for (or dazzlement by) "Monarchs . . . whose aim is to make the people . . . softest, basest, vitiousest, servilest, easiest to be kept under" (p. 460). The agenda of any such king is, Milton contends, to bring "upon our liberties thraldom, upon our lives destruction" (p. 410)— both ends designed to keep monarchy fixed and in perpetuity.

The notion of a fixed monarchy—of authority which is self-perpetuating rather than predicated upon the good of the people—is at the very heart of Satan's misconception of the Son's reign. As Radzinowicz observes (p. 211), Satan can think of governance only in terms of permanent regimes: at the beginning of the council in Pandaemonium he proclaims that the "fixt Laws of Heav'n / Did first create" him the rightful leader of the angels (*PL* II, 18–19). His self-described "fixt mind" (I, 97) is keenly suspicious of anything that even looks like innovation, as he whispers to Beelzebub his anxiety over what "new Laws" and "new Counsels" will follow in the wake of God's proclaiming "*Messiah* King anointed" (V, 664, 680–81).[36] Readers of *Paradise Lost* can respond to this fear of Satan's with the knowledge that the reign of the Son is not "fixt" at all. Along with the exaltation in service which is granted Messiah in Book III, there is also a promised abdication, despite his being invested with "all Power" that he might "reign for ever" (III, 317–18). As the Almighty tells Messiah, at the creation of new heaven and earth in the fullness of time

> thou thy regal Sceptre shalt lay by,
> For regal Sceptre then no more shall need,
> God shall be All in All. But all ye Gods,
> Adore him, who to compass all this dies.　　　　　(339–42)

As the last two lines, directed toward the assembled angels, suggest, universal godhead and universal sovereignty will make even the true monarchy based on service and self-sacrifice obsolete. A scriptural source for the abdication can be found in Paul's account of how, at the promised end, Christ "shall have delivered up the kingdom to God . . . [and] shall have put down all rule and all authority and power" (1 Cor. xv, 24). In *Paradise Lost*, Milton depicts the Son as something of a cosmic Cincinnatus, responding to his people's needs (in this case, even unto death) and holding office only as long as the need exists. The connection with Cincinnatus is made clearer by the reference in *Paradise Regained* II, 443–46, to the heathens that Christ deems "Worthy of Memorial": the first name in a list which further reveals the indebtedness of Milton's political thought to

Augustine (especially *De civitate dei* V, 18) is *"Quintius,"* one of those who "could do mighty things, and could contemn / Riches though offer'd from the hand of Kings" (448–49). It was the legendary Quintius Cincinnatus who abandoned power after he successfully guided Rome through its crises, and returned to his humble farm.[37] Christ's rejection of wealth, which Satan offers as a means to royal power, in this later poem is consistent with Milton's indictment of most kingly states as diabolic in *Paradise Lost*. The kingship which the Son represents reveals that service, even of "th'unwise, or him who hath rebelled / Against his worthier," consists in response to others' needs. When the disharmonies between God and his Creation, between Reason and Passion, which make governance essential and tyranny inevitable—"Though to the Tyrant thereby no excuse" (XII, 96)—vanish in the final conflagration, the eternal jubilee which results will require neither iron rod, nor even golden sceptre.

If the Primal Sin and the inconclusiveness of the angelic wars in *Paradise Lost* both have bases in a political, as well as a theological, misapprehension, other passages in the poem might also have a stronger political component than might otherwise be apparent. Even if we look at the politically charged language "tropologically"—as, for example, a part of Milton's efforts at theological accommodation—politics provides the terms so used, and a closer understanding of what these terms meant to someone as politically active as Milton must help in clarifying the tropological import. Beyond this, the monarchial and even courtly aspects of Eve's and Adam's temptations and falls suggest their eventual emulation of the Son's self-sacrifice can show a political as well as a moral regeneration. Their repentance has a foundation in Eve's passionate acceptance of Messiah's model of service, which could help further to explain both why, other than biological necessity, the Incarnation should spring from the "Woman's Seed," and why Eve is spared the lessons of male-dominated, tyrant-haunted history.[38]

We should recognize that the rebellion of "Hell's dread Emperor" with his "God-like imitated State" (*PL* II, 510–11) readily and easily reflects on the crimes and excesses of tyrannical "Demi-Gods" whom Milton presents as having plagued mankind throughout history and in his own age. *The Readie and Easie Way*, given its late, even desperate, composition and publication,[39] is especially applicable as a meditation on the nature of rule and specifically on the failures of the good old cause; these failures could well be reflected in the initial inability of the faithful angels to disallow fully the notions of service which fuel the satanic rebellion and tyranny. But whatever political disillusionment Milton may or may not have experienced in the early years of the Restoration, sparks of the old antimonarchial fire illuminate much of *Paradise Lost*. In his epic, Milton illustrates several long-held convictions about what does and does not constitute "true autority in men": even Satan seems to grasp that it is "true filial freedom" (IV, 294), though he cannot acknowledge that such freedom demands willing and sincere imitation of the Son and his approach to service and rule.

University of Nebraska, Lincoln

NOTES

1. In *A Defence of the English People;* see the *Complete Prose Works of John Milton,* 8 vols., ed. Don M. Wolfe et al. (New Haven, 1953–82). References to Milton's prose are from this edition, and subsequent volume and page references will appear in the text as YP. In the Latin of the *Defensio*—"*si plane vult esse dominus, esse simul Christianus non potest*"—Milton directly contrasts the *desire* to be a ruler with the *ability* to be a Christian; see the Columbia Edition (New York, 1931–38), vol. 7, p. 158. I am grateful to Michael Fixler, Christopher Grose, Neil Harris, Michael Lieb, and John Shawcross for timely reminders and to the editors of this volume for many points of argumentation and style.

2. Mary Ann Radzinowicz, "The Politics of *Paradise Lost*" in *The Politics of Discourse,* ed. Kevin Sharpe and Steven Zwicker (Berkeley and Los Angeles, 1987), pp. 210–11.

3. *John Milton: Complete Poems and Major Prose,* ed. Merritt Y. Hughes (New York, 1957). References to Milton's poetry are from this edition.

4. For the theological implications of this passage, see Albert C. Labriola, " 'Thy Humiliation Shall Exalt': The Christology of *Paradise Lost*," in *Milton Studies* XV, ed. James D. Simmonds (Pittsburgh, 1981), esp. pp. 30–33. See also John Steadman, *Milton and the Renaissance Hero* (Oxford, 1967), pp. 144–50.

5. Milton follows Christ's response only through verse 27; he does not, at this point of the *Defence*, want to deal with the question of whether King Charles can be seen as a Christian (or even Christ-like) martyr. All scriptural passages are taken from the Authorized Version.

6. The preceding verse in Philippians also provides another basis for distinguishing Christ's exaltation in humility (and humiliation) from Satan's attempt at exaltation through force: Christ "thought it not robbery to be equal with God" (ii, 6).

7. Francesco Berni, (additions to) Matteo Maria Boiardo, *Orlando innamorato* (Venice, 1545), fol. 27ᵛ. The passage can also be found in the selection from Berni, with commentary, by Severino Ferrari (Florence, 1971), p. 52. The translation here is adapted from that of Ruth Mohl for YP. Mohl has commented on Berni's influence on *Paradise Regained* II, 462–65; see *John Milton and His "Commonplace Book"* (New York, 1969), pp. 193–94.

8. In her translation for the *Complete Prose Works,* Ruth Mohl corrects the rendering in the Columbia Edition (XVIII, pp. 174–75), where *fattore* becomes "one who cheats." While the Columbia version does not accurately translate the actual language of the passage that Milton cites in the *Commonplace Book*—even in contemporary Italian usage, a *fattoria*

is a steward's office—it does give a rough sense of the stanza as a whole. *Scorticare*, in line 5, does suggest cheating or "fleecing" those entrusted to the ruler.

9. I have used William Chase Greene's text and translation in the Loeb edition (London, 1960), vol. 6, pp. 184–87.

10. As he quotes the first of these sentences from *De civitate dei*, Milton deletes the phrase regarding the faithful man's exile from the heavenly city.

11. Christopher Hill, *Milton and the English Revolution* (Harmondsworth, 1979), esp. pp. 365–75; Stevie Davies, *Images of Kingship in "Paradise Lost"* (Columbia, Mo., 1983), esp. pp. 9–50.

12. Georgia Christopher, *Milton and the Science of the Saints* (Princeton, 1982), p. 90.

13. *The Psalmes of David and Others. With M. John Calvin's Commentaries*, trans. Arthur Golding (London, 1571), vol. I, fol. 3^r. I have modernized the spelling and orthography of all excerpts from Golding's translation.

14. Ibid., fol. 3^v.

15. Ibid., vol. II, fol. 133^r.

16. Ibid., vol. I, fol. 105^v. Theodore Beza also presents certain psalms as teaching "Political Doctrine"; see Anthony Gilby's translation of Beza's paraphrases: *The Psalmes of David* (London, 1580), fol. viii^r. One of Beza's selections for this category, Psalm 101, receives a gloss in the Geneva Bible which comments on the frequency of certain vices— slander and pride, especially—among courtiers. "[T]hese vices," the editors note, "are moste pernicious in them that are about Kings"; see *The Bible and Holy Scriptures* (Geneva, 1560), fol. 256^v, reprinted as *The Geneva Bible* (Madison, 1969).

17. Christopher Hill, *God's Englishman* (London, 1970), p. 139.

18. *Writings and Speeches of Oliver Cromwell*, ed. Wilbur Cortez Abbott (Cambridge, Mass., 1945), vol. III, p. 61.

19. *Tudor and Stuart Proclamations*, ed. Robert Steele (Oxford, 1910), no. 3005.

20. Michael Fixler, *Milton and the Kingdoms of God* (Evanston, Ill., 1964), p. 182.

21. In his reference to the king of heaven's "Iron Sceptre" (*PL* II, 327), Beelzebub conflates the two different temporal and interpretative stages Abdiel describes.

22. William Empson, *Milton's God* (Cambridge, 1981), p. 103.

23. For Empson's central claim that Satan legitimately regards God as usurper, see *Milton's God*, pp. 94–97. It is, of course, arguable to what extent Milton intends—or is able— to keep the Father "above" politics. My emphasis here is on the potential significance of the Son's rule as the primary object of Satan's concern, misunderstanding, and resentment.

24. The term "Platonic politics" is used in connection with the court masque by Stephen Orgel and Roy Strong in *Inigo Jones: The Theatre of the Stuart Court* (Berkeley and Los Angeles, 1973), vol. I, pp. 50–52, especially.

25. See, for example, the analysis of Stuart "stiles" by Jonathan Goldberg, *James I and the Politics of Literature* (Baltimore, 1983), pp. 26–54.

26. *Political Works of James I*, ed. Charles Howard McIlwain (Cambridge, Mass., 1918), p. 307. I have modernized the usage of *u* and *v* in excerpts from this edition.

27. See Calvin, *Psalmes*, vol. I, fol. 4^v; vol. II, fol. 133^r; and for the claim that "almost all kings are drunk with their own gloriousness," vol. II, fol. 86^r. In this strategy, Calvin seems close to the English reformer William Tyndale, as described by Stephen Greenblatt; see *Renaissance Self-Fashioning* (Chicago, 1980), pp. 89–93. In the *Defence* Milton attacks the opposition of crown to papal tiara and with it the equation of kings with "gods" (YP IV, p. 481).

28. McIlwain, ed., *Political Works*, pp. 307–08.

29. John Dryden, *Tyrannick Love* III, i, 32 in volume 10 of the University of California Press edition of his *Works* (Berkeley and Los Angeles, 1970). The line, interestingly, is uttered by Placidius (the "quiet man"), the play's heroic lover and eventual tyrannicide.

30. *Tracts on Liberty in the Puritan Revolution*, ed. William Haller (New York, 1934), vol. II, p. 183.

31. Ibid., pp. 183–4.

32. As in the Son's amplification at *Paradise Regained* III, 78–83.

33. Satan here specifically rejects the Father's presaging of Philippians ii, 10, his announcement that to the Son "shall bow / All knees in Heav'n" (*PL* V, 607–8); he may also be recalling the temporary effect of Abdiel's blow.

34. See also the description of "*Moloch* furious King" and his encounter with Gabriel during the War in Heaven (*PL* VI, 353–361).

35. In the *Second Defence*, Milton expresses his disenchantment with the populace's tendency to "set up as gods over it the most impotent of mortals" (YP IV, p. 551).

36. In the "confession" in Book IV, Satan points to an offensive lack of discrimination implicit in the very basis of his own "Power to stand": "Heav'n's free Love dealt equally to all" (*PL* IV, 66, 68).

37. While the index to the Columbia Edition does not acknowledge a single direct reference to Cincinnatus by Milton or by his represented correspondents, David Masson correctly identifies him as the "Quintius" mentioned by Christ in *Paradise Regained*; see the notes to his edition of *The Poetical Works of John Milton* (London, 1890) vol. III, p. 576. Elsewhere, in *Of Prelatical Episcopacy*, Milton depicts Lucius Junius Brutus, the slayer of Tarquin, in terms suggesting strong affinities with Cincinnatus, while also noting different circumstances: "We see the same necessity in state affaires; *Brutus* that expell'd the Kings out of *Rome*, was for the time forc't to be as it were a King himself, till matters were set in order, as in a free Commonwealth" (YP I, p. 640). This early (1641) admission of what "Necessity" sometimes requires suggests that Milton might have been predisposed to increasing autocracy. We do find "necessity" later described, in *Paradise Lost*, as "the tyrant's plea" (IV, 394), but this is an abuse that may or may not, in Milton's view, take away the use.

38. In discussing Eve's repentance and her visionary lesson, Diane Kelsey McColley provides a useful overview of opinions relating Eve's subordination to Adam with Messiah's to the Father, tracing the tradition back to Chrysostom's commentary on the Pauline view of marriage as expressed in 1 Corinthians xi. See *Milton's Eve* (Urbana, Ill., 1983), pp. 209–16.

39. Beyond the escape and recapture of John Lambert and other immediate circumstances of the impending Restoration, a Royal Proclamation of 13 Aug. 1660 suppressed the first *Defence* and *Eikonoklastes*, ordering all copies to be "publicly burnt by the common hangman" (*Tudor and Stuart Proclamations*, no. 3239). The revised edition of *The Readie and Easie Way* predates this edict by only four months.

"AMONG UNEQUALS WHAT SOCIETY?":
STRATEGIC COURTESY AND
CHRISTIAN HUMILITY IN *PARADISE LOST*

Michael C. Schoenfeldt

Evil communications corrupt good manners.
—*1 Corinthians xv, 33*

IN HIS CRITIQUE OF *Paradise Lost*, Samuel Johnson complains that the "plan" of the epic "comprises neither human actions nor human manners. The man and woman who act and suffer, are in a state which no other man or woman can ever know." Consequently, argues Dr. Johnson, "the reader finds no transaction in which he [sic] can be engaged; beholds no condition in which he can by any effort of imagination place himself."[1] This is, I think, one of the rare moments when Dr. Johnson is absolutely wrong, for Milton regularly diffracts the experience of *Paradise Lost* through the prism of human manners. The rebellion of the fallen angels, for example, begins as a rejection of the courtly system of deference, gratitude, and praise operative in heaven—what Satan terms "knee-tribute" and "prostration vile" (V, 782).[2] Likewise, the various dialogues among unequals participate profoundly in the familiar rituals of human etiquette. The Fall, furthermore, is registered most intensely at the beginning of Book IX as a loss of familiar courtesy with heavenly beings. In turn, it is a particular kind of reformed courtly behavior—prostration before authority—which enables the reconciliation of Adam and Eve, and humans and God, to occur. Milton's universe may indeed be, as Raphael tells Adam, ultimately inscrutable, but it is also deeply stratified. The angels march under banners that "for distinction serve / Of Hierarchies, of Orders, and Degrees" (V, 590–91). Throughout *Paradise Lost*, manners synchronize moral and political status: in the heavens, "the vulgar Constellations thick, . . . from [God's] Lordly eye keep distance due" (III, 577–78), while at the other end of the cosmological and political hierarchy, the birds and beasts "pay" Adam "fealty / With low subjection . . . cow'ring low / With blandishment" (VIII, 344–45, 350–51). Vigorously suspicious of earthly hierarchies and the deferential conduct they enjoin, Milton nevertheless endows his representation of the Fall with the engaging transactions of human manners.

Milton's attitude to hierarchical behavior in *Paradise Lost* bears a curious and complicated relationship to his frequent repudiation in the controversial prose of liturgical and political systems which demand obsequious conduct. In *Of Reformation* (1641), for example, Milton's first major prose tract, he complains that the prelates err in approaching God with "servile and thral-like fear, . . . cloak[ing] . . . their Servile crouching to all *Religious* Presentments . . . under the name of *humility*."3 Likewise, Milton's final work of explicit political controversy, *The Ready and Easy Way* (1660), laments the same gestures when used in a political rather than religious realm, where

a king must be adored like a demigod, with a dissolute and haughtie court about him, of vast expense and luxury, masks and revels, to the debauching of our prime gentry, both male and female; not in their pastimes only, but in earnest, by the loose employments of court service, which will be then thought honorable. . . .

[He will] set a pompous face upon the superficial actings of state, to pageant himself up and down in progress among the perpetual bowings and cringings of an abject people, on either side deifying and adoring him, for nothing done that can deserve it. (Hughes, p. 885)

Milton unequivocally repudiates both Anglican worship and monarchical rule because of the cringing conduct and crouching postures they demand. He recasts the liturgy of deference imbuing church and state as a despotic formation demanding unjust subjection.

Sounding oddly and uneasily like the revolutionary Milton, Satan and the fallen angels abjure a system of political and religious worship exacting deference, and reproduce in their censure of heaven the terms of Milton's attacks on the fawning court of Charles I and the obsequious ceremonies of conformist worship. In his first speech in the epic, Satan repudiates the mollifying gestures of submission and obeisance that the heavenly monarch they have just rebelled against would demand as the terms of reconciliation:

> To bow and sue for grace
> With suppliant knee, and deify his power
> Who from the terror of this Arm so late
> Doubted his Empire, that were low indeed,
> That were an ignominy and shame beneath
> This downfall. (*PL* I, 111–16)

In the same vein, Mammon, when contemplating the possibility that God might issue something like the "Act of free and general pardon, indemnity and oblivion"⁴ that Charles II did in 1660, asks:

> Suppose he should relent
> And publish Grace to all, on promise made
> Of new Subjection; with what eyes could we
> Stand in his presence humble, and receive
> Strict Laws impos'd, to celebrate his Throne
> With warbl'd Hymns, and to his Godhead sing
> Forc't Halleluiahs; while he Lordly sits
> Our envied Sovran,
>   . . . .
>   how wearisome
> Eternity so spent in worship paid
> To whom we hate.   (II, 237–49)

For both Satan and Mammon, the revolt in heaven rebuffs a code of submissive behavior resembling that required in Renaissance courts and English churches.

Yet the bitter ironies suffusing Satan's term for submissive action towards God—"deify"—and Mammon's adverb for God's behavior— "lordly"—are confounded by the revelation of how the fallen angels physically "lie / Groveling and prostrate" even as they utter their renunciation of heavenly servility (I, 279–80). The angels have assumed the very "abject posture" they purport to reject, reclining "Prone on the Flood" as they renounce deferential conduct (322, 195). The ironies multiply ever further, moreover, as the fallen angels proceed to practice towards Satan just the kind of adulation that they refused to perform in heaven:

> Towards him they bend
> With awful reverence prone; and as a God
> Extol him equal to the highest in Heav'n.   (II, 477–79)

Satan, as Mary Ann Radzinowicz has recently argued, "usurps the language of freedom to servile cause."⁵ For Satan, perhaps, it is more liberating "to reign in Hell, than [to] serve in Heav'n" (I, 263). But the deification of Satan in hell certainly discredits both Satan's heroic refusal to "deify [God's] power" and Mammon's revolutionary claim to prefer the "hard liberty" of hell "before the easy yoke / Of servile Pomp" (II, 256–57).

Although these rampant ironies deflate the frequent pretensions to liberty on the part of the fallen angels, they do not fully assuage the anxiety generated by the proximity between Milton and Satan as revolutionary propagandists. Rather, this proximity invests Satan's rhetoric and cause with a political urgency and topical referentiality which invigorates Milton's characterization of rebellion, and which has led many readers to feel, in the words of William Blake, that Milton "was a true Poet and of the Devil's party without knowing it."[6] I do not think that Milton was of the Devil's party, even subconsciously; but he does give the Devil some of his own best arguments, and in the process compels his readers to experience the powerful attractions of revolutionary eloquence. As Stanley Fish asserts, "By first 'intangling' us in the folds of Satan's rhetoric, and then 'informing us better' in 'due season,' Milton forces us to acknowledge the *personal* relevance of the archfiend's existence."[7] I would argue that Milton urges us to acknowledge not only the *personal* relevance but also the *political* relevance of Satan's existence by folding into Satan's language Milton's own revolutionary convictions. In so doing, he entangles his audience and theology in the political upheavals of seventeenth-century England. "Milton's experience of propaganda," observes William Empson, "is what makes his later poetry so very dramatic; that is, though he is a furious partisan, he can always imagine with all its force exactly what the reply of the opponent would be."[8] Milton turns both the deepest conviction, and the bitterest sarcasm, on positions resembling those in which he had invested much of his life. Only in Book XII, after we have been made to feel the full force of Satan's rebellion, are we told explicitly that Satan, like the Stuart kings, is an "execrable Son so to aspire / Above his Brethren, to himself assuming / Authority usurpt, from God not giv'n" (64–66).[9]

Yet as Satan's rhetoric of rebellion is uncomfortably alluring, however undeserved the authority he derives from it, so is his account of heavenly behavior distressingly corroborated by the non-Satanic glimpses of heaven we are granted. Satan resents God's introduction of the Son into the court of heaven because this upstart will require "Knee-tribute yet unpaid, prostration vile, / Too much to one, but double how endur'd" (V, 782–83). God indeed announces the elevation of the Son by stressing the angels' need to advertise their subordination to him through just such venerative postures:

> your Head I him appoint;
> And by my Self have sworn to him shall bow
> All knees in Heav'n, and shall confess him Lord.   (606–08)

He declares, moreover, the terrifying consequences of disobeying this new court favorite:

> him who disobeys
> Mee disobeys, breaks union, and that day

> Cast out from God and blessed vision, falls
> Into utter darkness, deep ingulft, his place
> Ordain'd without redemption, without end. (611–15)

In the opening of *Reason of Church Government* (1642), Milton had indicted those rulers who "set [human laws] barely forth to the people without reason or preface, like a physical prescript, or only with threatenings, as it were a lordly command," for acting "neither generously nor wisely."[10] The arbitrary and imperious nature of the promotion of the Son—announced long before he will prove himself worthy of such exaltation by means of his willing humiliation—seems to call for such censure, and so to justify, at least in part, the ways of Satan to men and women of Parliamentarian conviction.

Satan's refusal to "bend / The supple knee" before this figure who "hath to himself ingross't / All Power, and us eclipst under the name / Of King anointed" (V, 787–88; 775–77), then, can be mapped onto Milton's own revolutionary aspirations. Indeed, Satan's account of heavenly existence continually returns to those gestures of submission and gratitude that Milton found so distasteful:

> I sdein'd subjection, and thought one step higher
> Would set me highest, and in a moment quit
> The debt immense of endless gratitude,
> So burdensome, still paying, still to owe. (IV, 50–53)

The lines contain at once a blind ambition we are meant to censure and a heroic fortitude we cannot help but admire. Yet they also describe accurately, in striking if partisan terms, the heaven we view, where

> lowly reverent
> Towards either Throne [angels] bow, and to the ground
> With solemn adoration down they cast
> Thir Crowns. (III, 349–52)

Even Satan's "God-like imitated State" (II, 511)—he copies God's throne as well as his mode of address—not only announces the deific ambitions lurking behind Satan's libertarian rhetoric but also whispers the political subjugation for which heaven can serve as a model.

Milton's portrait of the Father, then, is likely to reinforce rather than extinguish our sympathy for the Devil. As Anthony Low concedes in an essay largely intended as theodicy, "Even Milton's most sympathetic defenders have been somewhat uncomfortable about his characterization of the Father."[11] One of the reasons for this is, as Low astutely observes, that his "tone is stern, powerful, absolutely without humility or any of the formulae of self-deprecation that normally accompany human speech" (p. 25). But where the Father in Book III is almost totally lacking in the common courtesy that lubricates hierarchical relationships, the Son supplies the epitome of such behavior. In response to the Father's stern sentence that the angels "by thir own suggestion fell, / Self-tempted, self-deprav'd: Man falls deceiv'd / By th' other first: Man therefore shall find grace, / The other none" (III, 129–32), the Son praises the Father's mention of grace in order to encourage him to be merciful to mortals:

> O Father, gracious was that word which clos'd
> Thy sovran sentence, that Man should find grace;
> For which both Heav'n and Earth shall high extol
> Thy praises, with th' innumerable sound
> Of Hymns and sacred Songs, wherewith thy Throne
> Encompass'd shall resound thee ever blest. (144–49)

In this deeply courtly situation, the Son lauds the Father for just the trait he is hoping the Father will exhibit, and promises eternal praise when the trait is manifested. He offers, then, what Annabel Patterson in another context terms a kind of "conditional praise," a praise "subject to withdrawal if his advice be not taken."[12] Milton endorses this strategy—the common coin of Renaissance courtiers—in the *Areopagitica* (1644) as a way of dealing with authority while maintaining one's integrity, declaring that "he who freely magnifies what hath been nobly done and fears not to declare as freely what might be done better, gives ye the best covenant of his fidelity. . . . His highest praising is not flattery" (Hughes, p. 718). The Son continues to use God's innate goodness as a tool of persuasion in just this way, asserting that,

> should Man finally be lost, should Man
> Thy creature late so lov'd, thy youngest Son
> Fall circumvented thus by fraud, though join'd
> With his own folly? that be from thee far,
> That far be from thee, Father, who art Judge
> Of all things made, and judgest only right.
> . . . .
> or wilt thou thyself
> Abolish thy Creation, and unmake,
> For him, what for thy glory thou has made?
> So should thy goodness and thy greatness both
> Be question'd and blasphem'd without defense. (PL III, 150–66)

As Michael Lieb argues, this is a profoundly dramatic moment, in which the Son's words serve at once to challenge and to warn.[13] Brilliantly fulfilling the role of "Patron or Intercessor" of humanity, the Son deploys not only the promise of eternal praise but also the threat of perpetual blasphemy to cultivate the Father's mercy. If the Father truly wishes that his "goodness" and his "greatness both" not "Be question'd and blasphem'd without defence," he must, the Son suggests, behave graciously.

Indeed, the Son's willing sacrifice for humanity embodies what his words have already accomplished—mediation between an angry king and his disobedient subjects. By becoming human, moreover, the Son will display the essence of courteous behavior: a kind of gracious condescension to inferiors which ennobles both parties. As God promises the Son,

> Nor shalt thou by descending to assume
> Man's Nature, lessen or degrade thine own.
> . . . .
>   because in thee
> Love hath abounded more than Glory abounds,
> Therefore thy Humiliation shall exalt
> With thee thy Manhood also to this Throne.   (III, 303–14)

The Son's loving sacrifice is the source of his ultimate glory. As Paul writes in Philippians ii, 5–11 (AV), Christ is made absolute king because of his willingness to make "himselfe of no reputation"; by becoming a servant, he is made a monarch. "All Power / I give thee," declares the Father, "reign for ever, and assume / Thy Merits. . . . All knees to thee shall bow, of them that bide / In Heaven, or Earth, or under Earth in Hell" (317–22).

The Son's act of genuinely courteous condescension, then, endows him with just the kind of power, made his by merit, that Satan seeks. Indeed, in one of his more clear-sighted moments, Satan reveals a striking awareness of the manner in which his own experience inverts that of the Son whom he so envies:

> While they adore me on the Throne of Hell,
> With Diadem and Sceptre high advanc'd
> The lower still I fall, only Supreme
> In misery; such joy Ambition finds.   (IV, 89–92)

The meritocracy of hell mirrors in reverse that of heaven; as monarch of the fallen angels, Satan is "by merit rais'd / To that bad eminence" (II, 5–6). His own desire for exaltation results in degradation, just as Christ's willing humiliation provides the occasion for his coronation.

Satan's first words in the epic, addressed to a barely recognizable

Beelzebub, attempt to comprehend the shocking degeneration produced
by the fallen angels' aspirations:

> If thou beest hee; But O how fall'n! how chang'd
> From him, who in the happy Realms of Light
> Cloth'd with transcendent brightness didst outshine
> Myriads though bright.   (I, 84–87)

This change in social and moral status can also be gauged in the various
interactions between Satan and the unfallen angels—those who were formerly his peers or inferiors. When Satan meets Uriel in Book III, he
disguises himself as "a stripling Cherub, . . . Not of the prime," hoping to
hide in the anonymity of a minor angelic functionary (636–37). Nevertheless, as part of his disguise, Satan "to every Limb / Suitable grace diffus'd, so
well he feign'd," unintentionally parodying the theological and social grace
shown by the Son's willing descension of the celestial hierarchy. In his
"impressive capacity to get inside all classes of angelic society," proposes
Robert Hodge, Satan resembles the Son, "since the only other person who
changes status in the poem is Messiah. Messiah changes more completely,
actually becoming Man, where Satan can at best adopt a disguise. So Messiah transcends his class where Satan only briefly takes a holiday from his."[14]

Yet Satan does not so much "take a holiday" from his class as alter it in
order to further his class-conscious ambitions. Satan cleverly flatters Uriel
with a sense of his preeminence, practicing the kind of strategic praise we
have seen the Son exercising on the Father:

> Uriel, for thou of those sev'n Spirits that stand
> In sight of God's high Throne, gloriously bright,
> The first art wont his great authentic will
> Interpreter through highest Heav'n to bring,
> Where all his Sons thy Embassy attend.   (III, 654–58)

At the end of their conversation, we see "Satan bowing low, / As to superior
Spirits is wont in Heav'n, / Where honor due and reverence none neglects"
(736–38). Although the humble disguise does temporarily fool Uriel into
divulging what Satan wants—directions to earth—it also reveals more than
it hides. For Satan, who was formerly "of the first, / If not the first Arch-
Angel, great in Power, / In favor and preëminence," must now bow—
declare physically his inferiority—to his former subordinate (V, 659–61).
Ironically, the gesture he had refused to perform before God is now required by his plotting against God. Even as Satan manipulates the postures
of courtesy to cloak his motives and to further his designs against God,
manners disclose his true place in the political and celestial hierarchy.

Despite this pronounced ability to adopt a strategically submissive posture, Satan chooses to insult Gabriel by suggesting that he and his "gay Legions" would rather bow than fight; the good angels dare not do battle, he claims, because their

> easier business were to serve thir Lord
> High up in Heav'n, with songs to hymn his Throne,
> And practis'd distances to cringe, not fight. (IV, 942–45)

Satan implies that heavenly service is the product not of heroic obedience but rather of servile sloth. Gabriel, however, throws his insults right back at him:

> And thou sly hypocrite, who now wouldst seem
> Patron of liberty, who more than thou
> Once fawn'd, and cring'd, and servilely ador'd
> Heav'n's awful Monarch? wherefore but in hope
> To dispossess him, and thyself to reign? (957–61)

Gabriel sees clearly how Satan uses both the language of liberty and the tactics of courtesy to further his personal ambitions. He suggests, furthermore, that the dissociation between behavior and intention displayed in Satan's strategically submissive encounter with Uriel was already present in Satan's ostensibly prelapsarian gestures of obeisance to God. Rather than distinguishing between cringing servility and defiant rebellion, Gabriel conflates them. Yet he does so in order to establish the crucial distinction between his own sincere service to heavenly authority and the aggressively submissive behavior that Satan had displayed even before the actual rebellion against God.

The rituals of courtesy also supply Satan with a pretext for gathering the rebel forces. Like a good country magnate, Satan proposes that he and his troops haste to his northern estate "to prepare / Fit entertainment to receive our King" who "Intends to pass triumphant" on royal progress (V, 689–90, 693). Satan thus perverts the cultural ideal of household generosity to further his own selfish ends. The subsequent encounters between Abdiel and Satan dramatize the urgency and difficulty of distinguishing between the hospitality of Satan's words and the hostility they mask, between unfeigned humility and strategic submission. Satan tells Abdiel that when his rebel forces attack heaven,

> then thou shalt behold
> Whether by supplication we intend
> Address, and to begirt th' Almighty Throne
> Beseeching or besieging. (866–69)

His sarcastic final pun awakens the antagonistic and supplicatory possibilities of the deferential approach to superior power identified by Gabriel.
During the battle, moreover, he will offer to "entertain" the good angels
"fair with open Front / And Breast, (what could we more?)" while firing a
cannon at them (VI, 611–12). In Satan's highly rhetorical universe, be-
seeching and besieging are as alike in effect as they are in sound.

When Satan and Abdiel subsequently meet on the battlefield, Satan
projects his own aspirations onto Abdiel, accusing him of being "ambitious
to win / From me some Plume"; he attempts, furthermore, to appropriate
for his cause the values of heroic freedom in combat with the slothful and
festive troops of heaven:

> At first I thought that Liberty and Heav'n
> To heav'nly Souls had been all one; but now
> I see that most through sloth had rather serve,
> Minist'ring Spirits, train'd up in Feast and Song;
> Such hast thou arm'd, the Minstrelsy of Heav'n,
> Servility with freedom to contend.   (VI, 160–69)

Satan, in other words, characterizes God's troops as royalist cavaliers,
"debauch[ed]," in the terms of *The Ready and Easy Way*, "by the loose
employments of court service." Abdiel, however, will not allow Satan to
set the terms of the dispute, and redefines the distinctions between servility and service in relation to the merit of one's master:

> Unjustly thou deprav'st it with the name
> Of *Servitude* to serve whom God ordains,
> Or Nature; God and Nature bid the same,
> When he who rules is worthiest, and excels
> Them whom he governs. This is servitude,
> To serve th' unwise, or him who hath rebell'd
> Against his worthier, as thine now serve thee,
> Thyself not free, but to thyself enthrall'd.   (VI, 174–181)

Where in the *Utopia* (1515) Thomas More's Raphael Hythloday had suggested that the difference between service and servitude (Latin *servias*
and *inservias*) "is only a matter of one syllable," for Abdiel and Milton the
difference is not phonetically superficial but morally crucial, depending
upon the caliber of one's superior.[15] Abdiel, whose name means "Servant
of God" (VI, 29), strikes Satan at the end of this speech, driving him back
"on bended knee" (194), and so forcing him to acknowledge via his posture
the servility implicit in his rebellion against the worthy authority of God.

The aggressive potential of superficially submissive demeanor is manifested most clearly in Satan's courtly seduction of Eve. The posture he

adopts in his approach to her parodies the glozing behavior by which Renaissance courtiers capture the attention of their monarch or mistress. Satan is discovered, for example, "Squat like a Toad, close at the ear of *Eve*," literally toadying to a creature who would have been his subordinate.[16] Later in the guise of a serpent, "Oft he bow'd / His turret Crest, and sleek enamell'd Neck, / Fawning, and lick'd the ground whereon she trod" (IX, 524–26). He addresses her as "sovran Mistress," "Empress of this fair World," "Sovran of Creatures," and "Goddess humane," and tells her that she deserves to be "ador'd and serv'd / By Angels numberless" (532, 568, 612, 732, 547–48). Even as he ostensibly submits to her through postures of submission and gestures of praise, Satan acquires a kind of power over Eve. This power is manifested most explicitly in his physically conducting her to the Tree of Knowledge; "Lead then," says Eve to a creature hierarchically inferior to her (631). Satan's aggressive submission and Eve's passive superiority reverse the very hierarchy that the Serpent's adulation purports to advertise.

The politics of this courtly pattern approximate the inversion of earthly hierarchies that Christianity proclaims: "For whosoever exalteth himselfe, shalbe abased; and hee that humbleth himselfe, shalbe exalted" (Luke xiv, 11 [AV]; see also Matt. xxiii, 12 and Luke xviii, 14). Yet the distinction between humbling oneself as a tactic of self-exaltation, and sincere humiliation which results in exaltation, is difficult to sustain. Indeed, the same passage from which the *locus classicus* of Christian humility is taken—the parable of the wedding feast (Luke xiv, 7–14)—is in Castiglione's *Courtier* appropriated as a device for increasing one's status at court:

Yet ought man alwaies to humble him selfe somewhat under his degree, and not receive favor and promotions so easily as they be offered him, but refuse them modestly, shewing he much esteemeth them, and after such a sort, that he may give him an occasion that offereth them, to offer them with a great deale more instance.

Because the more resistance a man maketh in such manner to receive them, the more doth he seeme to the prince that giveth them to be esteemed. . . .

And these are the true and perfect promotions, that make men esteemed of such as see them abroad. . . .

Then said the Lord Cesar Gonzaga, me thinke ye have this clause out of the Gospel, where it is writen: When thou art bid to a mariage, goe and sit thee down in the lowest roome, that when he commeth that bid thee, he may say, Friend come higher, and so it shall bee an honour for thee in the sight of the guestes.[17]

Tactical deployments of deference blend well with Christian gestures of humility; indeed, the latter can give the appearance of a winning piety to cunning applications of the former. As another popular courtesy writer, Stefano Guazzo, asserts, courtiers should behave according to "that *philo-*

sophical and Christian saying, That the more loftie we are placed, the more lowly wee ought to humble our selves: which is in deed, the way to ryse higher" (my emphasis).[18] At once philosophical and Christian, strategic and submissive, humility is the avenue of social and theological aspiration.

Satan's shrewd use of humble demeanor betrays Milton's profound unease with the tactically courteous behavior required by life at court. In fact, his disguises—inferior angel, toad, snake—allow Milton to burlesque the entire courtly project of manipulating humble appearances for self-serving ends. Where the Son condescends to mortal flesh to earn human salvation, Satan descends to "bestial slime" to arrange human damnation (IX, 165). Yet by providing Milton with a conduit for the antiauthoritarian impulses implicit in his deep distrust of ceremonial behavior, Satan makes it possible for Milton to express through the interactions among Adam, Eve, Raphael, the Son, and God an authentic and morally positive mode of courteous conduct. Milton, then, consigns his suspicions about servility and of political systems that demand it onto Satan in order to reinvest hierarchical behavior with social and moral value. Where Castiglione and Guazzo assimilate the moral lessons of the Bible to courtly shrewdness, Milton rehabilitates the patterns of courtesy for the ideals of Christian conduct.

Adam's dealings with his heavenly superiors, for example, embody simultaneously an epitome and a reproof of courtly behavior. When greeting Raphael, he,

> to meet
> His god-like Guest, walks forth, without more train
> Accompanied than with his own complete
> Perfections; in himself was all his state,
> More solemn than the tedious pomp that waits
> On Princes, when thir rich Retinue long
> Of Horses led, and Grooms besmear'd with Gold
> Dazzles the crowd, and sets them all agape.   (V, 350–57)

Adam's "native Honor" and "naked Majesty" (IV, 289–90) implicitly expose the vain pomp and luxury with which Satan, and earthly princes, surround themselves. Adam, moreover, manages in his gestures towards Raphael to acknowledge his own inferiority while avoiding the cringing prostration that Satan deployed towards Uriel, and that Satan and Gabriel accuse each other of practicing:

> *Adam* though not aw'd,
> Yet with submiss approach and reverence meek,
> As to a superior Nature, bowing low.   (V, 358–60)

Raphael's journey to Eden is, as Barbara Lewalski remarks, "a kind of Progress," in which Adam functions "as the lord of one great province welcoming an even more exalted prince."[19] In striking contrast to the hostility masquerading as hospitality by which Satan gathers his troops in the north, Adam praises Raphael for the honor the angel bestows upon him in condescending to visit and sup with his earthly inferior:

> Since by descending from the Thrones above,
> Those happy places thou has deign'd a while
> To want, and honor these, voutsafe with us
> Two only, who yet by sovran gift possess
> This spacious ground, in yonder shady Bow'r
> To rest, and what the Garden choicest bears
> To sit and taste.   (363–69)

The care with which Adam "frame[s]" his "wary speech" to Raphael registers Adam's recognition of the hierarchical distance separating him from Raphael even as the act of sitting and eating together serves to close it. Raphael tells Adam that "Nor less think wee in Heav'n of thee on Earth / Than of our fellow servant" (VIII, 224–25). Raphael's gracious assertion of near equality between angel and human is nevertheless carefully hedged by a reminder of who resides on earth and who in heaven. Heavenly condescension at once traverses and reinforces the hierarchy separating human from angel, human from God.

In contrast to the affable deference with which Adam greets Raphael, his instinctive reaction to the "Presence Divine" just after his creation is to perform a gesture of absolute reverence:

> Rejoicing, but with awe,
> In adoration at his feet I fell
> Submiss: he rear'd me.   (314–16)

Adam's congenital courtesy provides an archetype of behavior among unequals, and presents an emblem in miniature of the story of *Paradise Lost*. Where Adam bows "low . . . though not awed" to Raphael, he *falls* in a gesture of total awe at the feet of his maker. His innate manners, significantly, are calibrated as finely as those of the most fastidious courtier, able to express not only the distance between earthly and heavenly beings but also the differences between angels and God. Yet the gesture advertising the distance between himself and God also provides God with the opportunity and motive for closing that distance: "he reared me." In courtesy as in theology, humiliation sanctions exaltation; falling before power licenses rising.[20]

The conduct of the creator in these scenes is very different from that of the remote, unsociable Father of Book III. God not only lifts his prostrate creature but also will "stoop" to take a rib from Adam to make Eve (VIII, 465).[21] Such gracious condescension encourages Adam to address his Creator with a boldness even he finds surprising. Indeed, as Adam implores this unexpectedly avuncular God to grant him a "consort," he exercises a blend of reverence and presumption which conjoins stooping and rising. His "humble deprecation" properly employs the deferential litotes used to ask favors of superiors: "Let not my words offend thee, Heav'nly Power, / My Maker, be propitious while I speak" (378–80). Yet his words also display a remarkable brazenness to his maker—a brazenness which measures not his inability to accept a position of subordination but rather the familiarity that God allows his creatures to exercise in a prelapsarian world. Like the Serpent approaching Eve, Adam grows "bolder" with his superior (IX, 523, 664); unlike Satan's tactical submission, however, Adam's audacious speech to his maker reinforces rather than threatens the hierarchy separating them: "Thus I embold'n'd spake, and freedom us'd / Permissive, and acceptance found" (VIII, 434–35).

In the midst of this colloquy, moreover, Adam asks God a question which will reverberate throughout Milton's universe: "Among unequals what society / Can sort, what harmony or true delight?" Although answered in part by the remarkably intimate repartee between creature and creator of which it is a segment, the question interrogates the very possibility of social life in a political hierarchy (383–84). Adam insists that social harmony requires greater equality than any of the asymmetrical relationships he knows—with animals and with God—permit; it

> must be mutual, in proportion due
> Giv'n and receiv'd; but in disparity
> The one intense, the other still remiss
> Cannot well suit with either, but soon prove
> Tedious alike.   (385–89)

Adam desires neither a superior nor an inferior—he is already surrounded by both—but an equal. His abiding hunger for what he terms "fellowship," "conversation with his like," "Collateral love, and dearest amity," and "Social communication" (389, 418, 426, 429) suggests an appetite for companionship that neither lower creatures nor an omnipotent God can satisfy. Adam seeks a being equal to him, one with whom he could converse freely, without having to seek the "leave of speech" that even prelapsarian manners demand of discourse with heaven (377).

I have elsewhere explored how God both frustrates and fulfills

Adam's insistent plea for an equal partner. Attention to the political nuances of terrestrial manners, I argue, allows us to calibrate the fluid authority of Adam and Eve's fragile relationship.[22] The Fall is, at least initially, an estrangement of the two central relationships in the epic: between man and woman, and between earth and heaven. The "mutual help / And mutual love" that Adam and Eve enjoy as "the Crown of all our bliss" before the Fall are supplanted by "fruitless hours" of "mutual accusation" after the Fall (IV, 727–28; IX, 1187–88). Moreover, Milton begins his magnificently tragic Book IX not by lamenting the entry of pain, debility, and blindness into the world but by mourning the loss of intimacy with heavenly creatures:

> No more of talk where God or Angel Guest
> With Man, as with his Friend, familiar us'd
> To sit indulgent, and with him partake
> Rural repast, permitting him the while
> Venial discourse unblam'd: I now must change
> Those Notes to Tragic; foul distrust, and breach
> Disloyal on the part of Man, revolt,
> And disobedience: On the part of Heav'n
> Now alienated, distance and distaste,
> Anger and just rebuke.   (1–10)

The action of disobedience—the ultimate statement of disregard for one's place in the hierarchy—displaces the exuberant sociability between humans and heavenly beings that Milton so values. Curiously, the hierarchy can be traversed by boldness and presumption only as long as the obedience that sustains the hierarchy persists. Once that is lost, however, tragic estrangement supersedes pastoral conviviality.[23]

The Fall, therefore, is a social breach whose effects are likewise registered in social terms. Milton carefully records the altered nature of the discourse between humans and God after the Fall. When the Son arrives to judge Adam and Eve, he is greeted not with the fruitful generosity Adam and Eve used to welcome Raphael; rather, they "from his presence hid themselves" (X, 100). The Son immediately acknowledges the lack of accustomed hospitality:

> Where art thou *Adam*, wont with joy to meet
> My coming seen far off? I miss thee here,
> Not pleas'd, thus entertain'd with solitude,
> Where obvious duty erewhile appear'd unsought.   (X, 103–06)

Remarkably, God does not withdraw from humans at the Fall; rather, mortal shame impels Adam and Eve to shrink from the divine presence.

"Entertain'd with solitude" rather than society, the Son nevertheless displays a humility toward his inferiors that is the essence of true courtesy, judging them but also clothing them. He

> disdain'd not to begin
> Thenceforth the form of servant to assume,
> As when he wash'd his servants' feet, so now
> As Father of his Family he clad
> Thir nakedness with Skins of Beasts
> . . . .
> Nor hee thir outward only with the Skins
> Of Beasts, but inward nakedness, much more
> Opprobrious, with his Robe of righteousness,
> Arraying cover'd from his Father's sight.   (213–23)

The *kenosis,* Milton suggests, epitomizes postlapsarian courtesy between heaven and earth. In clothing his subordinates, the Son rehearses the role of servant that he will later assume, and performs a gesture of beneficent condescension like that which will make possible his own, and humanity's, exaltation. He also dramatizes the disjunction between appearance and reality that the Fall inaugurates. As the Son alters his demeanor by assuming the role of a servant, and Satan by becoming a snake, so do Adam and Eve change appearance and roles. Yet the differences among the Son's service to his inferiors, Satan's seduction of humanity, and human shame before God underscore the hierarchy the disguises would deny.

In Book X we see the alienating effects of the Fall on the two primary relationships in the epic: that of Adam with Eve, and that of Adam and Eve with God. Yet in both relationships, reconciliation is made possible by a gesture of submission and humiliation of which Eve is the primary author. As Adam curses Eve, terming a "Serpent" and a "fair defect / Of Nature" the creature for whom he has chosen to fall, Eve "at his feet / Fell humble, and imbracing them, besought / His peace" (867, 891–892, 911–13). The vision of Eve "at his feet submissive in distress," combined with her trenchant declaration of "love sincere, and reverence in my heart," subdues Adam's anger, and he "with peaceful words uprais'd her soon" (915–16, 945–46). Eve's "fall" at Adam's feet begins to restore what was lost in her first fall. Where she had sought superiority and had fallen, here she humbles herself and is subsequently "upraised." Submission "disarm[s]" Adam's anger.

Extrapolating from the power that Eve's submission has exercised over him, Adam suggests that he and Eve initiate their reconciliation with God by returning to the place

> where he judg'd us, [and] prostrate fall
> Before him reverent, and there confess
> Humbly our faults, and pardon beg, with tears
> Watering the ground, and with our sighs the Air
> Frequenting, sent from hearts contrite, in sign
> Of sorrow unfeign'd, and humiliation meek.   (1087–92)

At the site of judgment for the original Fall, they will fall again. But this time the fall will genuinely be a blessed fall, since the humiliation and sorrow they express will ameliorate the effects of the first fall. By stressing both the social and moral aspects of this fall, Milton maps the postures of courtesy onto the structures of theology. As in Adam's initial prostrations before divine authority, ceremonial acquiescence at once acknowledges the distance between unequals and functions to close that distance. Assuming the palliative capacity of sincere submission, Adam proposes that "Undoubtedly [God] will relent and turn / From his displeasure" (1093). The "sorrow unfeign'd" of Adam and Eve contrasts with the "feign'd submission" that Satan contemplates but rejects (IV, 96). The need of such adjectives, however, registers the effect of the Fall on language and motive, and records the consequent difficulty of distinguishing Guazzo's strategic servility from Christ's kenotic humility. After the Fall, even the most submissive behavior has the potential to be rhetorical. The interiority opened up in the act of disobedience presupposes a disjunction between appearance and motive—a disjunction both countered and fulfilled by the Son's act of clothing the fallen couple. As the sighs of sorrow rise and the tears of repentance fall, they hypostatize the complex process by which sorrowful submission becomes an occasion for exaltation.

This pattern of concurrent rising and falling continues in the opening lines of Book XI; although we last see Adam and Eve in X having fallen prostrate, in XI we learn that "Thus they in lowliest plight repentant *stood / Praying*" (my emphasis).²⁴ After the Fall, falling submissive is the only way to stand before God. In striking contrast to the sociable intercourse that Adam shares with Raphael is the somber encounter with Michael, who has come to earth not to dine with him but to evict him from Paradise: "*Adam* bow'd low, [Michael] Kingly from his State / Inclin'd not" (XI, 249–50). Chilly gravity supplants warm affability. The "state" that Adam exuded in his welcome of Raphael has evaporated with the Fall. Adam has only gestures of humility—unacknowledged and unreciprocated by Michael, his stately superior—to remind him of the dilation of the social and moral distance between heavenly and earthly beings that results from his fall.

Furthermore, instead of the presumptuous prelapsarian banter with which he successfully implored God for a mate, Adam must now confront the stifling limitations of mortal supplication. At the beginning of Book XI, Milton traces the path of the sighs of repentance from Adam and Eve, investigating in the process the physics of human petition. The very impulse to repent, we learn, was the product of "Prevenient Grace descending" from "the Mercy-seat above" (XI, 2–3). Yet the sighs also exercise immense verbal power; they are "wing'd for Heav'n with speedier flight / Than loudest Oratory" (7–8). In heaven the Son, "thir great Intercessor," functions again like a courtly patron, presenting the petitions of his client "Before the Father's Throne"; he implores the Father to "bend thine ear / To supplication, hear his sighs though mute" (19–20, 30–31). In this first act of postlapsarian prayer, Adam is amazed at the capacity of mortal speech to interest God:

> that from us aught should ascend to Heav'n
> So prevalent as to concern the mind
> Of God high-blest, or to incline his will,
> Hard to belief may seem; yet this will Prayer,
> Or one short sigh of human breath, up-borne
> Ev'n to the Seat of God.   (143–48)

Yet Adam's inner experience of the success of his petitions suggests at once the power and impotence of mortal utterance:

> For since I sought
> By Prayer th' offended Deity to appease,
> Kneel'd and before him humbl'd all my heart,
> Methought I saw him placable and mild,
> Bending his ear; persuasion in me grew
> That I was heard with favor.   (148–53)

God does "bend" his ear, responding to Adam's petition with a gesture of gentle condescension, but the persuasive power that Milton seems to bestow upon prayer is directed at the interiority of the supplicant rather than at his divine audience: "persuasion *in me* grew." Beginning with prevenient grace from God and concluding with the supplicant's self-persuasion, prayer is at once remarkably potent and severely delimited.

Indeed, as Adam reluctantly contemplates God's command to leave Paradise, he considers what it might mean actually to try to exercise some form of persuasive verbal power over God:

> if by prayer
> Incessant I could hope to change the will
> Of him who all things can, I would not cease

To weary him with my assiduous cries:
But prayer against his absolute Decree
No more avails than breath against the wind,
Blown stifling back on him that breathes it forth:
Therefore to his great bidding I submit. (307–14)

Where before the Fall Adam "embold'n'd spake, and freedom us'd / Permissive, and acceptance found" (VIII, 434–35), Adam can now only "submit" to the "absolute decree" of his divine monarch. The very breath that one uses to beseech God becomes a cruelly literal parody of the heavenly inspiration that Milton continually seeks. Rather than the "unimplor'd" visitation of a "Celestial Patroness" who "inspires" Milton's "unpremeditated Verse" (IX, 21–24), Adam confronts the possibility of speech to God that only suffocates the ineffectual supplicant. Before the Fall, Adam enjoys "venial discourse unblam'd" with heaven. But after the Fall, Milton as divine poet nervously asks his sacred subject, "May I express thee unblam'd?" (III, 3). The grammatical instability of the terms of Milton's question—the way "unblam'd" modifies both "I" and "thee"—indicates the probability of a negative response. The self that blames its religious subject deserves blame.

Yet the "better Cov'nant" that will be offered to humanity through the sacrifice of the Son makes possible the restoration of a kind of venial discourse with and about God. The movement from the Old Testament to the New not only represents for Milton a progress "From shadowy Types to Truth, from Flesh to Spirit, / From imposition of strict Laws, to free / Acceptance of large Grace"; it also signals a change in the tone of the mortal relationship to God "from servile fear to filial" (XII, 303–06). Fear is not erased entirely, but the abasement present in Adam and Eve's falling prostrate is conjoined with something like the familiarity that Adam shares with Raphael and with God before the Fall. Indeed, the incarnation has its primary meaning for Adam in the physical proximity between mortal and God that it signals: "So God with man unites" (382).

The epic of the Fall appropriately ends with a series of descents which presage but do not perform the concomitant act of rising. Adam and Michael "descend" the hill from which Adam has been given a vision of Christian history to the bower where Eve passively sleeps but creatively dreams (606). "Hand in hand" but "solitary," together but alone, Adam and Eve in turn proceed "down the Cliff [of Paradise] . . . To the subjected Plain" (639–40, 648–50). Echoing the "dreary Plain" of hell (I, 180), the landscape Adam and Eve will inhabit bears the geographical signature of the sentence that their act of disobedience has incurred. Yet like all the other falls and acts of condescension in this text—all but one, that is—this descent also holds out the promise of ascent. The exile from Paradise will warrant that moment when, at the Last Judgment, "the Earth / Shall all be Paradise, far happier place / Than this of *Eden*" (XII, 463–65). The dilation of social and physical distance between heaven and earth that issues from the Fall will occasion the Incarnation, the moment of greatest physical intimacy between God and humanity. The end of time, moreover, is imagined by God himself as the termination of the institution that aroused such antipathy in Milton: monarchy. "Then thou thy regal Sceptre shalt lay by," declares God to the Son, "For regal Sceptre then no more shall need, / God shall be All in All" (III, 339–41).

   Paradise Lost promises but does not participate in such a democratic universe. Although profoundly disenchanted with earthly hierarchies, Milton nevertheless constructs his justification of divine authority from the materials of those political institutions and forms of courtly and liturgical conduct he despised. John Milton was, in Annabel Patterson's apt description, "*both* a radical who wrestled all his life against hierarchy and authority *and* an elitist who believed in a meritocracy for which there were no defining categories other than those of rank and class."[25] By displacing onto Satan both the urge to spurn submissive behavior and the strategic deployment of submissive demeanor, Milton at once reproves and reforms the Renaissance system of hierarchical conduct. For Milton, then, manners are both the gestures by which one acknowledges one's submission to a hierarchy, and a vehicle for attempting to bend a hierarchy to one's will; hierarchy implies both a tyrannical structure enjoining absolute servility and a beneficent order encouraging heroic obedience. Throughout *Paradise Lost* Milton exploits the fusion of Christian humility and tactical courtesy that preoccupied and troubled the Renaissance. The patterns of humiliation and exaltation that proliferate in the corollary discourses of Christianity and of courtesy allow Milton to ground theology in the dramatic energy and political complexity of human manners. Beginning with a figure who lies prone in hell because he refuses to prostrate himself before heavenly authority, and concluding with Adam and Eve's reluctant submission to divine ordinance, *Paradise Lost* reclaims the engaging transactions of human courtesy for the resonant patterns of Christian history.

University of Michigan, Ann Arbor

NOTES

1. *Selected Milton Criticism: Selections from Four Centuries*, ed. James Thorpe (New York, 1969), p. 80.

2. *John Milton: Complete Poems and Major Prose*, ed. Merritt Y. Hughes (Indianapolis, 1957). Unless otherwise indicated, all subsequent references to Milton's poetry and prose are to this edition.

3. Cited from *John Milton: Selected Prose*, ed. C. A. Patrides (Columbia, Mo., 1985).

4. This Act is excerpted in *The Stuart Constitution 1603–1688: Documents and Commentary*, ed. J. P. Kenyon (Cambridge, 1966), pp. 365–71.

5. Mary Ann Radzinowicz, "The Politics of *Paradise Lost*," in *Politics of Discourse: The Literature and History of Seventeenth -Century England*, ed. Kevin Sharpe and Steven Zwicker (Berkeley and Los Angeles, 1987), p. 226.

6. William Blake, *The Marriage of Heaven and Hell* (1793), cited from Thorpe, *Milton Criticism*, p. 353.

7. Stanley Fish, *Surprised by Sin: The Reader in Paradise Lost* (Berkeley and Los Angeles, 1967), p. 22.

8. William Empson, *Milton's God* (Cambridge, 1965), p. 123.

9. See Joan S. Bennett, "Satan and King Charles: Milton's Royal Portraits," in *Reviving Liberty: Radical Christian Humanism in Milton's Great Poems* (Cambridge, 1989), ch. 2, pp. 33–38. Bennett establishes in detail "the fundamental similarity between Charles and Satan" (p. 35).

10. Hughes, *Complete Poems*, p. 640. William Flesch, "The Majesty of Darkness," in *John Milton: Modern Critical Views*, ed. Harold Bloom (New York, 1986), p. 295, likewise juxtaposes the preface of *Reason of Church Government* to God's announcement of the elevation of the Son.

11. Anthony Low, "Milton's God: Authority in *Paradise Lost*," in *Milton Studies* IV, ed. James D. Simmonds (Pittsburgh, 1972), p. 37, n. 1.

12. Annabel M. Patterson, *Marvell and the Civic Crown* (Princeton, 1978), p. 61. Patterson does not discuss *Paradise Lost* in this context, but she does refer to *Areopagitica*.

13. Michael Lieb, *The Sinews of Ulysses: Form and Convention in Milton's Works* (Pittsburgh, 1989), pp. 88–92.

14. Robert Hodge, "Satan and the Revolution of the Saints," *Literature and History* 7 (1978), 30.

15. I cite the translation and note of *Utopia*, trans. Robert M. Adams (New York, 1975), p. 9.

16. Under *toad*, sb. no. 3 (1605), the *Oxford English Dictionary* records the pejorative phrase "court tode," apparently deriving from the similar kneeling posture of courtly sycophant and croaking amphibian.

17. Baldassare Castiglione, *The Book of the Courtier* (1528), trans. Thomas Hoby (1561; rpt. London, 1928), p. 109.

18. Stefano Guazzo, *The Civile Conversation* (1574), trans. George Pettie (1581), ed. Edward Sullivan, 2 vols. (London, 1925), vol. I, p. 192.

19. Barbara K. Lewalski, *"Paradise Lost" and the Rhetoric of Literary Forms* (Princeton, 1985), p. 206. In "The Visit of Raphael: *Paradise Lost*, Book V," *PQ* 41 (1968), 36–42, John R. Knott analyzes the prelapsarian courtesy of this scene, and compares it to Virgil's account of the visit of Aeneas to Evander in Book VIII of the *Aeneid*.

20. The theological resonance of such patterns is expounded by Albert C. Labriola,

" 'Thy Humiliation Shall Exalt': The Christology of *Paradise Lost*," in *Milton Studies* XV, ed. James D. Simmonds (Pittsburgh, 1981), pp. 29–42.

21. Wendy Furman discusses this particular moment of divine condescension (along with a number of others) in the work of Mary Groom, a twentieth-century engraver and illustrator of *Paradise Lost*. See Furman's essay in this volume: " 'Consider first that Great / Or Bright infers not Excellence': Mapping the Feminine in Mary Groom's Miltonic Cosmos."

22. In "Gender and Conduct in *Paradise Lost*," forthcoming in *Sexuality and Gender in Early Modern Europe: Institutions, Texts, Images*, ed. James G. Turner (Cambridge, 1993).

23. On the generic implications of this change, see Lewalski, *"Paradise Lost" and the Rhetoric of Literary Forms*, pp. 196–253.

24. Milton similarly puns on the moral and physical aspects of standing in *Paradise Regained*, when the Son responds to Satan's temptation to throw himself from "the highest Pinnacle": "Also it is written, / Tempt not the Lord thy God; he said and stood. / But Satan smitten with amazement fell" (IV, 56–62). In " 'Stand' and 'Fall' as Images of Posture in *Paradise Lost*," in *Milton Studies* VIII, ed. James D. Simmonds (Pittsburgh, 1975), pp. 221–46, Nicholas R. Jones examines Milton's use of physical posture to represent moral decision.

25. Annabel Patterson, " 'Forc'd fingers': Milton's Early Poems and Ideological Constraint," in *"The Muses Common-Weale": Poetry and Politics in the Seventeenth Century*, ed. Claude J. Summers and Ted-Larry Pebworth (Columbia, Mo., 1988), p. 22.

MILTON'S DIALOGUE WITH PETRARCH

Ilona Bell

We feel ourselves under the influence of a mighty intellect, that the nearer it approaches to others, becomes more distinct from them.
—*William Hazlitt on Milton*

Milton absorbed precursors with a gusto evidently precluding anxiety.
—*Harold Bloom¹*

MUCH AS FREUD provided the twentieth century with a vocabulary for exploring the psyche, Petrarch provided the Renaissance with a vocabulary for talking about love. Renaissance love poetry could be Petrarchan or anti-Petrarchan or pseudo-Petrarchan (by twisting Petrarchan vocabulary to seductive purposes) but not a-Petrarchan; for Renaissance writers use Petrarchan discourse whether they endorse, challenge, parody, or exploit the Petrarchan posture. As Julia Kristeva pithily remarks, "The language of love is impossible, inadequate, immediately allusive when one would like it to be most straightforward"², in the Renaissance, love's allusions all harken back to Petrarch. *Paradise Lost,* the first epic in which the main subject is married love and the role of the hero is shared jointly by a man and a woman, is inevitably part of the Petrarchan debate. Since the ideology of desire posits a whole world view, and since a former world can only be recaptured through its textual constructs, challenges to the Petrarchan ideology of desire give us a penetrating view of challenges to the Renaissance world. For a poet steeped in Renaissance literature and living in a patriarchal society, Petrarchism posed an inevitable poetic temptation. For Adam and Eve, the original human temptation is posed in the discourse of Petrarchism: when Satan seduces Eve, first abortively in her dream and then successfully later, he offers her the "high exaltation" of Petrarchan adulation.³ Satan's rhetoric is indisputably Petrarchan, or pseudo-Petrarchan, but is the converse also true? Is Petrarchism ultimately Satanic in a seventeenth-century English Puritan epic like *Paradise Lost?*

Because changes in culture generate changes in genre, even as

91

changes in genre express and initiate changes in culture, it is important to consider how the Petrarchan convention adjusted as it passed from fourteenth-century Catholic Italy to seventeenth-century Protestant England. In Milton's divorce tracts, for instance, the Puritan ideology of marriage clashes with the Catholic—and Petrarchan—ideal of celibacy. Regretting that the "superstition of the Papist is, *touch not, taste not, when God* bids both," the *Doctrine and Discipline of Divorce* advances first the "solace and satisfaction of the minde" and then "the sensitive pleasing of the body."[4] The great English Renaissance love poets like Sidney, Spenser, Shakespeare, and Donne, decry Petrarchism's univocal, idealized, disembodied love only to approach its abysses, and then to reemerge, conscious of, and for the most part inoculated against its recurrent temptations. Following their course, Milton represents Petrarchan love as the obverse and test of paradisal love. "We writers must look to it that with a basis of similarity there should be many dissimilarities. And the similarity should be planted so deep that it can only be extricated by quiet meditation," wrote Petrarch to Boccaccio. Citing this letter, Thomas Greene argues that Petrarch's poetry requires "the activity of subreading" because it contains "enmeshed in, or half-buried beneath, the verbal surface," a conversation with the ancients, "reaching the reader from far off, from a remote and prestigious world radically unlike his own."[5] *Paradise Lost* may likewise be subread: beneath its vocal conversation with the ancients is a hushed conversation with Petrarch, buried so deeply that its complex blend of admiration and challenge has not been fully heard by modern critics. Milton's Petrarchan subtext attests to the continuing power of Petrarch's poetry, even as it asserts differences between the ideologies of Petrarchism and Puritanism.

The *Canzoniere* was not published in Renaissance England, but a small number of the sonnets, largely those *in vivo*, were translated and adapted by so many English poets that they became staples of Elizabethan discourse.[6] Although Milton's Petrarchan language relies heavily on sonnets known in England, he probably obtained the complete sequence in Italy, for he writes to his Italian friends about Petrarch's poetry as if it had been a familiar topic of conversation between them. In a 1638 letter Milton observes that he could "yet sometimes willingly and eagerly go for a feast to that Dante of yours, and to Petrarch, and a good few more" (YP I, p. 35), suggesting a youthful passion still capable ("can yet") of flaring up "sometimes" even as it is waning; and in 1647 he writes that above all the love poets he preferred "the two famous renowners of *Beatrice* and *Laura* who never write but honour of them to whom they devote their verse, displaying sublime and pure thoughts, without transgression" (YP I, p.

890). Milton's prose works from 1641 to 1645 also show a continuing intimacy with Petrarch. In *Of Reformation Touching Church Discipline in England* he cites Petrarch twice and translates five lines of *Rime* CXXXVIII. The *Apology Against a Modest Confutation* also mentions Petrarch, and in the *Commonplace Book* he notes a biography of Petrarch by Thomasinus of Padua.

Based on such substantial evidence, Parker, Smart, Honigmann, Samuel, and Prince assert Petrarch's influence on Milton's early poetry, his first seven sonnets, *The Passion, Elegia Septima,* and, to a lesser degree, *Lycidas.*[7] Milton's direct references to Petrarch end here, and critics have traditionally assumed that Petrarch's influence on Milton's poetry also ends at this time. Since love poetry is traditionally associated with the lyric, there have been few concerted attempts to connect *Paradise Lost* and Petrarch's *Rime Sparse.*[8] But if, as Barbara Lewalski demonstrates, *Paradise Lost* is a compendium of literary forms,[9] the Petrarchan lyric could well be among them, although the very transfer of lyric to epic would constitute a significant questioning of Petrarch's principled insistence "on the purity of each genre, unmixed with another" (Colie, p. 19).

Petrarchan love poetry has long been admired for its capacity to explore and express the dominant male point of view, but that very focus reduces Laura to a mirror and an idol.[10] As Nancy Vickers notes, the *Rime* "suppresses [Laura's] voice, and it casts generations of would-be Lauras in a role predicated upon the muteness of its player."[11] That Milton represents "a meet and happy conversation [as] the chiefest and the noblest end of mariage" (YP II, p. 246) in both *Paradise Lost* and the divorce tracts has been frequently remarked. That this mutual, dialogic love language represents an English critique of Petrarchan self-absorption has not been noted. "Since by definition the cultural monuments and masterworks that have survived tend necessarily to perpetuate only a single voice in this class dialogue, the voice of a hegemonic class," Fredric Jameson writes,

they cannot be properly assigned their relational place in a dialogical system without the restoration or artificial reconstruction of the voice to which they were initially opposed, a voice for the most part stifled and reduced to silence, marginalized, its own utterance scattered to the winds, or reappropriated in their turn by the hegemonic culture.[12]

Petrarchism's single-minded, tormented, male self-exploration, and its concomitant idolatrous worship of an absent, angelic lady is at odds not only with modern feminism but also with Renaissance defenses of women and Puritan iconoclasm.[13] The critique of Petrarchism remains a subtext throughout *Paradise Lost* which signifies patriarchy's power to marginalize women's voices, even as it suggests Englishwomen's readiness to raise their voices to criticize Petrarchism's silencing of women—in Queen Elizabeth's empowering transformation of Petrarchan discourse; in Mary Sidney's translation of Petrarch's *Triumph of Death*, where Laura finally speaks out and explains her suppressed love for the poet; in the spaces between Spenser's *Amoretti*, or Daniel's *Delia*, or Donne's *Songs and Sonnets*, where the poet's rhetoric is momentarily silent and the woman's implicit responses comment on what he has said and influence what is to come; in sonnet sequences like Lady Mary Wroth's *Pamphilia to Amphilanthus*, or romances like her *Urania*, which empower and voice the women's point of view; and in defenses of women like Mary Tattle-well's and Ioane Hit-Him Home's *Women's Sharp Revenge*, where women are taught to laugh at the pseudo-Petrarchan poet who

> would sweare that his life or death were either in my accepting or rejecting his suite, he would lye and flatter in prose, & cogge and foyst in verse most shamefully; he would sometimes salute me with most delicious Sentences, which he alwayes kept in sirrup . . . hee was never unprovided of stew'd Anagrams, bak'd Epigrams, sows'd Madrigalls, pickled Round delayes, broyled Sonnets. . . . an enamoured Toade lurks under the sweet grasse, and a faire tongue hath been too often the varnish or Embrodery of a false heart.

One can well imagine why a poet/lover might prefer a woman's discreet silence![14]

As John Halkett has noted, for the seventeenth century, *conversation* means most broadly, living together in society and intimacy; however, the more specific meanings of spiritual intercourse, familiar discourse or talk, and sexual intercourse or intimacy, are all central to *Paradise Lost*. Eve has not only a spirit, but also a mind, a body, and a voice.[15] While Laura remains largely silent, enigmatic, and altogether inaccessible, an idealized, angelic mistress, Eve lives her paradisal existence as an outspoken, practical woman, at ease with her own body and walking firmly on the originary earth of Eden. As she prepares dinner, tends the garden, and makes the bed, she is continually conversing with Adam, for the heart of their relationship is dialogue—their rich conversation ranging from casual chat, to serious speculation about the planets, to the shared pleasure of telling and hearing familiar stories.[16] Noting the oddly unchronological construction of Book IV, Mary Nyquist describes Adam and Eve's conversation as a series of set speeches, unconnected by any underlying purpose: "[I]t hardly seems appropriate to refer to their speech as dialogue. Their conversation has practically none of the purposeful qualities that we expect of literary dialogue."[17] But, I would respond, the purpose *is* conversation, conversation that is simultaneously verbal, spiritual, and physical. Indeed, their dialogue is much like that of all lovers: they share experiences, establish intimacy, jockey for power, and all the while they talk of love, until they are in the mood for making love.

In Eden sexual fulfillment emerges from conversational pleasure, and conversational pleasure leads naturally to sexual fulfillment:

> Nor gentle purpose, nor endearing smiles
> Wanted, nor youthful dalliance as beseems
> Fair couple, linkt in happy nuptial League. (*PL* IV, 337–39)[18]

Edenic love combines "purpose," meaning conversation, and "dalliance" meaning amorous play. It makes conversation sensual and sensuality conversational, for "speaking of love is in itself a *jouissance*," as Lacan writes, and "To make love, as the term indicates is poetry. Only there is a world between poetry and the act"—the fallen world which Adam and Eve have not as yet entered.[19] When in his divorce tracts Milton argues that marriage was "instituted to the solace and delight of man" (*YP* II, p. 235) to prevent "the loneliness which leads him still powerfully to seek a fit help" (*YP* II, p. 253), he implicitly rejects the self-absorption, solitude, contradictions, and misery of Petrarchism.

Petrarchan love, "Begotten by despair upon impossibility" (to cite Marvell's "Definition of Love"), is riddled with *if only's*, with desire that is always already impossible. For Petrarchan man and woman, like Lacanian man and woman, and like Milton's Satan, there can be lust or love but there is no loving sexual relation, because desire is defined by lack, absence, frustration.[20] For Adam and Eve, as for the couple in the Song of Solomon, there is no lack; and the natural abundance makes desire as satisfying as the fruit and honey. Unlike Petrarchan sonnets where desire and frustration founder in an eternal oxymoronic stasis, or anti-Petrarchan sonnets where lust is "Enjoyed no sooner but despisèd straight" (Shakespeare Sonnet CXXIX), the plot of Book IV is the eternal plot of mature love, the movement of desire towards consummation—although Miltonic desire is paradisal precisely because consummation increases and sweetens desire. Choreographed to bring them closer and closer together until they retire for the night, still mingling physical pleasure and pleasurable talk—"talking hand in hand alone they pass'd / On to thir blissful Bower" (*PL* IV, 689–90)—Adam and Eve's conversation derives imaginative pleasure by recollecting and reenacting their first sexual encounter; in contrast, the *Rime* endlessly eternizes that first miraculous but distant vision of Laura.

From the very start Edenic love is presented as the obverse of Petrarchan love. As his first speech demonstrates, Adam does not suffer from that obsessive fixation on the lady which, thanks largely to Petrarch, we think of as the *sine qua non* of love poetry. Adam's brief references to Eve are exceedingly tender ("Dearer thyself than all"), but he says less about Eve than about God. In *The Doctrine and Discipline of Divorce* Milton argues that Christian life should be dedicated to joy and peace, since "the dignity & blessing of mariage is plac't rather in the mutual enjoyment" (YP II, p. 252). In the *Canzoniere* Petrarch is tormented by the conflict between human and divine love; he begins and ends, "weeping for [his] past time, which [he] spent loving a mortal thing without lifting [himself] in flight." *Paradise Lost*, in contrast, characterizes Adam and Eve's love as a mutually delighting intimacy which finds its natural expression in their mutual love of God.

The poem's first view of Adam and Eve, a divine one, shows them "Reaping immortal fruits of joy and love, / Uninterrupted joy, unrivall'd love" (*PL* III, 67–68). The *Canzoniere* constantly struggles with the conflict between love and duty, but Adam extols and enjoys the intimacy of their joint labors:

> our delightful task
> To prune these growing Plants, and tend these Flow'rs,
> Which were it toilsome, yet with thee were sweet.   (*PL* IV, 437–39)

The *Canzoniere* describes the male poet/lover's feelings incessantly; the "vario stile in ch' io piango et ragiono / fra le vane speranze e 'l van dolore" (I, 4–5) ("varied style in which I weep and speak between vain hopes and vain sorrows"),[21] explores *his* hopes and sorrows, not Laura's. But plural pronouns come spontaneously to Adam's lips, suggesting that he thinks about their common feelings and experiences. Although Eve was created after Adam, and as tradition would have it, for Adam, at this point he simply says, God "raised *us* from the dust and placed *us* here / In all this happiness" (my emphasis).

In the *Canzoniere* Petrarch celebrates Laura's beauty over and over again: "Erano i capei d'oro a l'aura sparsi, e 'l vago lume oltra misura ardea di quei begli occhi" (XC, 4–5) ("her golden hair loosed to the breeze, the lovely light that burned without measure in her eyes"). But Adam's poetry does not dwell upon Eve's appearance—at least not until Book VIII, when Adam describes the disconcerting effect of Eve's Petrarchan dream. Petrarchism debases the poet/lover, "et del mio vaneggiar vergogna e l'frutto, / e 'l pentersi" (I, 12–13) ("of my raving, shame is the fruit, and repentance") and exalts the woman, "uno spirto celeste, un vivo sole" (XC) ("some angelic form . . . a celestial spirit, a living sun"), creating an insurmountable distance between them. By contrast, when Adam echoes God's bequest, "all the Earth / To thee and to thy Race I give; as Lords / Possess it, and all things that therein live" (*PL* VIII, 338–40), he speaks directly, warmly, openly to Eve and stresses their equality, their shared power over others:

> so many signs of power and rule
> Conferr'd upon us, and Dominion giv'n
> Over all other Creatures that possess
> Earth, Air, and Sea.   (*PL* IV, 429–32)

When Eve responds to Adam's first speech, she addresses him as "my Guide / And Head" (IV 442–443), thereby acknowledging the historical conditions that make patriarchy the expected discourse in seventeenth-century epic as in seventeenth-century England—except in those instances where the text concertedly alters that discourse, and this is not one of them. Still, there is an edge to Eve's comment which makes her seem as much a discriminating judge as an awestruck acolyte: she approves not only because Adam is her guide and head but also because she thinks what he "said is just and right" (IV, 443). Indeed, she has good reason to approve, for Adam's remarks about the "many signs of power and rule / Conferr'd upon us, and Dominion giv'n / Over all other Creatures" (IV, 429–31) offer a remarkably equal vision of Edenic gender, perhaps the most thoroughly developed statement of egalitarianism in the poem.

"But what if the object began to speak?," Julia Kristeva asks. Eve does. Although placed in a creation narrative plotted by Adam and before that, God, she does not simply echo and affirm Adam's discourse.[22] She introduces a new topic for conversation, perhaps the only topic upon which her authority and knowledge is indisputably greater—the memory and experience of her own birth: "That day I oft remember, when from sleep / I first awak't" (*PL* IV, 449–50).[23] Adam might have broached the story of his creation here, for he was created first;[24] or he might have silenced Eve by telling her story for her, since he observed her birth: "Abstract as in a trance methought I saw . . . Under his forming hands a Creature grew" (*PL* VIII, 462–70). However, Eve seizes the occasion to tell her creation story first, thereby disrupting biblical chronology and preempting Adam's more conventional account. Given this unexpected priority, Eve's narrative bears a heavy interpretive burden, especially since, as Mary Nyquist observes, it "lacks any immediately discernible connection with the Genesis creation accounts on which the narratives of both Raphael and Adam draw."[25] Thus it is important to ask, how does Eve's story supplement or alter the standard biblical version?

Some critics have argued that this divine voice is not God's but an angelic minister's because the narrator says a "genial Angel to our Sire / Brought her in naked beauty more adorn'd" (*PL* IV 712–13); but Adam explicitly asserts that Eve was "Led by her Heav'nly Maker though unseen, / And guided by his voice" (VIII, 485–86). In the absence of additional textual clarification, why not infer that Eve was guided by God's voice while being led by an attendant angel? Regardless of how one chooses to resolve the textual difficulty, the divine voice demonstrates that God has taken charge of Eve's education—unless, of course, one starts with the ideological assumption that God's relation to Eve is, and must be, mediated through Adam. But then, one would need to counter, the divine voice addresses Eve before she even meets Adam, thereby bestowing upon her a direct, unmediated, divine account of her identity. That fact repositions Eve in history and discourse: not only is *our* experience of her creation defined by her and her unmediated encounter with the divine voice, but so is Adam's subsequent account of her birth, for he hears this story from her before he recounts it to Raphael (much as he converses with her about astronomy before discussing it with Raphael).

If *Paradise Lost* were a Petrarchan poem, this conversation would have begun with Adam describing *his* first sight of Eve, for the *Canzoniere* derive their vitality from Petrarch's originary vision of Laura, miraculously transformed by the imagination and constantly recreated by the poetry. Eve's first image of herself not only recalls but inverts the anniversary poems which commemorate Petrarch's first sight of Laura as well as Sonnet XLV familiar to English readers in Daniel's lovely adaptation, *Delia* XXIX. After banishing the poet from his place in her eyes and sentencing him to deadly despair, Laura/Delia gazes at herself in a mirror and falls in love with herself. Although Petrarch chastises Laura for being self-absorbed, for loving her own reflected beauty more than him, her narcissism is the inevitable result of his idolatry. Indeed the Petrarchan ideology of love rests upon her capacity to mirror his thoughts and desires. In banishing the poet, theoretically she could create a space to look at herself by herself, to define herself to herself—though that would have to occur outside the poem, or in the space between the poems as it does in the *Amoretti* or *Astrophel and Stella*. Yet even in banishment Petrarch remains imaginatively present, looking over her shoulder, telling her what she sees, in effect, reducing her to the image of his inordinate desire and unbounded praise. "More than the other senses, the eye objectifies and masters," Irigaray writes. "It sets at a distance, maintains the distance. In our culture, the predominance of the look over smell, taste, touch, hearing has brought an impoverishment of bodily relations. It has contributed to disembodying sexuality. The moment the look dominates, the body loses in materiality."[26] Trapped by the male gaze and later by the male critique in an infantile stage of self-absorbed narcissism, Laura, Delia, and all Petrarchan ladies are objectified and subjugated by Petrarchism.

Petrarch's outraged statement of wounded pride, "harsh and proud to my harm," reveals, though it never acknowledges, that Laura's female narcissism is a reflection of his male anxiety and self-absorption. More a lugubrious punishment for what will happen because it has in effect already happened than a suasive warning against what need not happen ("questo et quel corso ad un termino vanno" (XLV, 12–13) ("this and that course lead to one goal"), the very terms of the fantasy reveal its futility. For Laura as for Narcissus, the destruction dissolves into a final sigh of admiration: "ben che di sì bel fior sia indegna l'erba" (XLV, 14) ("the grass is unworthy of so lovely a flower"). The Petrarchan dilemma begins with adulation which is unbounded and ends with desire which is unquenchable because impossible.

By empowering Eve to narrate her creation first, *Paradise Lost* inverts the premises upon which Petrarchism was founded. Since Eve's narrative has no biblical source, it is an innovation, a story which marks our ancestral mother's emergence as a speaker in language. "[M]uch wond'ring where / And what I was, whence thither brought, and how" (*PL* IV, 451–52), Eve experiences a moment of solitary self-examination when she *is not* and *has never been* the object of the male gaze; therefore, unlike Laura and Narcissus, she rejects narcissism before she rejects love. The Lacanian child's first sight of itself in the mirror is "the symbolic matrix in which the I is precipitated in a primordial form, before it is objectified in the dialectic of identification with the other, and before language restores to it, in the universal, its function as subject" (1977, p. 2); Eve looks back at this moment as the beginning of selfhood, as that formative encounter with self which precedes her entrance into the symbolic and rhetorical order of language, and its ensuing desire for the other—in her case, Adam.[27] In this prelapsarian world, where language is *not* marked by the oedipal triangle because Adam and Eve have no human mother or father, Eve's identity develops along the course which Lacan associates with the male subject: from the mirror image to the other, the object of desire.

In her penetrating critique of *Paradise Lost*, Christine Froula argues that the mirror scene educates Eve to accept her subordinate position as object: "As the voice interprets her to herself, Eve is not a self, a subject at all; she is rather a substanceless image, a mere 'shadow' without object until the voice unites her to Adam—'hee / Whose image thou art.' "[28]

Basically, Froula sees Eve as an epitomal Petrarchan lady, a shadowy, reflected image of a desirous male gaze; however, Froula's critique takes into account only the first part of what the divine voice tells Eve. Initially, of course, the voice presents Adam as the subject:

> but follow me,
> And I will bring thee where no shadow stays
> Thy coming, and thy soft imbraces, hee
> Whose image thou art   (PL IV, 469–72)

for Adam was formed first and Eve was created in his image as the answer to his desire. At least, that is what Adam will later assert, understandably, since love poetry conventionally describes what the male poet/lover desires: " 'woman' [who] is the poet's most constant creation."[29] Since "no shadow" is the subject of "stays / Thy coming, and thy soft imbraces," in reading Eve's story we naturally assume "he" begins a new independent clause that will proceed to characterize Eve as the object of Adam's desire. But contrary to all conventional expectations, the divine voice veers suddenly, transforming Adam from the subject of the discourse to the object of Eve's desires: "hee / Whose image thou art, him thou shalt enjoy / Inseparably thine" (PL IV, 471–73). Remarkably (though generally unremarked), the voice woos Eve away from her own reflection by telling her about the pleasure *she* will find in love, thus divinely authorizing *her* independent subjectivity.

The surprising syntactical breach that divides "he" from "him" creates a gap into which all our expectations—biblical, Petrarchan, patriarchal—suddenly fall, making Eve's narrative one of those revelatory moments which differentiates *Paradise Lost* from the Petrarchan and biblical texts whose traces it contains. Jameson's political theory—that literature "tilts powerfully into the underside or *impensé* or *non-dit*, in short, into the very political unconscious, of the text [which directs] us to the informing power of forces or contradictions which the text seeks in vain wholly to control or master" (p. 49)—helps to explain the historical implications of this startling syntactical turn. Whereas traditional patriarchal discourse allows "woman" no subjectivity and no voice, Milton's divine voice deploys a prelapsarian language that enables Eve to awaken from shadow and image to the subject of the inspiring discourse she now retells and makes her own. As Eve's narrative supplements its biblical source and alters its Petrarchan pretexts, *she* becomes the subject and *he* becomes the object of *her* gaze and *her* desire.

Eve's introduction to God may seem to pale by contrast with Adam's because she only hears a voice, whereas he sees an image. But hearing—

what T. W. Adorno calls that "most abstract of all the senses"[30]—was privileged over sight by Protestantism, which replaced the images of Catholicism with the words of Scripture made audible to the individual by the inner voice of the Spirit upon whom Milton's blind bard relies so deeply.[31] When Adam receives his final history lesson, Michael begins with more accessible visual images ("*Adam*, now ope thine eyes, and first behold" [*PL* XI, 423]), but switches to spoken words when it is time to explain the more difficult matters of Book XII. Furthermore, voice is the original primal bond between mother and child, who hears the mother's voice in the womb and responds to it immediately at birth and throughout infancy. Hélène Cixous argues, "all the feminine texts that I have read are very close to the *voice*, are very close to the flesh of the language, much more than in masculine texts."[32] Like a newborn infant turning to track mother's voice with its eyes, or a reborn Puritan hearing the inner voice of the Holy Spirit interpreting a phrase of Scripture, Eve is closer to God, one might argue, because she begins her life hearing a "maternal" voice within.[33]

In the divorce tracts Milton writes that marriage was first created for "apt and cheerfull conversation of man with woman . . . not mentioning the purpose of generation till afterwards" (YP II, p. 235). In Eden the divine voice likewise teaches Eve to value conversation in both its verbal and sexual senses, not mentioning generation until afterwards. Emerging from the waters of the maternal stream, Eve becomes a newly born woman—newly born with the independent capacity to desire, to speak, to see, to choose, to act: "to him shalt bear / Multitudes like thyself, and thence be call'd / Mother of human Race" (*PL* IV, 473–75). At this crucial moment, Eve is not the object of others' actions, but the subject of her own active verbs. Moreover, Eve's and Adam's children are created in her image, which implicitly makes her the bearer of God's image for posterity, much as Adam is the bearer of God's image for her.

At this point Eve's narrative not only lacks a biblical source, but it actually alters standard biblical commentary in her favor; for Genesis ii, 23 says that Eve only receives her name, with its etymological meaning of *mother*, after the Fall.[34] Furthermore, in Genesis it is Adam who names Eve *Hawwah*: "The man, in giving her this particular name, further determines the character: Eve is imprisoned in motherhood. There is no more question of the sexual attraction celebrated earlier" (Bal, p. 39). To be sure, in *Paradise Lost* naming is Adam's prerogative: he has already named all the other creatures in the garden (although, it seems, Eve is allowed to name the flowers). But here it is God who first names Eve, thereby symbolically preempting Adam's traditional power to name and define her, and creating a bond between God and Eve as creators: "the fact that she is appointed as the future creator/provider of 'all living,' " Bal writes, "may very well be signified in the resemblance between her name and Jahweh's, the consonants H and W being the phonetic actant which oppose the creators to the creatures, signified by D and M in Adam and ha-damä, meaning earth" (p. 24). Milton's God names Eve just after he has promised her the sexual joys of marriage, thereby making her doubly blessed, blessed first in desiring her husband and blessed later in creating children in her image.

Traditional theories of kinship present marriage as a patriarchal institution in which the father gives the daughter to the husband. Mary Nyquist notes that Milton's *Tetrachordon* emphasizes Eve's status as "divinely bestowed gift" (1987, p. 114), but here in Eden the Father also gives the son to the wife. Here the divine voice, as incorporated by Eve's narrative, presents *Adam* as a divinely bestowed gift: "Inseparably thine." Set off and emphasized by their position at the beginning of the line and magnified by their powerful preeminence as Eve's birthright, these two divine words fundamentally redefine woman's position in the order of exchange and the symbolic order of language. Adam will later claim that Eve was created for him, in his image and in response to his wishes, but Eve's creation narrative—told first and from the unmediated point of view the divine voice gives her—suggests that she was also created to have Adam as her own, to enjoy him as a marital right/rite, the object of her desire, already created for her pleasure, much as he was created to enjoy the riches that had already been created in Eden to fulfill his desires and needs: "all the Earth / To thee and to thy Race I give; as Lords / Possess it" (*PL* VIII, 338–40).

Once the syntax shifts course, turning Eve into the subject of the following sentence, the preceding clause, "hee / Whose image thou art," becomes an afterthought, a postscript added to the previous dependent clause which can now be glossed thus: I will bring thee where no shadow stays thy coming, but where he, who is no shadow, stays thy coming and thy sweet embrace. Here "coming" alludes to Eve's arrival as well as her origin; from the perspective of the marital joys promised her, however, "coming" also alludes to her forthcoming sexual fulfillment, as Juliet's thoughts about her marriage night illustrate: "Come, civil night, . . . And learn me how to lose a winning match, / Play'd for a pair of stainless maidenhoods. . . . Come, night, come, Romeo, come, thou day in night" (*Rom.* III, iii, 10–17). Thus, Eve learns, Adam is awaiting not only the embraces she confers upon him, but also the joy she derives from him and shares with him. That Eve's divinely inspired self-definition is based upon her marriage right is historically significant because Renaissance marriage doctrine comes closest to declaring equality for the sexes when it grants "due benevolence" to the wife as well as the husband.[35]

Because of the way in which Eve's response—"what could I do, / But follow straight?" (*PL* IV, 475–6)—is formulated, feminists have complained that Eve is forced to submit; but as I hope my reading of the scene makes clear, Eve follows "straight," eagerly, directly, because Milton's God teaches her to seek her own joy, something that Petrarch never ventures to suggest. At first sight Adam seems "Less winning soft, less amiably mild" (IV, 479) than her own reflection, and instead of instantly throwing herself into Adam's arms, Eve withdraws. By keeping her narcissism in reserve, Eve maintains her self-sufficiency and exercises her freedom of choice, though, one must add, she soon yields.[36] Kerrigan and Braden argue that her "sweet reluctant amorous delay" (IV, 311) shows the continuing power of the Petrarchan love convention, and certainly the language calls the convention to mind. Petrarchan delay is unmitigated, however; it impedes intimacy, suspends passion, and pivots hope upon despair, longing upon frustration, love upon solitude. Paradisal delay, by contrast, is itself reluctant, reluctant to delay. The phrase is by now so familiar that, I suspect, we no longer notice how odd it is that "reluctant" modifies "delay." In Eden delay defers only briefly and hesitantly, just long enough to heighten the amorous sweets with which it is syntactically intertwined, just long enough to establish the difference between Miltonic and Petrarchan love. Perhaps "Milton absorbed precursors with a gusto evidently precluding anxiety" (as Harold Bloom suggests, p. 50) because he was so ready to appropriate their poetry and discard their ideology.

The fact of the matter is that Eve yields because she finds Adam more physically appealing than herself: "from that time [I] see / How beauty is excell'd by manly grace / And wisdom, which alone is truly fair" (*PL* IV, 489–91). If Eve discovers that female beauty is excelled by manly grace which is in turn excelled by manly wisdom, as many critics have assumed, there is reason for a feminist to object once again. If, however, Eve discovers (as Kerrigan, Braden, and Shullenberger point out) that beauty is excelled by manly grace, and that manly grace is in turn excelled by wisdom which is available to both Eve and Adam since birth ("in thir looks Divine / The image of thir glorious Maker shone, / Truth, Wisdom, Sanctitude severe and pure" [IV, 291–93]), Eve has every reason to yield. Her yielding redefines love from the female point of view, and undercuts the governing assumptions of Petrarchan and Neoplatonic love in which the lady's beauty leads the poet's thoughts from earth to heaven. Here, the man's beauty allows the woman to fulfill her physical desires and to heighten her mental pleasures through conversation with her lover, but only after she has been allowed to discover her self independently so that she can choose him freely. "The first and more important point" in marriage, Milton argues in *Christian Doctrine*, "is the mutual consent of the parties concerned, for there can be no love or good will, and therefore no marriage, between those whom mutual consent has not united" (YP VI, p. 368). By rejecting the shadowy, unfulfilled, idolatrous love experienced by Narcissus, Laura, Petrarch and all their imitators, *Paradise Lost* highlights the radical mutuality and physicality of Edenic love.

After Eve finishes her story, Adam and Eve embrace thus:

> half her swelling Breast
> Naked met his under the flowing Gold
> Of her loose tresses hid: hee in delight
> Both of her Beauty and submissive Charms
> Smil'd with superior Love.   (*PL* IV, 494–99)

Citing this passage, Aers and Hodge complain that "this relationship feels intolerable in many ways, flawed with unacknowledged antagonisms, negative responses, manipulative, unfree and half-concealed sexuality" (p. 28). This seems unduly harsh (do we really need a full-frontal to demonstrate our ancestor's sexual openness?), although to a modern sensibility the combination of "superior" love and "submissive charms" does sound disturbingly patriarchal. Even though Eve does not immediately fall on her knees and declare allegiance to Adam, her "submissive charms" parallel Adam's response to his first sight of God, "at his feet I fell / Submiss" (*PL* VIII, 315–16), thus reminding us of her place in the divine hierarchy: "he for God only, she for God in him." "Desire must always be transgressive," Jameson writes, "must always have a repressive norm or law through which to burst and against which to define itself. Yet it is a commonplace that transgressions, presupposing the laws or norms or taboos against which they function, thereby end up precisely reconfirming such laws" (p. 68). At precisely the moment when Eve's independence seems strongest (and potentially most disruptive), patriarchal discourse seems to, or threatens to, reassert itself as a strategy of containing the dangerously empowering desire that Eve acquired from the divine voice. Mutuality does not guarantee equality: "though both / Not equal, as their sex not equal seemed."[37]

Yet the ironies of a Petrarchan subtext persist even here, making the description of Eve embracing Adam more empowering and less demeaning than Aers and Hodge imply, precisely because it radically transforms the classic Petrarchan imagery of Sonnet XC, Petrarch's inspired, remembered, first vision of Laura: "Erano i capei d'oro a l'aura sparsi / che 'n mille dolci nodi gli avolgea" ("Her golden hair was loosed to the breeze, which turned it in a thousand sweet knots"). To cite just a few of the most prominent allusions, this image was adapted by Spenser's "What guyle is this, that those her golden tresses"; parodied by Shakespeare's "My mistress' eyes are nothing like the sonne"; and played with by Donne's "Aire and Angels" ("Every thy hair for love to work upon/ Is much too much, some fitter must be sought; / For, nor in nothing, nor in things / Extreme and scatt'ring bright, can love inhere"). For Elizabethans Sonnet XC was almost synonymous with Petrarchism—and ideal love.

Yet the Miltonic text represents Eve obliquely, from the side, which creates a moment of unease that Aers and Hodge describe. By slightly altering the aesthetically acclaimed form that creates a particular and oppressive mode of sexual recognition (her golden hair and submissive charms), the visual image presents woman from a new angle. Eve only half reclines on Adam because she half retains the independence gained from her encounter with the divine voice. Laura's hair deceives and entraps—"Tra le chiome de l'or nascose il laccio / al qual mi strinse Amore" (LIX, 5–6) ("Amid the locks of gold Love hid the noose with which he bound me")—and thus, like her veil, symbolizes the distance between men and women. By contrast, Eve's golden tresses bind her and Adam together, signifying that little is hidden between them. Perhaps Adam's love is not superior to Eve's; perhaps instead their mutual dialogic, physical love is "superior" to clandestine, unrequited, unsatisfying love like Petrarch's, as the concluding reference to Jupiter and Juno suggests. In the *Canzoniere* Petrarch constantly invokes Jove's powerful thunderbolt and forcible, extramarital excursions; by contrast, Milton cites Jupiter's superior love for his wife Juno, thereby making Adam and Eve both like gods, freely enjoying a fertile love that flowers in smiles and "kisses pure." In so doing, Milton redefines "superior" to suggest not that Adam's love is higher than Eve's, but that his prelapsarian love for her, like hers for him, is transcendent or superhuman (O.E.D., 4).

Their embrace provides a visible contrast to Petrarchan love, which becomes even clearer when we re-view it through Satan's alienated gaze and discover that he has been standing apart, observing "these two / Imparadised in one another's arms," transported by admiration for Eve "whom my thoughts pursue / With wonder, and could love" (*PL* IV, 362–63).[38] Feeling the pangs of unrequited love, determined to pursue Eve even though she is married and unattainable, Satan is caught in the archetypal Petrarchan—and Lacanian—dilemma: "neither joy nor love, but fierce desire, . . . / Still unfulfill'd with pain of longing pines" (IV, 509–11). When the text differentiates, not "love, but fierce desire," it posits an ideology of love less Petrarchan than Donnean: "It cannot bee / Love, till I love her, that loves mee" ("Loves Deitie").

Satan's desires have always been Petrarchan, or rather pseudo-Petrarchan, as his relationship with Sin illustrates. Sin, "shining, heav'nly fair, a Goddess" (*PL* II, 757), represents herself in the classic Petrarchan language of Sonnet XC, the recurrent subtext of Book IV that Satan will himself exploit in his forthcoming seduction of Eve. Just as Laura's narcissism reflects Petrarch's self-absorption, Sin accepts the definition of herself as a reflection of Satan's narcissistic self-love: "Likest to thee in shape and count'nance bright" (II, 756). Springing out of Satan's heady imagination, Sin is the allegorical figure of the passions that fill his head with "flames thick and fast" (II, 754). She represents the uncontrolled, destructive nature of Petrarchan desire, figured repeatedly in images of fire, burning, and melting: "e 'l desir foco" ("desire a fire"), "mi punge Amor, m'abbaglia, et mi distrugge" (CXXXIII, 8–10) ("Love pierces me, dazzles me, and melts me").

When the conjunction of Satan's desire and Sin's reflected narcissism spawns Death, the picture is complete; for Petrarchan love produces not only sin but also symbolic death, figured in those quintessential and highly imitable oxymorons—"O viva morte, o dilettoso male" (CXXXII, 7) ("o living death, o delightful harm")—that became the sign of Petrarchism in its European reign and the cliché of Petrarchism in its decline. Sin's description of Satan's passion includes all the faded Petrarchist images in Sidney's famous parody: "Of hopes begot by fear, of wot not what desires, / Of force of heavenly beams, infusing hellish pain, / Of living deaths, dear wounds, fair storms and freezing fires" (*PL* VI, 2–4). Indeed, as Christopher Grose suggested to me, Sidney's language sounds very much like the physical ecology of hell in Book II.

Because he cannot escape his own self-absorption, Satan epitomizes the univocal monomania of Petrarchism, incapable of the love and empathy that enables Adam and Eve's verbal and corporeal conversation. Except for the grotesque parody of a conversation with Sin and Death discussed above, Satan speaks either in soliloquy, where, like a Petrarchan lover, he bemoans his solitude, frustration, and fierce desire, turning his self-absorbed Petrarchan gaze into solitary poetry of remarkable power; or in apostrophe, where he projects his feelings onto the distant, silent sun, much as the Petrarchan poet/lover projects his feelings onto the distant, silent heavenly figure of his beloved; or in oratory, calculated to persuade and deceive, like those cynics who used pseudo-Petrarchan poetry as a tool of seduction and thus incurred the wrath of seventeenth-century defenders of women such as Mary Tattle-well and Ioane Hit-Him-Home. The ensuing conversation between Adam and Eve again stands in sharp contrast to the standard discourse of Petrarchism. Adam's remarks about "th'hour of night" recall Petrarch's recurrent nighttime complaints— especially Sonnet XXII, which bemoans the nocturnal solitude that sets the Petrarchan poet/lover apart from the animals which "labor . . . while it is day." While Petrarchan poet/lovers neither work nor sleep, Adam and Eve sleep soundly together because they work well together:

> the timely dew of sleep
> Now falling with soft slumbrous weight inclines
> Our eye-lids; other Creatures all day long
> Rove idle unemploy'd, and less need rest.   (*PL* IV, 614–17)

Petrarch's canzone concludes with one of his most explicit (and unattainable) sexual fantasies, but Adam and Eve converse as they approach "their blissful bower" and the fulfillment of the unfulfillable Petrarchan dream.

Eve's response, a beautiful paean to the seasons (*PL* IV, 635–58), also recalls and inverts the familiar Petrarchan Sonnet CCCX (and its countless English imitations including Surrey's much-admired "The Soote Season"), which describes the returning delights of spring only to conclude: "Ma per me, lasso, tornano i più gravi / sospiri" ("But to me, alas, come back heavier sighs"). The convention has already been evoked at least twice: first, in those plangent lines from the invocation to light—"Thus with the Year / Seasons return, but not to me returns / Day, or the sweet approach of Ev'n or Morn" (III, 40–42)—which show just how alluring Milton found the poetry of Petrarchism apart from the ideology of Petrarchism; again, when Satan enters Eden to discover the joys of nature, "all delight of human sense" (IV, 206) through eyes that cannot enjoy: "the Fiend / Saw undelighted all delight, all kind / Of living Creatures new to sight and strange" (IV, 285–86). Like Petrarch's canzone, Eve's hymn praises the sky, the meadows, the flowers, the nightingale; but she gives the plaintive Petrarchan convention a happy turn when she concludes that none "without thee is sweet." Her pleasure in the shared experience is inseparable from her pleasure in sharing the conversation, which she praises ("with thee conversing I forget all time") and deliberately extends by repeating the entire catalogue and ending with a question calculated to prolong the conversation.[39]

Before retiring for the night, "both stood, / Both turn'd, and under op'n Sky ador'd / The God that made both Sky, Air, Earth and Heav'n" (*PL* IV, 720–22). "Imagine doing that," Diane McColley writes. "Could any-

thing be more engaging than the mutual, spontaneous production of poetry and song, made possible by shared rapture and established structure?" (p. 116). Like the courtship sonnet Romeo and Juliet coauthor, this
hymn, "said unanimous," proves that Adam and Eve are, as they claim,
united in their just adoration of God and their perfect understanding of
each other: "happy in our mutual help / And mutual love" (IV, 727–28).
Perhaps, though, the best comparison is Donne's "Extasie," where the
lovers experience such a unison of thought and feeling that their silent
"dialogue of one" leads, without a word having been spoken aloud, to a
consummation that is at once sexual and spiritual.

When Adam and Eve finally retire for the night, moreover, Milton
pauses to offer his own hymn extolling "wedded love," and for the first
time, to denounce Petrarchan love poetry openly: the "Serenate, which
the starv'd Lover sings / To his proud fair, best quitted with disdain" (*PL*
IV, 769–70). The starved lover, the proud fair, disdain: all these Petrarchist clichés, capped with the word "serenade" (especially the Ital-
ianate variant, "*serenate*" which occurs in some texts) appear that we
might see and know the temptation of Petrarchism, and yet abstain.[40] At
this climactic moment, Cupid turns up, not hiding treacherously in the
lady's eyes, or fleeing to take refuge in the poet's heart—as in Petrarch's
Sonnet CXL or Sidney's "Fly, fly, my friends" (XX)—but right out in the
open, reveling in this consummate experience: "Here Love his golden
shafts imploys . . . waves his purple wings, / Reigns here and revels" (IV,
763–65).

This pronouncement, made as the scene changes to reveal the lovers
lying together in their blissful bower bedecked with flowers, recalls another of Petrarch's most glorious, visionary memories of Laura sitting on
the ground while a rain of flowers descended upon her: one on her skirt,
one on her braids, one on the ground, one on the water; and "one, with a
lovely wandering, turning about seemed to say, 'Qui regna Amore. Quante
volte diss' io / allor, pien di spavento: / 'Costei per fermo nacque in
paradiso!' " (CXXVI, 51–55) (" 'Here reigns Love.' How many times did I
say to myself then, full of awe: 'She was surely born in Paradise' "). The
quotation, "Here reigns love," the flowers falling all about, the paradisal
birth: all this seems as close as we ever get to Petrarchan language that
could be called a direct inspiration for *Paradise Lost;* but it is actually less
notable as a source than as an allusion that critiques, even as it evokes,
Petrarch's canzone. In reading *Paradise Lost*, as Hazlitt remarked, "we feel
ourselves under the influence of a mighty intellect, that the nearer it approaches to others, becomes more distinct from them."[41] The serenade that
the Petrarchan lover sings, the appearance of Love which reigns here and

revels—these composite allusions to Canzone CXXVI remind us once again that Renaissance love poetry cannot be a-Petrarchan, that all formulations of love—even prelapsarian wedded love—encounter Petrarchism as a temptation to be faced and resisted. Laden with forgetfulness, lost in a visionary dream, thinking he is in heaven, Petrarch is divided from Laura, the true image, by his own imagination: "sì diviso / da l'imagine vera." Alluding to Petrarch's separation from Laura at the very moment when the text dramatizes Adam and Eve's verbal, sexual, spiritual union, *Paradise Lost* again uses Petrarchan imagery to reject Petrarchan ideology.

Indeed, at this very moment active resistance to Petrarchism is urgently required for the first time in the poem; for as the lovers are falling asleep, Satan is plotting to transform their fill of "bliss on bliss" into the endless frustrations of Petrarchism: "enjoy, till I return, / Short pleasures, for long woes are to succeed" (*PL* IV, 534–35). The guardian angels discover Satan, "Squat like a Toad, close at the ear of *Eve*" (IV, 800), trying to insinuate "distemper'd, discontented thoughts, / Vain hopes, vain aims, inordinate desires / Blown up with high conceits ingend'ring pride" (IV, 807–09), echoing the vain hopes and vain sorrows, "vane speranze e 'l van dolore," that Petrarch immortalizes in his opening sonnet. If only Eve could have read (as Milton himself might have) Mary Tattle-well and Ioane Hit-him-Home's warning about the duplicity of poet/lovers: "I wish all women and maids in generall, to beware of their gilded Glosses; an enamoured Toade lurks under the sweet grasse, and a faire tongue hath been too often the varnish or Embroidery of a false heart; what are they but lime-twiggs of Lust, and Schoole-masters of Folly?" (pp. 69–70).

Steeled to suffer the lengthy frustrations inherent in the role he has chosen, not to be dissuaded by temporary banishment, Satan is a committed Petrarchist love poet. He returns in Book V to disturb Eve's peaceful sleep with a Petrarchan dream, symbolically enacting the Petrarchan assumption that whatever pleases in the world is a brief dream: "che quanto piace al mondo è breve sogno" (I, 14). When he addresses Eve as a Petrarchan lady, "happy Creature, fair Angelic *Eve* . . . Thyself a Goddess, not to Earth confin'd" (*PL* V, 74, 78), Satan offers her the "high exaltation" (V, 90) of Petrarchist idolatry—every innocent (or gullible) Renaissance girl's fantasy, I suppose. Satan's pseudo-Petrarchan rhetoric is easily identifiable, for once again it plunders and violates *Rime* XC, that most famous commemoration of Petrarch's first sight of Laura to which Milton and Renaissance poets constantly return (as Petrarch does himself). Since "ravishment" meant both mystical transport and forcible abduction or violation of a woman, Satan's flattering description of Eve as "Nature's desire, / In whose sight all things joy, with ravishment / Attracted by thy beauty still to gaze" (*PL* V, 45–47), reveals that Satanic seduction, like Petrarchan idolatry, violates the woman it so mystically exalts by subjecting the woman's independent vision of herself to the admiring male gaze. Alas, Satan's Petrarchism is beginning to insinuate itself; *now* we see and judge Eve through the male gaze: seeing her "discomposed" and "glowing," Adam "Hung over her enamor'd, and beheld / Beauty, which whether waking or asleep, / Shot forth peculiar graces" (V, 13–15). "Peculiar" is usually glossed as "particular," while "graces" means both female charms and divine favor; but Eve is suspiciously "discomposed," reminding us that "peculiar" also meant strange, odd, or queer. When Eve first appeared "with native Honor clad," in her "looks Divine / The image of thir glorious Maker shone" (IV, 289, 291–92). Now "glowing" with the "ravishment" of Satan's Petrarchist idolatry, her original divine incandescence momentarily obscured, Eve resembles Petrarch's idolatrous vision of Laura, shining and resplendent like a sun or a goddess.

Stirred by Eve's beauty as never before in the poem, demonstrating the powerful temptation Petrarchism held for all Renaissance poets, including Milton, Adam utters his most passionate and poignant love language yet. Awakening to his tender profession of love, Eve recounts her dream without hesitation, confirming the continuing conversation and complete trust that enables them again to sing a hymn of praise, "Unmeditated, such prompt eloquence / Flow'd from thir lips" (*PL* V, 149–50). Their hymn epitomizes the experience of mature, mutual love, that experience Kristeva describes as "miraculous—the experience of having been able to exist for, through, with another mind" (Kristeva, p. 4). Adam and Eve had better seize the day and enjoy their time together before Satan's Petrarchist persuasion destroys their perfect happiness. This is the last time their conversation will end in such perfect unanimity. Having defined married love as the obverse of Petrarchan love, the second half of *Paradise Lost* proceeds to confront, toy with, and finally, though not conclusively, to ward off the powerful temptation to Petrarchize.

Even in Eden Milton could not imagine a world (or a God) that did not require men and women to strive to resolve that central challenge for Renaissance culture (as for our own): the difficulty of gender relations. In Book VIII while Adam can still clearly perceive and defend the incalculable advantages of mutual, conversational love, the conversation with Raphael shows Adam struggling to rebuff the allure of Satan's Petrarchan temptation, prefiguring the even more powerful temptation Petrarchism poses for him (and us) in the postlapsarian world. As anyone wishing to defend Milton's idea of women would surely want to point out, God allows Adam to formulate his wish for a helpmeet—"To see how [he could] judge of fit and meet" (*PL* VIII, 448)—and then agrees to fulfill this "wish, exactly to [his] heart's desire" (VIII, 451)—much as Eve approved Adam's first speech because it was "just and right" and suasively egalitarian— precisely because Adam understands that "a meet and happy conversation is the chiefest and the noblest end of marriage" (YP III, p. 391); because he believes "true delight . . . must be mutual"; and because he requests a wife "fit to participate / All rational delight," capable of sharing the "fellowship" and "conversation" of equals (*PL* VIII, 390–391).

Yet Adam was in fact wrong to think that Eve is the result of his desire, as God tells him in no uncertain terms: "I, ere thou spak'st, / Knew it not good for Man to be alone" (*PL* VIII, 444–45), and here, I think, "man" is a generic rather than a masculine term. Adam's account of Eve's creation is a rare and enchanting literary moment because it shows how "lovely fair" the language of love can become when the beloved escapes objectification and mastery by the male gaze. Upon first seeing Eve (VIII, 474–77), Adam experiences a visionary transport as does Petrarch upon first seeing Laura; but for Adam (as for Milton and the Puritans who exalt the inner revelation of the spirit), the experience is less the result of sight than a revelation of sight's inadequacies. What does this beloved woman look like? Petrarch tells us in loving detail, again and again. Adam does not, although we see Eve here through his eyes.

Awestruck though asleep and passive, Adam watches as Eve is created, inspired, and empowered by God (not Adam): "Under his forming hands a Creature grew" (*PL* VIII, 470)—an independent subject. Attempting to regain control, Adam's narrative struggles to reduce her from the clear, undeniable subject of the sentence to the object of his gaze, the object of his desire, the object of his controlling and limiting prepositional phrases: "in her summ'd up, in her contain'd, / And in her looks" (VIII, 473–74). But the verbal ambiguity of "her looks," which first seems to represent her beauty rendering her the object of Adam's gaze, suddenly turns into *her* gaze, making her the subject of a subordinate clause so powerful that Adam becomes the object of a prepositional phrase controlled by "her looks, which from that time infus'd / Sweetness into my heart" and "into all things" (VIII, 474–75). Even as the parallelism gives her powerful looks unrestricted power, the sentence is pulled apart again: "and" becomes a conjunction extending the power of "her looks" over yet another clause: "And into all things from her Air inspir'd / The spirit of love and amorous delight" (VIII, 476–77). If we take air to mean "mien, look," the second prepositional phrase, "from her air," refocuses attention on her appearance and strives to reassert Adam's power over the sentence, to reduce her to the object of his gaze/his prepositions. Yet "air" could also mean "breath," which "gains support from the fact that in Milton's time the physical sense of inspired ('breathed') was still current"; Fowler concludes, in fact, that these lines are "radically ambiguous, [these] two main possibilities being separable."[42] I would argue, however, that both "her looks" (an ambiguity Fowler does not note) and "her air" should be read as *amphibologia*, a figure of speech that allows the sense to be construed two or three ways at once.[43] When the two readings converge, her beauty as it appears to Adam turns into her gaze as it expresses her subjectivity, her sexual desire, and her breath, her inner spirit. This moment of revelation conquers the Satanic Petrarchism that subjected Eve ("In whose sight all things joy, with ravishment / Attracted by thy beauty still to gaze" [V, 46–47]), even as it reenacts that earlier and equally momentous syntactical disruption of Book IV, where the divine voice transformed Eve from the object of our patriarchal expectations ("hee / Whose image thou art" [IV, 471–72]) to the subject of her own desire ("him thou shalt enjoy / Inseparably thine" [IV, 472–73]).

Quite simply, this transformative moment turns our mundane conceptions of love and women inside out, for Adam's words, passing over Eve's appearance pull our gaze irresistibly inward until, suddenly, we find ourselves looking back at Adam and the world, experiencing the sexual and spiritual power of Eve's desiring, inspiring love. As the divine voice explained to Eve—and she has already explained to Adam and us, both in the story of her creation and in her hymn to nature's joys (none of which "without thee is sweet")—it is her gaze, her birthright, her "love and amorous delight" at the sight of Adam, that produces "the spirit of love and amorous delight" in Adam and "in all things." Mary Nyquist asks, "Why, if Adam was formed first, then Eve, does Adam tell his story to Raphael last, in Book VIII?" (1987, p. 115). Nyquist suggests that Adam's creation narrative follows Eve's in order to provide an official male theory for her female praxis. I would argue instead that Eve's version, with its prominent narrative priority, provides (1) a precedent which helps us to assess the strengths and limitations of Adam's version; (2) a divine, authoritative voice which supplements and explains the ellipses in Adam's account; (3) an alternative point of view which shows that Adam's perspective is (like Eve's) a limited, singular point of view. For when Adam tells Raphael that he awakened to discover her walking toward him, he acknowledges that Eve's account of her birth constitutes the ellipsis that explains his account of her birth:

> Led by her Heav'nly Maker, though unseen,
> And guided by his voice, nor uninform'd

Of nuptial Sanctity and marriage Rites:
Grace was in all her steps, Heav'n in her Eye,
In every gesture dignity and love.   (*PL* VIII, 485–89)

To prepare Adam for the moment when Eve transforms desire into delight by gazing at him with dignity and love, God has taken Eve visibly and physically away from Adam's side. At the pool where Adam cannot see her, before his gaze can objectify and master her as Petrarch's poetry objectifies and masters Laura, Eve sees herself and hears God's divine voice. As Lynn Enterline notes (p. 46), when Eve disappears from sight, Adam seems to be in great danger of becoming a Petrarchan lover, always yearning for the unattainable image of his desire: "Shee disappear'd, and left me dark, I wak'd / To find her, or for ever to deplore / Her loss, and other pleasures all abjure" (*PL* VIII, 478–80). But the Petrarchan threat does not dissolve when Eve reappears, as Enterline assumes, because Adam's ensuing description of her reflects the disturbance created in her looks by her Satanic/Petrarchan dream.

Ever since hearing Eve's dream, Adam has felt dangerously distracted by her beauty. That creates the first breach in their perfect paradisal dialogue, for Adam tells Raphael what he did not and cannot tell Eve. Placing Eve on a pedestal that distances and isolates ("yet when I approach / Her loveliness, so absolute she seems / And in herself complete" [*PL* VIII, 546–48]), describing her and her effect on him rather than conversing with her as he did in Book IV, Adam momentarily sounds like a Petrarchist poet. Eve's poised self-sufficiency (like Laura's) tempts Adam to believe what Petrarch and his successors repeatedly proclaim: that the woman is the sole guardian of virtue and wisdom; "what she wills to do or say, / Seems wisest, virtuousest, discreetest, best" (VIII, 549–50).[44] Passion and adoration threaten to make him servile; he tells Raphael, "All higher knowledge in her presence falls / Degraded" (VIII, 551–52). In exalting Eve's beauty and virtue, Adam devalues himself—thus laying the foundation for the posture of the abject, embittered Petrarchan lover that he will assume temporarily after the Fall.

In the humorous exchange with Raphael that follows, Adam reasserts the difference between his connubial bliss and the distant, unfulfilled longing of Petrarchism, and shows that the temptations of Petrarchism can be faced and overcome. Raphael reprimands Adam for his servility and says that human love is the scale by which he should ascend to heavenly love; but Adam is not satisfied by Raphael's Neoplatonism, nor should he be, for Milton and Milton's God have both approved "nuptial Sanctity and marriage Rites" (*PL* VIII, 487). When Adam asks Raphael whether angels love "by looks only" as the *Petrarchisti* do, "or do they mix / Irradiance, virtual or immediate touch?" (VIII, 615–17), his blunt question prompts Raphael to admit that angels consummate their desires ("if Spirits embrace, / Total they mix, Union of Pure with Pure / Desiring" [VIII, 626–28]), and the threat of Petrarchism is again put to rest—for the moment.

   "[C]ourtly love. What is it?" Jacques Lacan asks. "It is an altogether refined way of making up for the absence of sexual relation by pretending that it is we who put an obstacle to it. It is truly the most staggering thing that has ever been tried. But how can we expose its fraud?" (1982, p. 141). Lacan attributes the absence of sexual relation to the symbolic phallic lack the oedipal complex creates. Asking much the same questions—what is courtly love? how can we expose its fraud?—*Paradise Lost* attributes the lack of loving, fulfilling sexual relationship to the Satanic Petrarchism that both precipitates and emerges from the Fall. Although there is no space (or need) here to reexamine the "fraudulent temptation" that finally succeeds in Book IX, suffice it to say that Eve, allured by Satan's Petrarchist promise of admiration, transcendence, and power, temporarily forgets the value of her more perfect Edenic love. We do not forget, however; for "exaggeration of the servile tone and compression into a few lines of so many hyperbolic words and images typical of the language of courtly love poetry," as Anne Ferry explains, "creates the effect of parody" and exposes the hollowness of Satan's fawning Petrarchan rhetoric (p. 141).

   After the Fall, Adam and Eve enter the abyss of Petrarchism that they have heretofore skirted and resisted; when they talk like self-indulgent, self-absorbed Petrarchist lovers, their experience of separation, recriminations, discord, and deceit, warns us that the Satanic temptations of Petrarchism make mutual, conversational love all the more vulnerable in the postlapsarian world.[45] Responding to Eve's fallen discourse, divided between narcissistic self-absorption and performative duplicity, Adam also begins to think one thing and say another. In lines 896–916, his admiring, loving thoughts resemble the more positive Petrarchist poems of praise. In lines 921–960 his harsh words echo the Petrarchist poems of recrimination and blame. The jarring fluctuation of tone shows that bliss has bled into woe, producing the wildly conflicting feelings that allow Petrarchan sonnet sequences to achieve stasis but not peace in oxymoronic tension. Misogyny rears its ugly head, not because Milton is a misogynist,[46] but because Adam, having fallen, needs a scapegoat for his misdeed. At the end of Book IX Adam withdraws from Eve, for the first time seeking solitude rather than "union and communion." Alone and self-pitying, haunted by a past before love turned his life to misery, Adam begins to sound like the bleakest of Petrarchist lovers, aggressively attacking female pride and cruelty ("O serpent") in terms that recall bitter Petrarchan complaints (like *Rime* CCCX or *Amoretti* XXXI) against women as "cruel, savage beasts."

Adam and Eve, like Spenser's poet/lover and his beloved Elizabeth but unlike Petrarch and Laura, emerge from the isolation and misery of Petrarchism through conversation and empathy that restore the understanding, if not the spontaneous unanimity, that made their original Edenic love so glorious. In Book X Eve comes to Adam, begs forgiveness, and offers to accept full punishment for the Fall. By humbling herself, she prompts Adam to talk to her once again, to recognize their mutual fault and mutual love. Adam learns from Eve's humility: her words and gestures teach him to join her in kneeling to God and begging his forgiveness. The Fall requires a new kind of conversation, a willingness to listen to each other. The word "helpmeet" takes on a new meaning, for now they need each other to see the errors of their own self-deceptions. They no longer speak in one voice, improvising unanimous hymns of praise, because now each must express repentance—and desire—separately. Eve and Adam's fallen discourse never regains its perfect unanimity; but purged of Petrarchist clichés, their renewed capacity for dialogue makes mutual love possible in the postlapsarian world they enter at the end of the poem.

As the poem prepares for its conclusion, God describes his purpose in saving Adam from Petrarchism:

> He sorrows now, repents, and prays contrite,
> My motions in him: longer than they move,
> His heart I know, how variable and vain
> Self-left.   (*PL* XI, 90–93)

The words "variable" and "vain" again recall, and finally reject, the "vario stile," the "vane speranze e 'l van dolore" (I, 5–6), the signature of Petrarchism. Appropriately (since her original appearance "infus'd / Sweetness into my heart, unfelt before, / And into all things from her Air inspir'd / The spirit of love and amorous delight" [*PL* VIII, 474–77]) at the end of the epic Eve puts into words—words learned not from Adam or an angelic messenger but from the inward, unmediated, divine inspiration of her dream—the empathetic, hopeful love that makes it still possible, though clearly more difficult, to continue their conversational intimacy in the postlapsarian world:

> Whence thou return'st, and whither went'st, I know;
> For God is also in sleep, and Dreams advise,
> Which he hath sent propitious, some great good
> Presaging.   (*PL* XII, 610–13)

Having escaped the isolation and monologic self-examination of Petrarchan poetry and broken the cycle of egotism, recrimination, and discord that succeeded the Fall, their conversation now moves toward the resolution of Elizabethan love poetry at its dialogic best, as Puttenham's 1589 *Arte of Poesie* (p. 60) instructs love poets to do: "in the ende laughing, rejoicing and solacing the beloved againe, . . . moving one way and another to great compassion." In her brief, hopeful speech Eve alludes to the highlights of their prelapsarian love. Her divine dream dispels the Satanic nightmare that first tempted her with Petrarchism; her willingness to go with Adam ("without thee here to stay, / Is to go hence unwilling" [*PL* XII, 616–17]) reenacts the rejection of Petrarchan narcissism with which her life began, and echoes the rapturous Edenic hymn to nature's joys (none "without thee is sweet") that distinguished their fulfilled, mutual Edenic love from Petrarch's frustrated, solitary complaint.

As they now prepare to leave the nuptial bower where Adam once "led her blushing like the Morn" (*PL* VIII, 511), Eve says, "but now lead on; / In mee is no delay" (XII, 614–15), inadvertently recalling "the sweet reluctant amorous delay" that enabled Edenic desire, always so freshly alluring, to withstand the temptations it now includes: lust, selfishness, narcissism, idealization, misogyny, and hostility. Their fall inscribes Petrarchism in human love and discourse, but their salvation reclaims conversation as an active alternative for postlapsarian relationships. Although writing within an inherited patriarchal discourse, Milton adds the part of the story silenced by the *Canzoniere* but recovered by Mary Sidney's translation of *The Triumph of Death:* Laura's part, Eve's part, women's parts. To insure that Eve's voice continues into the fallen world, she is given not only the first account of their meeting in Book IV but also the last human words to be spoken in Book XII; for "*Adam* heard / Well pleas'd, but answer'd not" (*PL* XII, 624–25). In the end Eve's love and God's grace save Adam from the Satanic, and all too human, temptation of becoming a narcissistic Petrarchist lover; and for this reason, when they leave Eden together, "hand in hand with wand'ring steps and slow" (XII, 648)—in a tableau for which, as Roland Frye has noted, there are no apparent precedents—Adam and Eve, still "hand in hand . . . the loveliest pair / That ever since in love's imbraces met" (IV, 321–22) represent the triumphant culmination of the English Petrarchan critique.

Williams College

NOTES

1. *The Collected Works of William Hazlitt*, ed. A. R. Waller and Arnold Glover (London, 1902), vol. V, p. 58. Harold Bloom, *The Anxiety of Influence* (London, 1973), p. 50. The present essay, written with support from the National Endowment for the Humanities, is part of a book-length study of courtship and Elizabethan poetry now in preparation. For invaluable suggestions in the development of my argument, I am grateful to Robert Bell, Anne Ferry, Dayton Haskin, and John Shawcross.

2. Julia Kristeva, *Tales of Love*, trans. Leon S. Roudiez (New York, 1987), p. 1.

3. Studies of Eve to which I am especially indebted are Anne Ferry, *Milton's Epic Voice* (Cambridge, Mass., 1963), pp. 141–45; Ferry, "Milton's Creation of Eve," *SEL* 28 (1988), pp. 113–32; Barbara Lewalski "Milton on Women—Yet Once More," in *Milton Studies VI*, ed. James D. Simmonds (Pittsburgh, 1974), pp. 3–20; Diane Kelsey McColley, *Milton's Eve* (Urbana, Ill., 1983). Studies of marriage which I have found helpful include David Aers and Bob Hodge, " 'Rational Burning': Milton on Sex and Marriage," in *Milton Studies XIII*, ed. James D. Simmonds (Pittsburgh, 1979), pp. 3–31; John Halkett, *Milton and the Idea of Matrimony: A Study of the Divorce Tracts and Paradise Lost* (New Haven, 1970); W. Haller and M. Haller, "The Puritan Art of Love," *HLQ* 5 (1941–1942), 235–72; and James Grantham Turner, *One Flesh: Paradisal Marriage and Sexual Relations in the Age of Milton* (Oxford, 1987).

4. Milton's prose quoted from *Complete Prose Works of John Milton*, 8 vols., ed. Don M. Wolfe, et al. (New Haven, 1953–82); cited here from II, p. 228 and II, p. 246; subsequent volume and page references will appear in the text as YP.

5. Thomas Greene, "Petrarch and the Humanist Hermeneutic," in *Italian Literature Roots and Branches: Essays in Honor of Thomas Goddard Bergin*, ed. Giose Rimanelli and Kenneth John Atchity (New Haven, 1976), pp. 212, 209–10.

6. See Stephen Minta, *Petrarch and Petrarchism: The English and French Traditions* (New York, 1980); Anthony Mortimer, *Petrarch's Canzoniere in the English Renaissance* (Bergamo, It., 1975); and George Watson, *The English Petrarchans: A Critical Bibliography of the Canzoniere* (London, 1967).

7. William Riley Parker, *Milton: A Biography*, 2 vols. (Oxford, 1968); John S. Smart, *The Sonnets of Milton* (Glasgow, 1921); E.A.J. Honigmann, ed., *Milton's Sonnets* (New York, 1966); and F. T. Prince, *The Italian Element in Milton's Verse* (Oxford, 1954). See also Irene Samuel's references to Petrarch in *Dante and Milton: The Commedia and Paradise Lost* (Ithaca, 1966), pp. 35–41, and Lynn E. Enterline's argument that Milton alters his Petrarchan sources to incorporate the lady's voice in " 'Myself / Before Me': Gender and Prohibition in Milton's Italian Sonnets," in *Milton and the Idea of Woman*, ed. Julia M. Walker (Urbana, Ill., 1988), p. 45.

8. The major exception is William Kerrigan and Gordon Braden's innovative essay, "Milton's Coy Eve: Paradise Lost and Renaissance Love Poetry," *ELH* 53 (1986), 27–51. For an alternative interpretation see B. A. Wright, *Milton's "Paradise Lost"* (London, 1966), pp. 55–56, and S. A. Demetrakopoulos, "Eve as a Circean and Courtly Fatal Woman," *MQ* 9 (1975), 105, who argues that "courtly love and Circean allusions merge into one powerful indictment of Eve."

9. Barbara Kiefer Lewalski, *"Paradise Lost" and the Rhetoric of Literary Forms* (Princeton, 1985).

10. See, for example, Giuseppe Mazzotta, *"The Canzoniere* and the Language of the Self," *SP* 75 (1978), 271.

11. Nancy Vickers, "Diana Described: Scattered Woman and Scattered Rhyme," *CI* 8 (1981), 278.

12. Fredric Jameson, *The Political Unconscious: Narrative as a Socially Symbolic Act* (Ithaca, 1981), p. 85.

13. Useful observations include those of Northrop Frye, "The Revelation to Eve," in *"Paradise Lost": A Tercentenary Tribute,* ed. Balachandra Rajan (Toronto, 1969), p. 28; Joan Kelly, *Women, History, and Theory: The Essays of Joan Kelly* (Chicago, 1984); and Joan Malory Webber, "The Politics of Poetry: Feminism and *Paradise Lost*," in *Milton Studies* XIV, ed. James D. Simmonds (Pittsburgh, 1980), p. 13.

14. Mary Tattle-well and Ioane hit-him home Spinsters, *The Womens Sharpe Revenge: Or an answer to Sir Seldome Sober that writ those railing Pamphelets called the Iuniper and Crabtree Lectures, etc.* (London, 1640), pp. 67–68. Thus, I would argue that Renaissance women, like "all women can (and do) think about, criticize, and alter discourse, and thus, that subjectivity can be reconstructed through the process of reflective practice," as Linda Alcoff writes, though not in relation to the Renaissance, in "Cultural Feminism Versus Post-Structuralism: The Identity Crisis in Feminist Theory," *Signs* 13 (1988), 425. For a related, but fuller argument, see Teresa de Lauretis, *Alice Doesn't* (Bloomington, Ind., 1984). On the problems facing feminism as a result of the postmodernist disappearance of the subject, see Alice A. Jardine, *Gynesis: Configurations of Woman and Modernity* (Ithaca, 1985); Ann Rosalind Jones, "Inscribing femininity: French theories of the feminine," in *Making a Difference: Feminist Literary Criticism,* ed. Gayle Greene and Coppélia Kahn (New York, 1985), pp. 80–112; and Nancy K. Miller, "Arachnologies: The Woman, the Text, and the Critic," *The Poetics of Gender,* ed. Nancy K. Miller (New York, 1986), pp. 270–95. On Renaissance women writers, see Elaine V. Beilin, *Redeeming Eve: Women Writers of the English Renaissance* (Princeton, 1987); *Silent But for the Word: Tudor Women as Patrons, Translators, and Writers of Religious Works,* ed. Margaret P. Hannay (Kent, Ohio, 1985); *Women in the Middle Ages and the Renaissance: Literary and Historical Perspectives,* ed. Mary Beth Rose (Syracuse, N.Y., 1986).

15. In addition to the studies cited above (notes 3, 8, and 13), see Marilyn R. Farwell, "Eve, the Separation Scene, and the Renaissance Idea of Androgyny," in *Milton Studies* XVI, ed. James D. Simmonds (Pittsburgh, 1982), pp. 3–20, and Lana Cable, "Coupling Logic and Milton's Doctrine of Divorce," in *Milton Studies* XV, ed. Simmonds (Pittsburgh, 1981), pp. 143–159.

16. See Lewalski, "Milton on Women," pp. 6–8. For a thoughtful study of the topic, though not in relation to Milton, see Roy Roussel, *The Conversation of the Sexes: Seduction and Equality in Selected Seventeenth- and Eighteenth-Century Texts* (New York, 1986).

17. Mary Nyquist, "Reading the Fall: Discourse and Drama in *Paradise Lost*," *ELR* 13 (1983), 203. Similar reservations are expressed by Georgia B. Christopher, *Milton and the Science of the Saints* (Princeton, 1982), p. 149, and Christopher Kendrick, *Milton: A Study in Ideology and Form* (New York, 1986), 210–11.

18. *Paradise Lost* quoted here and throughout from *John Milton: Complete Poems and Major Prose,* ed. Merritt Y. Hughes (Indianapolis, 1957).

19. Jacques Lacan, *Female Sexuality: Jacques Lacan and the école freudienne,* ed. Juliet Mitchell and Jacqueline Rose, trans. Jacqueline Rose (New York, 1982), pp. 154, 143. This is why Eve prefers Adam's "grateful digressions" to Raphael's message (*PL* VIII, 55).

20. My argument has been influenced by Jessica Benjamin's critique of psychoanalysis, *The Bonds of Love: Psychoanalysis, Feminism, and the Problem of Domination* (New York, 1988).

21. Quoted throughout in Italian and English from *Petrarch's Lyric Poems, The Rime sparse and Other Lyrics*, trans. and ed. Robert M. Durling (Cambridge, Mass., 1976).

22. See Diane McColley's illuminating discussion in *Milton and the Idea of Woman*, p. 108.

23. On the symbolic significance of this moment, see Patricia Parker, *Inescapable Romance: Studies in the Poetics of a Mode* (Princeton, 1979), pp. 114–23.

24. Mieke Bal, "Sexuality, Sin and Sorrow: The Emergence of the Female Character: (A Reading of Genesis 1–3)," *Poetics Today* (1985), 21–42, argues compellingly that Eve was in fact created before Adam, but this was certainly not the understanding of the biblical text either in the seventeenth century or in *Paradise Lost*.

25. Mary Nyquist, "The Genesis of Gendered Subjectivity in the Divorce Tracts and in *Paradise Lost*," in *Re-membering Milton: Essays on the Texts and Traditions*, ed. Mary Nyquist and Margaret W. Ferguson (New York, 1987), p. 119.

26. Quoted in Stephen Heath, "Différence," *Screen* 19 (1978), 84.

27. Turner, *One Flesh*, p. 238.

28. Christine Froula, "When Eve Reads Milton: Undoing the Canonical Economy," *CI* 10 (1983), 328. Comparing Eve's memory of her creation with Adam's, Maureen Quilligan, *Milton's Spenser: The Politics of Reading* (Ithaca, 1933), p. 228, values Eve's moment of selfhood but regrets its brevity.

29. Jardine, *Gynesis*, p. 39. On the male gaze, see Laura Mulvey, *Visual and Other Pleasures* (Bloomington, Ind., 1989).

30. Quoted in Jameson, *Political Unconscious*, p. 239.

31. For a discussion of this preference, see my essay, " 'Setting Foot into Divinity': George Herbert and the English Reformation," *MLQ* 38 (1977), 219–41; rptd. *Essential articles for the study of George Herbert's Poetry* (Hamden, Conn., 1979), pp. 63–83.

32. Hélène Cixous, "Le sexe ou la tête?" quoted by Heath, p. 83, connects Cixous's and Montrelay's emphasis on the voice with Irigaray's distrust of "the eye [which] objectifies and masters."

33. Janet E. Halley, "Female Autonomy in Milton's Sexual Poetics," in *Milton and the Idea of Woman*, p. 248, acknowledges Milton's "historically innovative insistence on female conversation. At least part of the importance of Eve's speech is that she *does* speak patriarchal discourse, *as* an autonomous subject." I am suggesting that at moments her discourse is more matriarchal than patriarchal.

34. For a summary of feminist theories of mothering, see Coppélia Kahn, "The Hand That Rocks the Cradle: Recent Gender Theories and Their Implications," in *The M(other) Tongue: Essays in Feminist Psychoanalytic Interpretation*, ed. Shirley Nelson Garner, Claire Kahane, and Madelon Sprengnether (Ithaca, 1985), pp. 72–88.

35. For this point, I am indebted to Heather Dubrow, *Happier Eden* (Ithaca, 1990); see also Turner, *One Flesh*, p. 216.

36. In "Women and Representation: a discussion with Laura Mulvey," *Wedge* 2 (1978), 51, Mulvey says that she wanted "to set up narcissism and a sense of the female as something quite strong in opposition to the Oedipus complex."

37. In "Wrestling with the Angel: *Paradise Lost* and Feminist Criticism," *MQ* 20 (1986), 76, William Shullenberger argues for Eve's significant difference from Adam, rather than her "inherent inferiority."

38. For the view that Satan is conceived as a "spectator/gazer" in both *Paradise Lost* and *Paradise Regained*, see Christopher Grose, *Milton and the Sense of Tradition* (New Haven, 1988), p. 107.

39. Irene Samuel, *Dante and Milton*, p. 107, discusses Eve's hymn as an embedded sonnet, "too self-contained, too exclusionary, as sonnets traditionally had been."

40. The Petrarchan critique is strengthened by the imagery of the Song of Solomon and the lyric epithalamium tradition, as Sara Thorne-Thomsen argues in " 'Hail Wedded Love': Milton's Lyric Epithalamium," in *Milton Studies* XXIV, ed. James D. Simmonds (Pittsburgh, 1988), pp. 155–85.

41. William Hazlitt, *The Collected Works of William Hazlitt*, ed. A. R. Waller and Arnold Glover (London, 1902), vol. 5., p. 58.

42. *Paradise Lost*, ed. Alastair Fowler (Harlow, Eng., 1971), p. 421.

43. See George Puttenham, *The Arte of English Poesie* (Kent, Ohio, 1970), p. 267.

44. Fredson Bowers, "Adam, Eve and the Fall in 'Paradise Lost'," *PMLA* LXXXIV (1969), 270, criticizes this moment as "effeminacy [which] consists in the exchange of places in the divinely appointed order by which Adam allowed Eve to become the guide of his judgment."

45. Suzanne Woods, "How Free are Milton's Women?," in *Milton and the Idea of Woman*, p. 15, writes: "Far from being a misogynist, Milton was ahead of his time in granting to women a dignity and responsibility rarely conceded in the seventeenth century." Marcia Landy, " 'A Free and Open Encounter': Milton and the Modern Reader," in *Milton Studies* IX, ed. James D. Simmonds (Pittsburgh, 1976), p. 23, says, "Adam displaces his anger with himself onto Eve; Eve plays the penitent in order to appease Adam's anger."

46. The point has been most forcefully argued by John Reichert in " 'Against His Better Knowledge': A Case for Adam," *ELH* 48 (1981), 83–109, an essay that has fundamentally shaped my reading of Adam and Eve's conversation. Most critics credit Eve with leading Adam toward repentance, but Georgia Christopher (*Milton and the Science of the Saints*, p. 163), argues that Adam's rehabilitation occurs through a "radically different kind of illumination—and not through the prompting of Eve's love."

"CONSIDER FIRST, THAT GREAT / OR BRIGHT INFERS NOT EXCELLENCE": MAPPING THE FEMININE IN MARY GROOM'S MILTONIC COSMOS

Wendy Furman

IN *PARADISE LOST*, writes Stevie Davies, a "mind is equated with a world, a world with a womb. In attributing the female creative function to the closed structures of his cosmos, Milton . . . implicitly use[s] the feminine as a measure of all things."[1] Over the past two decades, gender issues have gradually but steadily become very nearly the measure of things in Milton studies, whether those studies have been of Milton's domestic politics (James Turner and Maureen Quilligan); his alleged archrepresentation of a patriarchal canon (Sandra Gilbert and Christine Froula); his theology (Mary Nyquist and Philip Gallagher); his creative neuroses (Jackie Di Salvo); or his affiliation with his female readership (Joseph Wittreich).[2] But the centrality of the gender issue itself is virtually the only point upon which these Miltonists and a number of others have been able to agree. As Diane McColley has forcefully argued, when it comes to this most politically charged of topics,

The intimate relation between reader and text in *Paradise Lost* can be a prolific marriage, but it can also become a rape. And whenever there is a rape of the text, Eve gets the worst of it. Whatever our gender, if we are inclined to appropriate the poem for our own textual politics, or project our own devices and desires into it, we exploit Eve as a text object.[3]

In so doing, she suggests, we run the risk of mirroring Satan's mental state: in our inability to *imagine*, to be transformed by another's vision, we deconstruct and ultimately destroy it.

The last decade's deconstruction of Milton's Eve and her creator has been fruitfully discussed—several years ago by William Shullenberger[4] and most recently by Philip Gallagher, who set out to lay to rest, once and for all, the myth of Miltonic misogyny (pp. 7–8). But it is still something of a shock to revisit Eve the "divine afterthought" of radical feminist readings, a character whose inborn sinfulness is as complete as that of the

121

snake, and who resembles no other character in the epic so much as Sin (Gilbert, p. 3). It is still a shock, too, to find the assertions, altogether un-Miltonic, that childbearing is Eve's sole function; that sexual pleasure is legitimate only at the service of procreation; that Eve is by nature vain and silly, engaging only in housework while Adam is instructed in what makes him (not her) sufficient to stand; that at the end of the epic she is merely "put to sleep" while Adam learns, proleptically, the whole outline of salvation history.[5]

In the intervening years, and often in response to such readings, Eve and the feminine in Milton's poem have also been more fully and fairly treated: first by Barbara Lewalski and Joan Webber; more recently by Diane McColley, Douglas Anderson, Anne Ferry, and Stevie Davies, among others.[6] These readers have discovered a poem far more consistent with the great lesson Raphael teaches Adam—when he asks, with many recent readers, how "this Earth, a spot, a grain, / An atom" could be so favored by God. "Consider first," Raphael replies,

> that Great
> Or Bright infers not Excellence: the Earth
> Though, in comparison of Heav'n, so small,
> Nor glistering, may of solid good contain
> More plenty than the Sun that barren shines,
> Whose virtue on itself works no effect,
> But in the fruitful Earth; *there* first receiv'd
> His beams, unactive else, thir vigor find.
>
> (VIII, 90–97; emphasis mine)[7]

More than merely rehabilitating Eve, indeed, these readers—often in an effort *both* humanist and feminist to mediate in the vain contést between defensive humanist orthodoxy and feminist assault—have begun to discover an alternative, and potentially reconciling, *Paradise Lost:* a poem in which a divinely and joyfully gendered universe is the very center of meaning. The feminine in that universe—as well as in the human characters, male and female, who reflect its nature—is vulnerable, but not weak or intrinsically fallen; powerful, but not intrinsically threatening; life-giving before the Fall and, by mirroring the Son's *kenosis,* redemptive after. The creative principle in this universe, moreover, is far less the coercive Patriarch whose specter is nearly as old as the poem, than an androgynous divine Eros who is lovingly and, as Davies has best demonstrated, "*sensuously* pictured" (p. 206).

Visual artists have been as inclined as other Milton critics to read *Paradise Lost* as patriarchal epic—perhaps because they too have drawn upon previous traditions, in this case largely iconographic ones, at the expense of the nuances of Milton's text. Vain and prefallen Eves—not to mention prefallen Edens—abound both in biblical illustrations and, not coincidentally, in those of *Paradise Lost*. As early as 1505, for instance, one sees in a French Bible an illustration with Eve and the serpent having almost identical faces.[8] Frequent too are fierce and anthropomorphic conceptions of God. No one who has seen Carlotta Petrina's 1936 Milton illustrations, for example, can fail to remember the fascist power of her chariot of paternal deity.[9] But among Milton's best illustrators, Mary Groom is distinctive—not only for the most coherent visual reading of the epic since Blake's, but also for the reading most attentive to the two great sexes that animate Milton's cosmos.[10] Indeed, in twenty-nine wood engravings designed for the 1937 Golden Cockerel edition of *Paradise Lost*, she re-constructs, recreates Milton's text, giving visual form to something very much like the redemptive fertility myth which critics such as Anderson and especially Davies have discovered in the poet's words. Groom's designs of Milton's muse, of his Godhead, of Adam and Eve, of Eden, of Satan, of the Fall and Restoration exemplify indeed a "prolific marriage"— not only between word and image, but also between Milton's text and a reader responsive to its simplicity, sensuousness, and passion.

I

Mary Elizabeth Groom was a little-known British wood engraver, active in the nineteen-twenties and thirties, who died in 1958.[11] She illustrated two books, both published in 1937 by the Golden Cockerel Press: *Paradise Lost*, a reprint of the first impression of the ten-book first edition (1667) with twenty-nine of her wood engravings, and *Roses of Sharon*, a selection of "Poems Chosen from the Flower of Ancient Hebrew Literature," with twelve. Before World War II, a number of her prints, including several of the book illustrations, were shown at exhibitions in London. In 1985, a sale in London of some of the studio contents from her home in Suffolk brought "high-ish prices." Today several of her engravings are in the British Museum; others are at the Ashmolean Museum, Oxford; and an unknown number of prints and paintings are in the hands of relatives, friends, and buyers whose names are not recorded.

A friend and fellow artist, the late Joan Ellis White, once described Mary Groom as "a deeply rooted country woman." During and after her art studies in London she was regarded by teachers and associates as having fine talent and potential, but she apparently had mixed feelings about pursuing an artistic career. For some years she was part of a circle of British artists and wood engravers whose work was highly innovative and distinguished. The influence of some of her associates—especially Leon Underwood, the sculptor-painter-writer who was her teacher, and sculptor Henry Moore, who was her fellow student, as well as a number of other fellow wood engravers—is reflected in her fresh and original *Paradise Lost* illustrations. After their publication in her mid-thirties, however, she apparently did not take on other such projects. She made visits to Holland and Mallorca after World War II, where she completed a few paintings and sold them to North Americans; she also sent some of her work to small local exhibitions in Southwold, near her home.

Mary Groom was born in 1903 at the Old Hall, Corringham, Essex, the third child of Captain J. Bax Groom, R.D. and Mrs. C. D. Groom of Chediston Grange, Chediston, Halesworth, Suffolk. She was educated at St. Felix School, Southwold; the Royal College of Art; and the Slade School of Fine Art in London. The Grooms were a large old Suffolk farming family, who for a time moved to Harwich, went into business and became prosperous, with members of the family serving as mayors of Harwich and otherwise engaging in community life. One of Mary's brothers was the late Rev. William Groom, rector of Hoseley. Her sister, L. Rowena Groom, read English literature at Oxford during the years Mary worked on her designs for *Paradise Lost,* and shortly before her death remembered assisting the artist in making her selection of texts for illustration.[12] Mary Groom was a person of independent means, described by a relative as "forthright, very strong-minded, very kind." Joan Ellis spoke of her as having "a marvelous sense of humour and the fun of life," a quality often seen in her art, and credited her as well with "a deep spiritual side which one sees in her religious subjects"—a spiritual side, as we shall see from her engravings, which seems to have been no more literal, patriarchal, or conventional than Milton's own. For most of her life Mary Groom lived at Chediston Grange, amid the rural scenes that had inspired the lyrical work of Constable and Gainsborough, both of whom were born nearby. It was there, living quietly, that she carved the sensuous and exuberant blocks for *Paradise Lost.*[13] Her father died in 1931, her mother in the 1940s—and at that time Mary Groom moved to the Mill House at Wenhaston, where she lived until, unmarried at the age of fifty-five, she died after undergoing surgery for cancer. Her grave is in Chediston Churchyard.

In the early twenties, when she was just past twenty herself, Mary Groom studied drawing with Leon Underwood at his private Brook Green School, then located at the western end of Girdler's Road in Hammersmith. Underwood usually accepted only postgraduate students whom he regarded as especially promising. Among those also studying with Underwood was Henry Moore, on a scholarship at the Royal College of Art—whose renown as a sculptor was still ahead and whose early wood engravings, not to mention his later sculpture, show considerable affinity to Groom's own work. Also at the school, and destined to be two of her closest friends, were Blair Hughes-Stanton and Gertrude Hermes, who became leaders among English wood engravers and were later associated with the Gregynog Press. The group's interest in wood engraving was stirred, according to Thomas Balston, by a North American woman named Marion Mitchell, who had been introduced to the technique while studying with Robert Gibbings, already well established by the early twenties as a wood engraver. [14] Underwood himself, along with Henry Moore and a number of other students, took up this exciting untried medium. Thus Mary Groom became a member of an unusual circle, with Underwood as its artistic and philosophical mentor.

Most of the members of the circle showed their work at exhibitions held by the Society of Wood Engravers, which had been founded by Gibbings and others in 1920. For several years some of the Underwood group and others broke away from the original society. The two groups remained friendly, however, and later reunited. Groom showed prints at eight exhibitions between 1928 and 1938. In 1934 she was recognized as an associate member of the Society of Wood Engravers, and in 1951, the only year she exhibited after World War II, she was listed as a full member.

Mary Groom's illustrations are white-line on black. It is the "white-line" technique that distinguishes many twentieth-century wood engravings from the woodcuts that date back to the fifteenth century. Woodcuts are primarily black-line work, in which the cut is made with a knife on the side-grain, or plank, of a block of soft wood, and requires cutting away the surface of the wood on both sides of the line to be left black. In contrast, white-line wood engravings are often much finer work, done on the end-grain of a hard wood, usually box, with an assortment of pointed tools used to cut away all parts of the design that are to appear white, like chalk lines on a blackboard. (See, for example, figures 1 and 3.) As Dorothea Braby describes it, the artist "begins from utter blackness, and knows the satisfaction of saying 'Let there be light.' "[15]

Both the black-line and white-line techniques had been used in the nineteenth century, especially for commercial work. But Albert Garrett wrote in 1978 of the "excitement" felt by the post–World War I generation in "the rediscovery of a medium that had lain dormant for so long under the avalanche of commercialism . . . concepts were being clarified . . . [and the] white-line aesthetics were firmly established."[16] More recently, Simon Brett, one of the present generation of wood engravers creating

distinguished illustrations in the eighties and early nineties, has attrib-
uted to the generation of the twenties and thirties the invention of "a new
fine art medium." "A journeyman's craft," Brett writes, "which had become a Victorian industry was taken up as a potential art form for the
young modern movement. Its appeal was as a direct, vigorous alternative
to etching, similar to the appeal of carving to sculptors reacting against the
era of modelling for bronze; carving, like engraving, had become little
more than an imitative technique."[17] Similarly, Balston observes that the
wood engravers between the wars "created what was essentially a new art,
and in this new art, owing to their comparative independence of tradition
or of any central influence, produced works of remarkable variety."[18]

In the mid-thirties, when Groom was invited to illustrate *Paradise
Lost*, the Golden Cockerel Press was outstanding among the private
presses engaged in fine printing of limited editions. Books by Golden
Cockerel were so much prized by collectors that in 1931 they were sold
out a year in advance of publication. In turn, the private presses' demand
in the twenties and thirties for wood engravings to illustrate their books
helped to foster the striking growth of innovative wood engraving during
these years in England, on the continent, and in the United States. The
vogue for fine printing and the "remarkable variety" of the illustrations of
the period can be seen in the three editions of *Paradise Lost* published in
the thirties.[19] Preceding the Golden Cockerel Press's 1937 edition, which
Mary Groom illustrated, were Cresset Press's 1931 edition—published in
London, with wood engravings by D[imitrov] Galanis, a French artist who
was said to have exercised "a strong influence over American and English,
as well as French engraving";[20] and John Henry Nash's *Paradise Lost*—
published in 1936 for the Limited Editions Club of San Francisco with
plates by Carlotta Petrina (Charlotte Kennedy), a North American who
exhibited paintings and prints in the United States, France, and Italy.
Like Groom's work, the illustrations by Galanis and Petrina are interpretive rather than merely decorative, but the twelve plates that each drew
are less strongly narrative and generally reflect Milton's text less subtly
than Groom's twenty-nine engravings.

Groom had been introduced to the Golden Cockerel Press by her
close friend and colleague Blair Hughes-Stanton, and it may have been
Robert Gibbings who asked her to illustrate *Paradise Lost* before he left
the press in 1933.[21] Gibbings, the most influential figure in the fine press
movement, took over the Golden Cockerel Press in January 1924, from its
founder Harold Taylor, who had become ill. The stream of beautiful
books, many of them literary classics newly illustrated, that came from the
press in the next decade resulted from Gibbings's own considerable tal-

ents as artist, wood engraver, sculptor, and book designer as well as from his success in attracting and fostering gifted illustrators—including Eric Gill, the artist, sculptor, and wood engraver who would also soon attain great distinction as a type designer. All the titling and type used for the Groom-illustrated edition of *Paradise Lost* belonged to the Golden Cockerel font, designed by Eric Gill and cut by Caslon. And as in all the Golden Cockerel books, a great effort was made to integrate illustration and typography. By 1933, the Golden Cockerel Press had been sold to Christopher Sandford, Owen Rutter, and Francis Newbery, who continued the Press's tradition of excellence. Working with her husband was Lettice Sandford, who illustrated with wood, copper, and zinc engravings seven books for Golden Cockerel as well as a number of books for other presses. Recently Lettice Sandford recalled that although she herself had never met Mary Groom, her late husband had much admired Groom's work.[22] Apparently, in any case, it was about the time of the ownership change of Golden Cockerel Press that Groom began her work on the blocks for *Paradise Lost*. And by 1935, two years before publication of the book, she had shown versions of five of her *Paradise Lost* illustrations in an exhibition held at the Redfern Gallery by the Society of English Wood Engravers.[23]

More than a hundred male artists had illustrated *Paradise Lost* in the 247 years since the first illustrated edition of 1688. Groom appears to have been the first *woman* to design such illustrations, with some of her plates exhibited about a year before Petrina's were published in 1936. In any case, according to an endnote in the book, work on the edition was begun "on the 22nd January, 1935, and finished on the Eve of the Coronation of King George and Queen Elizabeth of England on the 12th May, 1937." The edition was limited to two hundred copies, with numbers 1–4 printed on lamb vellum full bound in white pigskin, and 5–200 printed on Batchelor paper "hand-made from pure linen rag with an appropriate Tree & Serpent watermark," and half-bound in black pigskin. The binding was by Joseph Zaehnsdorf, and the cloth sides were marbled by Sydney Cockerell in a design of red, orange, beige, and gray to suggest the flames of the "lake of fire" on which Milton's Satan and his fellow rebels find themselves after their expulsion from heaven. Reviews of the volume were enthusiastic, although most centered on its technical excellence and few undertook a critique of Groom's interpretation of the poem. One reviewer, however—Humbert Wolfe of *The Observer* for 8 August 1937—suggested that Groom was perhaps somewhat ahead of her time, and that an appreciation of her work might require a special degree of sophistication in the viewer: "Did that admirable engraver Miss Groom see Milton plain—or did she perhaps see him coloured? Or, if we criticise, is it because . . . we are too ridden with our own conceptions of Milton to see him with other eyes?"[24]

Mary Groom's engravings do indeed require "other eyes," eyes able to see beyond the patriarchal surface of Milton's text to its deep structure of feminine consciousness. It is perhaps partly for that reason (along, of course, with the rarity of the book in which her illustrations appear) that she has been largely overlooked for the past fifty years.[25] But it is also for that reason that I believe her work is especially valuable to us now. In these times so uncertain and divisive for women and men—as for Miltonists of both genders and all persuasions—Groom's silent voice, like Eve's audible one in Book X and like Milton's throughout the poem, sues for "peace, both joining, / As join'd in injuries" (924–25). Her vision, at once humanist and feminist, takes us into the womb, as Davies would put it, of Milton's cosmos—a cosmos which reflects a gentle, kenotic, and androgynous Godhead, and which supports a strong, mutually supportive humanity. At last (because with Milton she must turn her notes to tragic) Groom also expels us onto the subjected plain we know too well. But first she shows us clearly the role of the feminine in repairing the ruins wrought by a patriarchal satanic consciousness (a kind of consciousness to which we all, men and women, are too easily inclined). And in the end she shows us an Expulsion—in contrast to most Expulsions in the visual tradition, whether preceding or inspired by Milton's poem—uniquely attuned to Milton's redemptive and reconciling vision: though driven forward by the "flaming brands" of angelic anger, our first parents walk hand in hand with a restored harmony born of mutual responsibility and love.

II

The "closed structure" of Groom's Miltonic cosmos, the womblike world within which all the action is contained, is represented even in the decorative headpieces repeated for each of the ten books of the Golden Cockerel edition (see fig. 1). At first glance the design appears to be merely a profusion of leaves, stems, grass, flowers, and fruit. But almost hidden in the upper corners, involved in the natural environment as Satan will become involved with the nature of the snake he employs, the faces of Adam and Eve gradually emerge. Eve gazes thoughtfully at an enormous apple swelling beneath her—magnified like the apples, as Groom will later show them, in her dream. The apple itself is in turn involved in what looks to be foliage, but is actually the tail of a serpent, whose fanged head is disguised as a pear. Adam responds to this pear-serpent with a gesture

BOOK ONE

Figure 1. Decorative headpiece, Books I through X

of surprise, raising his leaflike hands. From the apple on the left, the serpent's body winds across the bottom of the illustration, his body partially hidden by flowers and leaves until his head emerges in its pear shape on the right side of the design. The enemy is "now hid, now seen," as is Milton's serpent in Book IX (510–14), where the poet hides Satan's name in an acrostic. Groom's serpent, indeed, moves very much like Milton's acrostic one: "With tract oblique / At first, as one who sought access, but fear'd / To interrupt, side-long he works his way" (510–12). And both his motion and his disguises perfectly demonstrate Milton's great lines from *Areopagitica:*

Good and evil we know in the field of this world grow up together almost inseparably; and the knowledge of good is so involved and interwoven with the knowledge of evil, and in so many cunning resemblances hardly to be discerned, that those confused seeds which were imposed on Psyche as an incessant labor to cull out and sort asunder, were not more intermixed. It was from out the rind of one apple tasted, that the knowledge of good and evil, as two twins cleaving together, leaped forth into the world. And perhaps this is that doom which Adam fell into of knowing . . . good by evil. (Hughes, p. 728)

But for all his capacity to deceive and dismay, to insinuate himself into the lushness of a good and fertile creation, the serpent is balanced by the also nearly hidden figure at the top-center of the design, where a gentle-faced deity—somewhat reminiscent of Blake's *Ancient of Days,* but without a trace of his patriarchal fierceness—extends leaflike hands in a gesture of prevenient blessing: "Man . . . shall find grace, . . . Mercy first and last shall brightest shine" (III, 131, 34).[26]

The mythic and "primitive" aspects of Groom's style are also well illustrated in this first and recurring decorative design. One reviewer noted the influence of the Flemish Primitives in her work (Sandford, p. 16), and some illustrations (few of those especially relevant to my discussion here) do indeed show what seems the direct influence of Rogier van der Weyden, Dirk Bouts, Hugo van der Goes, Quintin Metsys, and possibly others. Groom and her circle also explored a variety of other "primitivisms." Both Underwood and Moore, for instance, like many artists of the twenties and thirties, were deeply interested in tribal sculpture—whether African, Egyptian, Etruscan, Mexican, or Polynesian. Such models, they believed, could help them attain a mythic and spiritual quality not allied to any particular culture or creed; and what Leo van Puyvelde says of the Flemish painters resonates with the effect of Groom's work, especially as mediated through African and Polynesian influences: "A human face took on a quality of universality and became the face of a person who, though certainly an individual, was at the same time an image of humanity. A landscape was a corner of nature, but also a concentrated image of the universe."[27] Moreover, the non-European quality of some of Groom's faces and figures would not have to be entirely a matter of a search, however timely, for a more universalized human image; it would also be a matter of the medium itself, and its special appropriateness to a particular human type. As Robert Gibbings explained,

Wood engraving is essentially white on black. For dark-skinned people it is a perfect medium, because with them it is a matter of engraving lights on dark. But for light-skinned people one needs dark accents on white, and you cannot engrave dark accents; you can only engrave around them; and I have always disliked the black line.[28]

In any case, throughout Groom's work a consistent mythic synthesis can be found—as she brings together traditions both European and non-European, patriarchal and matriarchal—in an effort, perfectly suited to her chosen medium, to reveal the universality and humanity of Milton's universal epic of humankind.

The first textual illustration in the volume, Groom's portrayal of the descent of Milton's muse (see fig. 2), continues the mythic synthesis begun in the headpiece. First, and most simply, the muse embodies a conflation of Milton's first and third invocations, and probably his second. To her right are three images of the Hebrew and patriarchal figure whom Milton says she inspired "on the secret top / Of *Oreb* or of *Sinai*." "That Shepherd, who first taught the chosen Seed, / In the Beginning how the Heav'ns and Earth / Rose out of *Chaos*" (I, 6–7, 8–10) is pictured (1) seated in the foreground with the harp of sacred song (and with a crown, perhaps connecting his identity with that of the other divine singer-shepherd, David); (2) farther back holding the tablets of the Law; and (3) yet farther back, encountering the burning bush of Yahweh's self-revelation. The singer's toe touches a sprig of foliage, suggesting not only the "chosen Seed" but also Groom's continual emphasis on the natural, life-giving earth, while behind the three Moses figures rises Jerusalem's temple—summing up the Judaic and patriarchal side of Milton's inspiration. That this muse is also *Urania*, the Heavenly Muse whose meaning, not name, Milton calls in Book VII, is made clear by the figures to her left: the "Muses nine," attending to a bearded poet-figure in a classical chair before a classical temple, strongly reminiscent of the great altar of Zeus in the acropolis of Pergamum.[29] And if the poet represents, as seems likely, the *Maeonides* (Homer) figure of Book III, all three invocations are represented in Groom's design for the first.

OF MANS FIRST
DISOBEDIENCE,
AND THE FRUIT OF THAT FOR-
BIDDEN TREE, WHOSE MORTAL
TAST BROUGHT DEATH INTO THE WORLD,
AND ALL OUR WOE, WITH LOSS OF EDEN, TILL
ONE GREATER MAN
RESTORE US, AND REGAIN THE BLISSFUL SEAT,

5

Figure 2. Book I: *The Invocation to the Muse*

If Groom's muse brings together Milton's muses and invocations, she embodies a profounder synthesis as well: that of the male and female aspects of the Godhead. She sweeps down through the center of the design in a rain of dew on rays of "holy Light," propelled by dovelike wings so vast they fill the entire top of the design; like the wings of the muse Davies pictures verbally, they are "stretched out in imagination to occupy the entire cosmos" (p. 195). In the midst of her descent, moreover, she looses from her hands a fast-descending dove, showing Groom's attentiveness to the Muse's identity with the Spirit that "from the first" was "present, and with mighty wings outspread / Dove-like satst brooding on the vast Abyss / And mad'st it pregnant" (I, 19, 20–22)—an androgynous image which "unites a sensation," as Davies says, "of infinite gentleness with terrifying power." The Spirit's mysterious dual nature, both brooding and impregnating, calls the poet to brood upon divine generation itself— to surrender to the mighty imaginative feminine within, as she visits his slumbers, governs his song, and gives it answerable style—in the scroll and pages upon which the quaintly garbed poet stands, and through the pen that he raises for blessing. Thus Groom, like Milton, fuses classical and Hebraic; feminine and masculine; the engendering of universe, prophecy and song into one richly gendered and universal image.

No design of Groom's makes her view of divine gender clearer than the illustration accompanying Milton's second invocation: that to Light, at the beginning of Book III (see fig. 3). Here, in fact, Groom makes her definitive statement on Milton's God, portraying him not as the stiff, unyielding Patriarch many readers have claimed to find in the text, but rather, to use Joan Webber's words, "a much ampler idea or power, a force of life that is neither anthropomorphized or sexed . . . a God beyond God, certainly beyond rational expression" (p. 9). To portray God at all, of course, the visual artist must have recourse to visual images, and surely the human image (given its source) is the most appropriate form of accommodation to the limits of the medium. But Groom's God shows the artist's very close reading of the text, as he sits in tender colloquy with his beloved Son, the very Light Milton invokes: "Bright effluence of bright essence increate" (III, 6). The Father's posture—seated on the ground like a Madonna of Humility,[30] leaning gracefully to one side as he ponders the words of his Son—balances his traditional patriarchal crown and beard. Moreover, a comparison of the faces on the two divine figures reveals that, in portraying the Son, Groom has clearly attended to Milton's lines:

> in him all his Father shone
> Substantially express'd, and in his face

> Divine compassion visibly appear'd,
> Love without end, and without measure Grace.   (III, 139–42)

The Son's posture, his androgynous appearance (*Ecce Homo*, not *Ecce Vir*), and the tiny figures of Adam and Eve in his hands identify those "substantially express'd" values as maternal, archetypally feminine ones. His gesture also indicates his multiple roles with regard to humankind: (1) Creator (as his hands can be seen to have shaped the tiny human figures); (2) sustainer and nurturer (as he holds and seems almost to caress them); and (3) Redeemer (as he appears to lift them up to the attentive Father, in an act of supplication on their behalf). The surrounding figures—eight rejoicing angels, at least three of them playing musical instruments—also suggest that the Son has just completed his "dearest mediation" (226) on behalf of humankind, just at the point where

> His words here ended, but his meek aspéct
> Silent yet spake, and breath'd immortal love
> To mortal men, above which only shone
> Filial obedience: as a sacrifice
> Glad to be offer'd   (266–70)

and "Admiration seiz'd all Heav'n," leading eventually to the "Jubilee, and loud Hosannas" (348), pictured here and again, as main subject, two illustrations later.

The sweetness of the colloquy between Father and Son, moreover, seems calculated to remind us not only of the love of God (Father and Son, as that of the Spirit pictured in Groom's illustration for the first invocation) for humankind, but also of the love between the persons in the Godhead—expressed first in the Son's going forth as the Father's "creative might" (suggested lightly in the Son's artist hands) and then in his voluntary offer to redeem humankind—which is the mysterious and generative original of all human love. McColley has argued, in fact, that for Milton "the entire cosmos is expressed in full reciprocity as an interanimation of the sexes corresponding to the microcosm of human marriage" (*Milton's Eve*, p. 46). In Groom's work we repeatedly find the same insight "visibly express'd."

Indeed, in Milton's epic as read by Groom, human marriage is the very center. For her, as for McColley, it is marriage that makes up Eden: its freedom, its meaningful labor, its delicious, innocent sensuousness. But "among unequals," as Adam has asked the Father,

> what society
> Can sort, what harmony or true delight?
> Which must be mutual, in proportion due
> Giv'n and receiv'd.   (VIII, 383–86)

HAIL HOLY LIGHT, OFSPRING OF HEAV'N FIRST-BORN, OR OF TH' ETERNAL COETERNAL BEAM MAY I EXPRESS THEE UNBLAM'D? SINCE GOD IS LIGHT, & NEVER BUT IN UNAPPROACHED LIGHT DWELT FROM ETERNITIE, DWELT THEN IN THEE, Bright effluence of bright essence increate. Or hear'st thou rather pure Ethereal stream, Whose Fountain who shall tell? before the Sun,

71

Figure 3. Book III: *The Divine Colloquy*

Groom's Adam and Eve are two strong, responsible individuals—each
sufficient to stand, though intended, like the persons of the Godhead, to
act out of love in complementary ways. In her illustration of their initial
meeting with Raphael (see fig. 4), we find, as usual, Groom's careful
attention to Milton's text. In this design, she has simplified the
"lovely . . . Lantskip" (IV, 152–53) which, when she moves to her portrayal of the couple's erotic bond, will become her central focus. But even
here, where her emphasis is more upon their "fellowship" and "rational
delight" (VIII, 389, 91), our first parents are surrounded by rich grass and
teeming vegetation, and accompanied by a friendly pair of responsive
dogs—images of their fidelity, of their friendship, and of their need, with
all creatures, to "converse" and "rejoice / Each with thir kind" (396, 392–
93). Like the dogs, too, whose sexes are distinguishable by their hair and
body type, the couple are differentiated very much as Milton has differentiated them in Book IV: Adam's body *is* taller and harder in outline; Eve's
hair *is* longer ("thir sex not [identical] seem'd" [296]). But *both*, Groom
visually insists, are "Godlike," of "nobler shape erect and tall"; and in both
"thir looks Divine / The image of thir glorious Maker" shines (IV, 288,
291–92), as they stand side by side before their angel guest. Both "in
naked Majesty [seem] Lords of all" (290); both greet the angel visitor and
both, not just Eve, are hailed in his annunciationlike gesture as the parents of humankind.

     Anderson remarks that in Milton's first introduction of Adam and Eve
in Book IV, the "stability of both genders within the framework of human
perfection is carefully established before specialization of gender is announced" (p. 209). Groom seems equally intent on suggesting an essential
equality between the sexes—and she would have found this feminist idea
not only in Milton, but also in the work of her friends and contemporaries.
Indeed, several interesting analogues exist in engravings made by members of what Mary Groom's brother has called her "gang": Leon Underwood, Blair Hughes-Stanton, and Gertrude Hermes. Groom's Adam and
Eve are reminiscent, for instance, of the two "erect and tall" figures in a
1925 wood engraving by her mentor and teacher, Leon Underwood, aptly
entitled *Co-Eternal*. And something of the feminist consciousness that
imbues Groom's depiction of Adam and Eve also can be seen in Blair
Hughes-Stanton's *Emancipation of Woman* (1929) and Gertrude Hermes's
beautiful *Tree of Life* (1930). In the designs of Mary Groom and the artists
of her circle, as well as in their comments upon their own work, one finds
a common and recurring emphasis on the divinity revealed in human
form—as "God created man in his own image, in the image of God created he him; male and female created he them" (Gen. i, 27)—coeternal

DESCEND FROM HEAV'N URANIA, BY THAT NAME IF RIGHTLY THOU ART CALL'D, WHOSE VOICE DIVINE FOLLOWING, ABOVE TH' OLYMPIAN HILL I SOARE, ABOVE THE FLIGHT OF PEGASEAN WING. THE MEANING, NOT THE NAME I CALL: FOR THOU
Nor of the Muses nine, nor on the top
Of old Olympus dwell'st, but Heav'nlie borne,
Before the Hills appeerd, or Fountain flow'd

199

Figure 4. Book V: *The Arrival of Raphael*

and codependent on the (coeternal and codependent) vigorous sun and fruitful earth.[31] The "two great Sexes animate" their world as well as Milton's.

Once Groom, like Milton, has established their equality and mutuality, it is Eve and Adam's erotic connection, their physical and spiritual oneness in diversity, that most fully represents the nature both of the Godhead and of Eden. Thus in her design for Book IV (see fig. 5), Groom most fully embodies the essence of Paradise—a great deal of paradise within a tiny space, on a very human scale. She represents the "fruitful Earth" of Raphael's lines, to which the rest of the cosmos is "officious" (as Adam is to Eve)—a garden which becomes, as Davies puts it, "an externalisation of the fruitful person of Eve" and perhaps, at least on some level, "an allegory . . . of the psyche itself" (p. 210). Like the headpieces to each book, this design is womblike in its perfect and protective enclosure. And for the moment Groom chooses not to remind us of the scoptophilic gaze of Satan, without which we could not enter, past the rural mound's "hairy sides / With thicket overgrown" (135–36), to visit this "delicious Paradise."[32] She will attend to his destructive agony—born of the perverse love he conceives for the trusting, fecund Eve upon whom he spies—in later designs. But looking at this illustration we do not yet fully attend to the thoughts such a scene must arouse in the Satanic mind:

> O Hell! what do mine eyes with grief behold,
> Into our room of bliss thus high advanc't
> Creatures of other mould,
> . . . .
>   whom my thoughts pursue
> With wonder, and could love, so lively shines
> In them Divine resemblance, and such grace
> The hand that form'd them on their shape hath pour'd.
> Ah gentle pair, yee little think how nigh
> Your change approaches, when all these delights
> Will vanish and deliver ye to woe,
> More woe, the more your taste is now of joy.   (IV, 358–69)

Rather Groom allows us to revel with the lovers in the sheer delight of their innocent, though vulnerable, love. Her Eden like Milton's, like heaven and unlike Satan's mind, is a world in which there is no tragic gap between desire and fulfillment. To love in this world—the world also of the Song of Songs, which Groom and other members of her circle illustrated—is to possess and be possessed by the beloved without jealousy, mistrust, or the anxiety of potential loss.

Indeed, the "youthful dalliance" (338) of Adam and Eve can be seen

More grateful, to thir Supper Fruits they fell,
Nectarine Fruits which the compliant boughes
Yeilded them, side-long as they sat recline
On the soft downie Bank damaskt with flours:
The savourie pulp they chew, and in the rinde
Still as they thirsted scoop the brimming stream;
Nor gentle purpose, nor endearing smiles
Wanted, nor youthful dalliance as beseems
Fair couple, linkt in happie nuptial League,
Alone as they. About them frisking playd
All Beasts of th' Earth, since wilde, and of all chase
In Wood or Wilderness, Forrest or Den;
Sporting the Lion rampd, and in his paw

110

Figure 5. Book IV: *Adam and Eve in Paradise*

as an earthly—and earthy—mirror of the eternal colloquy between the
Father and Son (III, see fig. 3). The human couple's sacred conversation is
also encircled by "jubilee," in this case that of birds and of lithe elephan-
tine proboscises. (It is typical of Groom's exuberance that she triples
Milton's solitary, "unwieldy" elephant.) The earthly lovers, like the heavenly Pair, are surrounded by lush vegetation. "[C]ompliant boughs /
[Yield] them" every kind of "Nectarine Fruit"; the "soft downy bank" on
which Eve reclines is "damask'd with flow'rs" (334); and their joy is attended not only by elephants, but by borrowed "birds of calm" who brood
on the "charmed wave" of their "brimming stream" (cf. Nativity ode, 68).
Clearly Mary Groom has read Milton closely and with delight.[33] Moreover, the way in which Adam and Eve make love, as Raphael later blush-
ingly tells Adam, is not unrelated to the way love is made in heaven. The
tenderness on all four faces and the self-giving postures of Eve and the
Son, though not literally alike, show a family resemblance: in the image of
his love created he their love.

In this womblike paradise, moreover, lovemaking is symbolically related not only to divine intercourse but also to the birth-giving it will
eventually bring about. Surely for Groom, as for the Milton of the divorce
tracts, such loving needs no external justification: it is also both innocent
play and a road to divine knowledge. ("I pray," writes St. Paul, "that ye
being rooted and grounded in love, may be able to comprehend . . . what
is the breadth, and the length, and depth, and height; And to know the
love of Christ, which passeth knowledge, that ye might be filled with all
the fullness of God" [Eph. iii, 17–19].) In sexual love Adam and Eve
celebrate a return to their original oneness, rejoining what has been
severed only to be reunited, but (as with all the divisions by which God
creates the universe) far happier for being both separate and one. Because, like Milton's Godhead, they are one in substance but not in personal essence, Adam and Eve are able to love freely—and in that very
freedom lies their capacity for love, a love which opens out not only one to
the other but also back toward its source in God. But Eve's birthing
posture also calls up her oneness with the fruitful, life-giving earth, and
her role as mediatrix between that earth and the spiritual realm.

Indeed, it is precisely such a connection that Groom's associate
Henry Moore sought to communicate with his huge reclining nudes, both
engraved and sculpted. "These reclining figures," writes Will Grohmann,
"are women in repose but also something more profound." The female
nude for Moore, as for Groom, is not primarily an erotic image; rather, she
is "the concept of fruitfulness, the Mother Earth." Indeed, Grohmann
goes on,

Moore, who once pointed to the maternal element in the "Reclining Figures," may well see in them an element of eternity, the "Great Female," who is both birth-giving nature and the wellspring of the unconscious. In the artist the unconscious is more highly developed than in others; he is dependent upon his ability to receive inspiration from the creative unconscious and is inclined to identify himself with motherhood and through it with the maternal as such. . . . Neither pagan nor Christian, these figures are neutral forms in which nature and spirit meet in accordance with their own laws. The pendulum swings now in one direction, now in the other, pointing at one moment toward the physical, the fruitful, the earthy and at another to the awakening of the unconscious, to spirit, to inner law.[34]

Groom's Eve—as McColley has shown us, the artist-poet-muse of Adam's paradise—is of course both pre-pagan and pre-Christian; conversely she reflects both Milton's Christianity and Groom's: a Christianity that reclaims the long-neglected sensuous pole of its birthright, and attempts to reconcile heaven and earth against an adversary who continually seeks to divide them—"Defaming as impure what God declares / Pure, and commands to some, leaves free to all" (IV, 746–47).

Groom uses this central image of a loving, birth-giving Eve in yet another way, to suggest yet another crucial parallel in Milton's vision. As the Paradise scene grows in meaning in juxtaposition to the divine colloquy between the Father and Son, it likewise takes on new meaning when juxtaposed with Groom's illustration of the creation of Eve (see fig. 6). Now we see not only her oneness with the Godhead and with the earth, but also her oneness with Adam, and the grace-linked reciprocity between them, which Milton borrowed from St. Paul's first letter to the Corinthians. Indeed, as Anne Ferry has recently noted, Milton plays down the hierarchical aspects of Paul's eleventh chapter, in favor of its reciprocal ones (p. 117), and Groom, as usual, has picked up Milton's cue. Her design does not show us Eve's creation out of Adam's rib (an image that has been used ever since the Fall as an excuse for misogyny); rather, she shows us the parallel to Eve's motherhood of Adam's seed (as seen in her birth-giving posture in fig. 5) in Adam's quite literal "motherhood" of Eve. "For," says Paul, "as the woman is of the man, even so is the man also by the woman, [and] all things of God" (1 Cor. xi, 12). Douglas Anderson's reading of Milton's text seems to recognize the poet's acute sensitivity to every nuance of the Pauline paradox:

Adam falls into a deep sleep as he does in the Bible, but it is a "sleep" like a trance in which he is able to watch what happens to his own body. . . . The detail Milton has added is just sufficient to suggest that this occurrence is, quite literally, the delivery of a child. In Genesis, the Lord simply takes what he needs to make what he desires. In Milton . . . God must stoop to his task like a midwife and deftly

The spirit of love and amorous delight.
She disappeerd, and left me dark, I wak'd
To find her, or for ever to deplore
Her loss, and other pleasures all abjure:
When out of hope, behold her, not farr off,
Such as I saw her in my dream, adornd
With what all Earth or Heaven could bestow
To make her amiable: On she came,
Led by her Heav'nly Maker, though unseen,
And guided by his voice, nor uninformd
Of nuptial Sanctitie and marriage Rites:
Grace was in all her steps, Heav'n in her Eye,
In every gesture dignitie and love.
I overjoyd could not forbear aloud.
  THIS turn hath made amends; thou hast fulfill'd
  Thy words, Creator bounteous and benigne,
Giver of all things faire, but fairest this

Figure 6. Book VIII (Golden Cockerel VII): *The Creation of Eve*

nurse the new creature with his forming hands. Adam's sensations of pleasure are immediate and at first wonderfully maternal. . . . [He] has shed his gender and done what no other man in history will ever do, much as God shed his gender in the birth of Adam. (pp. 136–37)

Groom also shows her deep attentiveness to the text by the addition of several striking visual details. First, Adam lies not on his side but on his back, making his posture more like one of birth-giving than in other illustrations of Eve's creation.[35] What is more, the divine Midwife, taking on an archetypally feminine role, does not so much shape our first mother with his "forming hands" (VIII, 470) as tenderly draw her forth, limp but complete, from Adam's life. And the three are encircled, indeed entangled, by a cordlike ribbon that suggests their profound connection and mutual dependency. She is of him; he is of her; both are of God. Thus Mary Groom, like Milton, has skirted all the potentially sexist implications of the Pauline text, finding instead the liberating and reconciling core of his thought.

But now Groom, with Milton, must turn her notes to tragic. Having lovingly depicted the dovelike brooding and impregnating act of Milton's muse—and the joyous fecundity of the cosmos it has seeded with its poetic power, whether that cosmos is the fruitful earth itself or the poet who recreates it—she must portray the satanic perversion of that love- and life-making act: the destruction of that same creation. Like other spirits, and indeed like Milton's muse, Satan "can either Sex assume, or both"; but psychologically, as Joan Webber and others have noticed, he is "the perfect example of a patriarchal, domineering figure" (p. 16), the masculinist ideal in its purest, most aggressive form. He cannot understand the relational principle, so aptly expressed by McColley, that "whenever beings are arranged in orders, the arrangement is made for the augmentation of each member, for greater individuation through manifold relations, and for the greater splendor of their mutual joy." Indeed, he cannot understand mutual joy at all because he does not know, as Milton and Groom do, that "the universe is not imaged" by the "static Ptolemaic chart and its 'degrees' are not exactly 'higher' and 'lower' " (*Milton's Eve*, pp. 39, 37). Unlike Milton's God, he would sooner be destroyed than shed the superficial power archetypally embodied in his gender—whether to serve, to create or to redeem; thus in a horrible parody of the brooding, impregnating Muse-Word-Spirit, he must become a cosmic rapist.

Groom's view that Satan's incursion into Eden parodies the Muse's generative act, can best be seen (as can her connection between divine and human love) by a juxtaposition of images, in this case figures 2 and 7.

While the vast but gentle wide-winged Muse (see fig. 2) glides down in inspiring rays of light and dew, the grim, sickle-winged Satan (see fig. 7) swoops over the earth in scorching rays of sun. While she hovers, dew-robed, over the poet in a gesture of brooding concern, he hovers naked over the earth's fruitfulness in a posture not unlike that of sexual inter-course. But his swooping action is more a dive than an embrace; his expression is fiercely inquisitional rather than tender and nurturing; and as he examines an unsupported stalk, he seems about to deflower it with a plucking motion of his hand. At the upper-left corner of the design, a rather discompos'd Uriel gestures frantic but unheeded warning from his station in the sun, while within the initial capital *O* of the text, a small bird—(possibly a nightingale?) oddly thrust on its back—cries out in alarm, as Satan begins to sow his seeds of death in the good "field of this world."[36] When the "one apple" he will offer our first parents has been tasted, the seeds will, until the last trumpet, be "intermixed": the darnel by the wheat; the "knowledge of good by evil." But the sower's sickle-shaped wings also remind us of that end: when his son the grim reaper will come back to harvest the evil he now begins to sow.[37]

The same unsavory inquisitiveness that Satan expresses toward the earth in Groom's design of his arrival is also displayed in his first spying on, then leering at, Eve. How different, Groom shows us, is that leer from Adam's loving, solicitous gaze. In her design where he awakens Eve from her satanically induced dream (see fig. 8), the husband leans tenderly, with "cordial love . . . enamor'd," over his sleeping wife (V, 12–13)—and Groom gives us our parting glimpse of prelapsarian human love, the kind of love we have seen first within the Godhead itself. Like most rapists, Satan is incapable of such healthy, life-giving love; but—because, made in God's image, every creature must long to connect itself with another—he is tormented by love's shadow in a nature insufficiently androgynous to experience its tender (and divinely origined) reality. "I to Hell am thrust," he has cried upon seeing the happiness of the human pair, "Where neither joy nor love, but fierce desire, / Among our other torments not the least / Still unfulfill'd with pain of longing pines" (IV, 508, 509–11). There is only one form of release for such desire; and Davies, like Groom, has ex-pressed it powerfully, calling Satan's act a "rapist penetration of the uni-verse [that] resembles the journey of semen carrying a potentiality for contaminated growth" (p. 210). As he has made his way through chaos, to this vulnerable "pendant world," to the *hortus conclusus* of Eden and of the first Eve, his journey has become a travesty not only of Milton's muse, but also of the fructifying Dew in April that will come "all so stille to his moder's bour."[38] Yet the travesty, by grace, is also the forbear; the Anti-

FOR THAT WARNING
VOICE, WHICH HE WHO
SAW TH' APOCALYPS,
HEARD CRY IN HEAVEN ALOUD,
Then when the Dragon, put to second rout,
Came furious down to be reveng'd on Men,
Wo to the Inhabitants on Earth! that now,
While time was, our first Parents had bin warnd
The coming of thir secret foe, and scap'd
Haply so scap'd his mortal snare; for now
Satan, now first inflam'd with rage, came down,
The Tempter ere th' Accuser of man-kind,

99

Figure 7. Book IV: *Satan's Incursion into Eden*

OW MORN HER ROSIE STEPS IN TH' EASTERN CLIME

ADVANCING, SOW'D THE EARTH WITH ORIENT PEARLE, WHEN ADAM WAK'T, SO CUSTOMD, FOR HIS SLEEP WAS AERIE LIGHT, FROM PURE DIGESTION BRED, And temperat vapors bland, which th' only sound Of leaves and fuming rills, Aurora's fan,

135

Figure 8. Book V: *Adam Waking Eve After Her Dream*

christ, the ante-Christ: the seed of the woman, thanks to his rape, will first grow up into Cain; but ultimately, it will come back to earth as Dew, the Word that gives eternal life.

Thus it is not surprising that Groom includes the *protevangelion* even in her portrayal of the Fall (see figs. 9 and 10). And as Satan at last reaches the aim of his incursion, she has also responded to other, often overlooked, nuances of Milton's text, remaining faithful to it (as few other illustrators have) in the face of an overwhelmingly misogynic visual tradition. First and importantly, unlike most illustrators of *Paradise Lost*, she follows Milton in portraying two separate falls: Eve's and then Adam's.[39] In so doing, she picks up his clear assertion of their individual responsibility, their sufficiency to stand, as well as showing us an Eve who is not only temptress, but *tempted*. Moreover, as Henry A. Kelly pointed out in 1971, and as Roland Frye and Diane McColley have both since demonstrated, snakes with women's heads were rife in medieval and Renaissance iconography of the Fall.[40] A famous and classic example is Raphael's depiction in the Vatican apartments (1517–19/20), where, as is typical, only Adam's fall (in patriarchal terms, *the* fall) is shown. Adam and Eve stand on either side of the tree, with the serpent wound in its branches between them—separating them, as it were, by a kind of spiritual adultery. However, the rival love object for Eve here is obviously her own image; the snake's face is not only a woman's, but Eve's own, suggesting rather vividly that Eve's natural narcissism has made her from the beginning especially prone to sin. Groom's snake, on the other hand, in keeping with Milton's description, is triumphantly and leeringly male.[41] He "addresses" his way "toward Eve"

> not with indented wave,
> Prone on the ground, as since, but on his rear,
> Circular base of rising folds, that tow'r'd
> Fold above fold a surging Maze, his Head
> Crested aloft, and Carbuncle his Eyes;
> With burnisht Neck of verdant Gold, erect
> Amidst his circling Spires, that on the grass
> Floated redundant: pleasing was his shape,
> And lovely.   (IX, 496–504)

Milton's Eve, in Groom's design, is also faithfully represented. When Satan surprises her, she is, as the poet tells us, in the midst of thick and glowing roses, where she—innocent, "yet sinless," as Milton repeats several times during their encounter—is busy propping them, not lost in narcissistic revery. Groom seems to have captured an early moment of the

Beyond his hope, Eve separate he spies,
Veild in a Cloud of Fragrance, where she stood,
Half spi'd, so thick the Roses bushing round
About her glowd, oft stooping to support
Each Flour of slender stalk, whose head though gay
Carnation, Purple, Azure, or spect with Gold,
Hung drooping unsustained, them she upstaies
Gently with Mirtle band, mindless the while,
Her self, though fairest unsupported Flour,
From her best prop so farr, and storm so nigh.
Neerer he drew, and many a walk travers'd
Of stateliest Covert, Cedar, Pine, or Palme,
Then voluble and bold, now hid, now seen
Among thick-wov'n Arborets and Flours
Imborderd on each Bank, the hand of Eve:

257

Figure 9. Book IX (Golden Cockerel VIII): *Eve's Temptation*

So faithful Love unequald; but l feel
Farr otherwise th' event, not Death, but Life
Augmented, op'nd Eyes, new Hopes, new Joyes,
Taste so Divine, that what of sweet before
Hath toucht my sense, flat seems to this, and harsh.
On my experience, Adam, freely taste,
And fear of Death deliver to the Windes.
SO saying, she embrac'd him, and for joy
Tenderly wept, much won that he his Love
Had so enobl'd, as of choice to incurr
Divine displeasure for her sake, or Death.
In recompence (for such compliance bad
Such recompence best merits) from the bough
She gave him of that fair enticing Fruit
With liberal hand: he scrupl'd not to eat

275

Figure 10. Book IX (Golden Cockerel VIII): *Eve Tempting Adam*

Serpent's attack—when Eve is surprised not so much by his flattering address to her as "sov'ran Mistress," as by an encounter with a talking snake—or perhaps even the very first instant, when he "Curl[s] many a wanton wreath" until "His gentle dumb expression turn[s] at length / The eye of *Eve* to mark his play" (517, 527–28). In any case there is not yet a trace of cupidity in her face: she is beguiled, perhaps—surprised, certainly—but not yet sinful. Her look is kind, frank, and free of the guile she cannot, in her innocence, see in Satan: "Hate . . . under show of Love well feign'd" (492).

To portray Eve as innocent at the moment of her temptation shows in itself, as Gallagher suggested (p. 80), a remarkable and rare attentiveness to Milton's account of the Fall. But Groom's interpretation goes even further: as at other points in her illustrations, she reminds us of recovery at the very moment of loss; for Eve's lines at the end of the poem are proleptically portrayed here, in the illustration of its climax:

> This further consolation yet secure
> I carry hence; though all by mee is lost,
> Such favor I unworthy am voutsaf't,
> By mee the Promis'd Seed shall all restore.   (XII, 620–23)

In the next few moments Eve will indeed admit the bad seed of satanic pride and guile. Moreover she will display that pride and guile in the next illustration (see fig. 10), where she seduces a sorrowful-looking Adam as the snake gloats erect in the foreground. But she also reveals, in her posture of surprise before the serpent, the very image of her saving counterpart. As Satan's arrival on earth both parodies and foreshadows the coming of the Spirit-Word-Muse, so his *Ave* to Eve both parodies and foreshadows the coming of Gabriel to "Mary, second Eve."[42] Groom's Eve is surrounded, as she is in Milton's text, by Mary's emblematic flower; and as in an Annunciation by Botticelli or Lippo Lippi, she responds to the snake's salutation with the Virgin's classic iconographic gesture of disquiet, "cast[ing] in her mind what manner of salutation this should be" (Luke i, 29). Surely the arrow-shaped blossoms aimed at her womb, almost like a quiver of Cupid's arrows, suggest Groom's wry awareness that the effect of this encounter will be very different from the divinely generative encounter that will balance and redeem it (when the dovelike "Holy Ghost shall come upon [Mary], and the power of the Highest shall overshadow [her]" [Luke i, 35]). Nonetheless, in her images throughout the poem from the headpiece on, Groom has visibly underscored the mercy underlying every judgment, the redemption that is offered before—and thus enwraps in prevenient, regenerative grace—the very moment of loss. Groom's Miltonic God would gather his "children together, even as a hen gathereth her chickens under *her* wings" (Matt. xxiii, 37); the terrible masculine figure in Groom's work is never God—but rather Satan, the brutal phallic parody of God's androgynous creative and redemptive generativity.

If Paradise is lost through "Language of Man pronounc't / By Tongue of Brute" (IX, 553–54), it is to be regained through the Word of God pronounced by tongue of humankind: immediately by Eve, ultimately through the incarnate divine Logos himself, and mediately through the singer's inspired poem. In each case, however, the hearer must be responsive, as Milton was afraid his readers would not be; as Adam clearly is not, at first, to Eve. Groom chooses to portray the moment in Book X when Eve finds Adam "afflicted" with grief and attempts to make amends. Seeing his misery, the poet tells us,

> Desolate where she sat, approaching nigh,
> Soft words to his fierce passion she assay'd:
> But her with stern regard he thus repell'd.
>   Out of my sight, thou Serpent, that name best
> Befits thee with him leagu'd, thyself as false
> And hateful
>   . . . .
>   But for thee
> I had persisted happy, had not thy pride
> And wand'ring vanity, when least was safe,
> Rejected my forewarning, and disdain'd
> Not to be trusted, longing to be seen
> Though by the Devil himself, him overweening
> To over-reach, but with the Serpent meeting
> Fool'd and beguil'd, by him thou, I by thee,
> To trust thee from my side, imagin'd wise,
> Constant, mature, proof against all assaults,
> And understood not all was but a show
> Rather than solid virtue, all but a Rib
> Crooked by nature, bent, as now appears,
> More to the part siníster from me drawn,
> Well if thrown out, as supernumerary
> To my just number sound. O why did God,
> Creator wise, that peopl'd highest Heav'n
> With Spirits Masculine, create at last
> This novelty on Earth, this fair defect
> of Nature, and not fill the World at once
> With Men as Angels without Feminine,
> Or find some other way to generate
> Mankind?   (X, 864–95)

Groom, however, makes clear in her design (see fig. 11) that unlike a number of readers, including both traditional humanists and radical feminists, she does not confuse Adam's misogynic outburst with Milton's own view of women. Rather, she reads in his text a warning against the masculinist, satanic refusal of "sweet attractive Grace"—whether that grace is found in Eve, in her divine counterpart the Son, or in the gentler nuances of Milton's poem. As Eve raises her hands to plead mercy for sin, Adam clearly chooses the worse part: to pull rank; to project his own guilt on another; to divide what God has joined; and to persist in his isolation. His attitude, in Groom's design, is shown literally in the fact that he lies lower than the anguished, suppliant Eve; it is also vividly mirrored in the now-fallen cosmos, where rain pelts them mercilessly out of a glowering sky, and two stags are locked in a fierce contest for dominance behind him. As Adam covers one eye and turns his back to their combat, he does not yet see what the world he has wished for in his tirade, a world without the feminine, would be like. But in rejecting Eve he rejects the possibility that she, in her sorrow and penitence, has begun to represent: the redemptive possibility of a "humiliation that exalts." And in rejecting that possibility he ironically places *himself* in league with the competitive, projective violence of the snake. For the moment he, too, is the abject image of a hell within—a hell sputtered out in syntax reminiscent of Satan's in Book IV, where "conscience wakes despair" (23).

Adam's despair, however, is not the last word, as Groom suggests even in this design. Though Adam recoils from his wife, turning his head away and covering one eye with his right hand, his left (right-brained?) hand seems to reach out to her for the succor and reconciliation the better self within him wants. Even here "from the Mercy-seat above / Prevenient Grace descending" is removing "the stony" from Adam's heart, as it has already removed the corresponding stony from Eve's. Eve's role, or lack of one, in this spiritual sea change within Adam has been the subject of some debate.[43] But for Groom it is clear that her role is a pivotal one. Kneeling above Adam and raising her hands toward heaven, in fact, she echoes not only the posture but the cadences and words of the Son, as he appeals to his Father in Book III:

> Between us two let there be peace, both joining
> As join'd in injuries,
>   . . . .
>   On me exercise not
> Thy hatred for this misery befall'n,
> On me already lost, mee than thyself
> More miserable; both have sinn'd, but thou

With other echo late I taught your Shades
To answer, and resound farr other Song.
Whom thus afflicted when sad Eve beheld,
Desolate where she sate, approaching nigh,
Soft words to his fierce passion she assay'd:
But her with stern regard he thus repell'd.

OUT of my sight, thou Serpent, that name best
Befits thee with him leagu'd, thy self as false
And hateful; nothing wants, but that thy shape,
Like his, and colour Serpentine may shew
Thy inward fraud, to warn all Creatures from thee
Henceforth; least that too heav'nly form, pretended
To hellish falshood, snare them.   But for thee
I had persisted happie, had not thy pride
And wandring vanitie, when lest was safe,
Rejected my forewarning, and disdain'd
Not to be trusted, longing to be seen
Though by the Devil himself, him overweening
To over-reach, but with the Serpent meeting
Fool'd and beguil'd, by him thou, I by thee,

313

Figure 11. Book X (Golden Cockerel IX): *Eve Suing Adam for Reconciliation
After the Fall*

Against God only, I against God and thee,
And to the place of judgment will return,
There with my cries importune Heaven, that all
The sentence from thy head remov'd may light
On *me*, sole cause to thee of all this woe,
Mee mee only just object of his ire.

                    (X, 924–36, emphasis mine; cf. III, 236–38)

For Groom this offer of "dearest mediation" seems clearly to have the theological significance Georgia Christopher, for one, would deny. It seems, moreover, to have an archetypal mythic significance—a significance underscored by an arresting analogue in the work of Groom's close associate Gertrude Hermes. Indeed, the similarities between her 1930 *Tree of Life* and Groom's illustration of Eve's plea to Adam are remarkable. Hermes' design shows the form of a woman growing up into that of a lustrous, leafy tree, her arms raised above her head (here in a *literally* life-bearing posture) like Eve's in Groom's engraving. She has grown from a seed in the ground that, on close inspection looks like an amniotic sac holding a child, and in turn from a smaller, pubescent girl. Behind her to the right, the sun floods the sea and land with light; and a rainbow, linking sun and moon, spans a sky filled with joyous birds. To her left, the moon shines—"communicating," with its inseparable consort, the sun, "Male and Female Light" (VIII, 150); and in the moonlight stands a peaceful, solitary stag, a vivid contrast to the death-dealing stags of Groom's postlapsarian vision. Woman, Hermes seems to suggest, is the mythic embodiment of peace: giving life in response to both sun and earth, and reconciling in herself all cosmic forces, masculine and feminine. She is very close, in short, to St. Paul's vision of the figure Matthew Fox has called "the Cosmic Christ":[44]

[He] is the image of the invisible God, the firstborn of every creature: For by him were all things created, that are in heaven, and that are in earth, visible and invisible, whether they be thrones, or dominions, or principalities, or powers: all things were created by him and for him: And he is before all things, and by him all things consist. . . . For it pleased *the Father* that in him should all fullness dwell; And, having made peace through the blood of his cross, by him to reconcile all things unto himself. (Col. i, 15–17, 18–20)

In any case, the restoration of Adam and Eve's marriage—foreshadowed in Groom's design and accomplished in the next few lines of the poem, where Eve's "lowly plight . . . in *Adam* wrought / Commiseration" (X, 937–40)—becomes the first step toward repairing the ruins of the cosmos. Rejecting the competitive violence that has begun to surround them in nature,[45] they recover a crucial, if fragile, understanding of their interdependence. And they decide, eschewing suicide and celibacy, to embrace their God-given "Labor": to earn their bread and to bear their children, which in spite of "Pains bringing forth" will ultimately be "recompens't with joy" (1051–54).

Not surprisingly, given Groom's emphases throughout the poem, Adam and Eve's restored relationship lies at the very center of her fine and unusual Expulsion (see fig. 12). As Frye, Prinz-Pecorino, and others have demonstrated, the Expulsion in biblical iconography was generally pictured very differently from the way Milton pictures it in *Paradise Lost*. The classic representation of the scene, and surely also one of the greatest, was Masaccio's Expulsion (c. 1425)—in the Brancacci Chapel, Church of the Carmine, Florence—which portrays our first parents' "loss of Eden" as unmitigated tragedy. In Masaccio's vision, and in a number of later images based upon it, the figures are driven forward by a sword-wielding angel, and are so caught up in their grief that there is, for the moment at least, no sign of connection between them. Adam, his shoulders hunched in grief, sobs into his hands; Eve's face seems caught forever in the middle of a wail, and as she walks beside Adam she covers her breasts and pudenda with shame. Indeed, Masaccio's great image is the very distillation of human agony: it is hard to imagine two beings more disconsolate than his Adam and Eve.

Ironically, however, Milton illustrators from the beginning based their work on visual tradition, ignoring the ways in which Milton's text consciously corrects, and in some ways even repudiates, it. So powerful, apparently, was the influence of Masaccio's image, and others based upon it such as Raphael's and Michelangelo's, that in 1688 Henry Aldrich— Milton's first illustrator, along with John B. Medina and Bernard Lens— ignored Milton's text completely to portray a disconnected Adam and Eve, he grieving and she traditionally ashamed, reconciled neither with one another nor with God. Dozens of later illustrators followed his lead. And even Milton's very best interpreters have rarely focused on the textual details to which Groom has attended. Blake and Petrina, for instance, have concentrated on the ways in which the Apocalypse is both embodied and foreshadowed in the scene.[46]

In Groom's design, Paradise is still, as it must be, "Wav'd over" by flaming brands, the gate still throng'd with "dreadful Faces" and "fiery Arms" (XII, 642–43). And as in Blake's Expulsion, the faces behind Adam and Eve suggest the four horsemen of the Apocalypse. But of all Milton's illustrators, Groom has chosen to depict the latest and most peaceful moment of the Expulsion. Here the Archangel Michael has already disappeared; Adam and Eve have already made their "fast descent" to the "subjected Plain," and have begun their sojourn out of the womb of Eden

They looking back, all th' Eastern side beheld
Of Paradise, so late thir happie seat,
Wav'd over by that flaming Brand, the Gate
With dreadful Faces throng'd and fierie Armes:
Som natural tears they drop'd, but wip'd them soon;
The World was all before them, where to choose
Thir place of rest, and Providence thir guide:
They hand in hand with wandring steps and slow,
Through Eden took thir solitarie way.

Figure 12. Book XII (Golden Cockerel X): *The Expulsion*

into a world that lies "all before them." They walk expressing the emotion
Milton's God has prescribed for them: "sorrowing, though in peace" (XI,
117), with small, sad smiles of hope on their thoughtful faces. Groom's
Adam and Eve, like Blake's and others in the tradition of Milton illustration, are accompanied by their inseparable companion, the snake. But he
is much chastened and reduced from the erect and phallic snake of their
temptation (going now upon the ground to suggest that his curse—set
forth in the *protevangelion* [X, 175–92]—has begun), and they seem
undismayed by his presence. He is going to be their continual adversary;
they may as well get used to him. He slithers along between them—as he
will no doubt often, after his first great success, renew his attempt to
come between them.

r hand, the snake moves exactly parallel to the curious, dog at Adam's left—not the first dog, by any means, in . He sniffs the ground, empirically finding his way, as will have to do, repairing gradually and by trial and error their fallen understanding. This dog is clearly not a dog from who must stay outside the gate of the New Jerusalem with the rs and murderers (xxii, 15). Rather, he appears again here as the archetypal image of the fidelity Adam and Eve will now need to struggle in order to maintain—a balance and recompense for the presence of the serpent. He is also, surely, an allusion to Tobias's dog from the Book of Tobit, who accompanies Tobias and "*Raphael,* the sociable Spirit, that deign'd / To travel with *Tobias,* and secur'd / *His* marriage with the seven-times-wedded Maid" (V, 221–24; emphasis mine). That biblical domestic comedy, too, is about a Providence-led journey through a difficult and hostile world; thus the dog here is a part of Groom's Miltonic theodicy—a gentle theodicy that, as is usual for her, makes room for allusions that are at once sophisticated and whimsical.

Groom has also attended, more than any other artist, to the last detail of Milton's poem: to the relationship, so central throughout the poem, between Adam and Eve. In a few other illustrations, notably Petrina's, they also hold hands; but when they do, that fact is almost lost in the terror of their apocalyptic experience. Here the couple's warm but loose connection—"hand in hand" but inevitably "solitary"—is the center, the point, and the greatest hope of the epic. Of them will come many seeds— some as faithful as their dog, some as evil as the snake—until at last the Seed of Woman comes, who will

> receive [his faithful] into bliss,
> Whether in Heav'n or Earth, for then the Earth
> Shall all be Paradise, far happier place
> Than this of *Eden* and far happier days.   (XII, 462–65)

Thus they find hope in the divinely generative figure who has shaped them and proleptically redeemed them, through the fallen love and history they will now begin to make. Indeed, they can be seen in this design as a slightly magnified close-up of the tiny figures that, from the Father's perspective, are always held up by the Son's loving and redeeming hands. But, as in their prelapsarian state, it is not the coming life alone—not even of the chosen Seed—that justifies and gives value to their bond. As diminished as their Edenic oneness is, and as difficult as its gradual recovery will be, at the end as at the beginning of the poem, they need each other above all, as Lewalski has gracefully put it, "to give . . . life human shape and make it bearable" (p. 19). For Groom more than for any other illustrator, the final meaning of the poem is the meaning of human marriage, in which the two great sexes, now reconciled, begin the slow process of reconciling a cosmos tragically at war with itself.

It is sad and somewhat ironic, perhaps, that the woman who could make such a sensuous response to Milton's joyously gendered universe—at a time, moreover, when to see Milton so was to see him "coloured"—died unmarried in middle age, and seems never to have been fully confident of her own artistic calling. Perhaps Mary Groom, like Milton himself, represented the paradox expressed by C. G. Jung: that it is often in losing the life that we find the meaning. Milton, in his long life of disappointment— in marriage and parenthood as well as in work, not to mention the lost light he invokes so poignantly in Book III—knew that paradox better than most human beings, and not only found the meaning but gave it compensatory life in the experience of our first parents. On one level his portrait of Eve and Eden, and perhaps of the Son as well, grows out of a deep sense of loss—out of his anguished search for the ever longed-for and ever elusive feminine within: the same desire indeed that leads his Satan to destroy, but his Father, Son, and Spirit to create and to redeem. What Groom saw and shows us, was that in *Paradise Lost*, if not in his life, he had found it—and gave it birth by his muse out of doubt, out of longing and darkness. Perhaps it was out of the disappointment in her own life that she was able to see him so clearly. But, whatever its biographical context, Mary Groom's loving response to the often-missed feminine in Milton's creation began a "prolific marriage" with the text—a marriage that can mediate its reconciling life to us as men and women and as readers.

Whittier College

NOTES

All illustrations are by Mary Groom, and were published in *Paradise Lost* (London: Golden Cockerel Press, 1937). Photographs of the illustrations were provided by the William Andrews Clark Library, UCLA.

1. Stevie Davies, *The Feminine Reclaimed: The Idea of Woman in Spenser, Shakespeare and Milton* (Lexington, Ky., 1986), p. 205.

2. James Grantham Turner, *One Flesh: Paradisal Marriage and Sexual Relations in the Age of Milton* (Oxford, 1987); Maureen Quilligan, *Milton's Spenser: The Politics of*

Reading (Ithaca, N.Y., 1983); Sandra Gilbert, "Milton's Bogey: Patriarchal Poetry and Women Readers," in *The Madwoman in the Attic* (New Haven, Conn., 1979); Christine Froula, "Pechter's Specter: Milton's Bogey Writ Small" and "When Eve Reads Milton," *Critical Inquiry* 10 and 11 (September 1984 and December 1985), 171–78; 328; Mary Nyquist and Margaret Ferguson, *Re-membering Milton* (New York, 1988); Philip Gallagher, *Milton, The Bible, and Misogyny*, ed. Eugene R. Cunnar and Gail L. Mortimer (Columbia, Mo., 1990); Jackie Di Salvo, "Fear of Flying: Milton on the Boundaries of Witchcraft and Inspiration," *ELR* 18 (Winter, 1988), 114–37; Joseph Wittreich, *Feminist Milton* (Ithaca, N.Y., 1987).

3. Diane McColley, "Subsequent or Precedent? Eve as Milton's Defense of Poesie," *MQ* 20 (December 1986), 132–33.

4. William Shullenberger, "Wrestling with the Angel: *Paradise Lost* and Feminist Criticism," *MQ* 20 (December 1986), 69–85.

5. Marcia Landy, "Kinship and the Role of Women in *Paradise Lost*," in *Milton Studies* IV, ed. James D. Simmonds (Pittsburgh, 1972), pp. 3–18.

6. Barbara K. Lewalski, "Milton on Women—Yet Once More," in *Milton Studies* VI, ed. James D. Simmonds (Pittsburgh, 1974), pp. 3–20; Joan Malory Webber, "The Politics of Poetry: Feminism and *Paradise Lost*," in *Milton Studies* XIV, ed. James D. Simmonds (Pittsburgh, 1980), pp. 3–24; Diane McColley, *Milton's Eve* (Urbana, Ill., 1983); McColley, "Subsequent or Precedent?" *MQ* 20 (December 1986), 132–36; McColley, "Eve and the Arts of Eden," in *Milton and the Idea of Woman*, ed. Julia M. Walker (Urbana, Ill., 1988), pp. 100–119; Douglas Anderson, "Unfallen Marriage and the Fallen Imagination in *Paradise Lost*," *SEL* 26 (Winter, 1986), 125–44; Anne Ferry, "Milton's Creation of Eve," *SEL* 28 (Winter, 1988), 113–32; Davies, *The Feminine Reclaimed*. Among the others, in my view, are Barbara K. Lewalski, Michael Schoenfeldt, Ilona Bell, and William Shullenberger as represented by the new essays in this volume.

7. This citation and all references to Milton's poetry are from *John Milton: Complete Poems and Major Prose*, ed. Merritt Y. Hughes (Indianapolis, 1957).

8. See Adam and Eve, in Vèrard's "Bible en Francoys" (1505) reproduced in Douglas Percy Bliss, *A History of English Wood Engraving* (London, 1928), p. 51. For a fine recent discussion of Edenic iconography—and specifically that of Eve—see Diane K. McColley, "The Iconography of Eden," in *Milton Studies* XXV, ed. James D. Simmonds (Pittsburgh, 1988), pp. 107–21. Also helpful is Jessica Prinz-Pecorino's "Eve Unparadised: Milton's Expulsion and Iconographic Tradition," *MQ* 15 (March 1981), 1–10. And of course Roland M. Frye's *Milton's Imagery and the Visual Arts: Iconographic Tradition in the Epic Poems* (Princeton, 1978) is the indispensable starting point for any such study.

9. For an excellent discussion of this illustration, see Michael Lieb's essay on the chariot tradition in *Milton and the Visual Arts*, ed. Edward Sichi and Albert Labriola (University Park, Pa., 1988), pp. 50–52. For Petrina's illustrations in general see Lloyd Dixon, "Against the Wiles of the Devil: Carlotta Petrina's Christocentric Illustrations of *Paradise Lost*," in *Milton Studies* XXV, ed. James D. Simmonds (Pittsburgh, 1989), pp. 161–90.

10. The comparison may seem a bold one in light of Groom's lack of stature as a "name" artist, but it is not a careless one. This essay has grown out of research for a book-length study of four illustrators of *Paradise Lost*, which I am coauthoring with Virginia Tufte and Eunice Howe. We have selected Mary Groom for detailed treatment along with the 1688 illustrators, William Blake, and John Martin not only because she is a twentieth-century artist and a woman, but also because of her penetrating and coherent "reading" of Milton's text.

11. Published references to Mary Groom are scanty. They include brief mentions (or a reprint of an illustration) in the following: Reproduction of Groom's *Girls Bathing in Craesor Cym, Creative Art* (March 1931), 159; *Roses of Sharon* (an announcement of the book), *Times Literary Supplement*, 8 January 1938; Bernard H. Newdigate, *The Art of the Book* (London, 1938), p. 169; Herbert Furst, "Wood-engraving in Modern Illustration," *The Penrose Annual* 41 (1939), 79; Thomas Balston, *Wood-Engraving in Modern English Books* (Cambridge, 1949), pp. 14, 15; Thomas Balston, *English Wood Engraving, 1900–1950* (London, 1951), pp. 12, 13; [Christopher Sandford], *Bibliography of the Golden Cockerel Press, 1919–1949*, 3 vols. in 1 (Folkestone, Kent, 1975), p. 15; Betty Clark, "*Shall We Join the Ladies?*" *Wood Engravings by Women Artists of the Twentieth Century* (Oxford, 1979); Brigid Peppin and Lucy Micklethwait, *Dictionary of British Book Illustrators: The Twentieth Century* (London, 1983), p. 132; [Simon Brett], *Engraving Then and Now*, catalogue of the retrospective 50th exhibition of The Society of Wood Engravers (1987), p. 14.

Simon Brett is also the author of an essay entitled "Wood-Engraving Then and Now," *Matrix* 8 (Andoversford, Eng., 1988), which includes Mary Groom's name and birthdate among a list of English wood engravers, as well as a thumbnail reproduction of Groom's "Agony in the Garden." Groom's *Paradise Lost* illustrations for Book IV are reproduced and discussed by Virginia Tufte in "Evil as Parody in the Paradise That Was Lost: Three Illustrators Interpret Milton's Book Four," *Mosaic: A Journal for the Interdisciplinary Study of Literature* 21 (Spring, 1988), 37–58. Groom's illustration of Milton's Expulsion is discussed and reproduced in my essay, " 'With Dreadful Faces Throng'd and Fiery Arms': Apocalyptic 'Synchronisme' in Three Illustrations of *Paradise Lost*," *Coranto* 25 (1990), 20–23.

Much of the biographical information included here comes from Simon Brett, chairman, the Society of Wood Engravers, London, in a letter dated 6 May 1990 to Virginia Tufte, generously responding to inquiries she had directed to John Randle, Hilary Paynter, and Simon Lawrence. Simon Brett sent notes that included titles and dates of prints exhibited by Groom, as recorded by the Society of Wood Engravers' catalogues, supplied to him by Hilary Paynter, honorary secretary of the society; information given by Mary Groom's brother to Anne Stevens of the Ashmolean; information given by the late Joan Ellis White (who died in August 1989) to Simon Brett; telephone conversations 5 May 1990 with A. R. Groom of Herne Hill Farm, Chediston; with E.T.P. De Lacroix of Ipswich; and with Mrs. L. R. Touquet of Wimbledon, Mary Groom's sister; telephone conversation 6 May 1990 with Betty Clark (of Studio One and *Shall We Join the Ladies?*).

Others who have replied to Virginia Tufte's inquiries with items of information or with suggestions that have been helpful are Sarah Manson (2 June 1989); Lettice Sandford (12 June 1989); Michael Bott, keeper of archives and manuscripts, The University of Reading Library (21 June 1989); Jean Spencer, tutor and secretary to The Slade School of Fine Art (21 May 1990); Roberta Waddell, curator of prints, New York Public Library (31 March 1990); and Mrs. L. Rowena Touquet, M.A. Oxon, Mary Groom's sister (July 1990). John Bidwell, reference and acquisitions librarian at the Williams Andrews Clark Library, has made many helpful suggestions, and the Clark library's collection of modern fine printing has been indispensable. Finally, as all the above amply indicates, *my* debt to Virginia Tufte herself is enormous.

12. From the July 1990 letter from Mrs. Touquet to Virginia Tufte.

13. Two letters by Mary Groom to Owen Rutter, written from Chediston Grange while she was working on the blocks for *Paradise Lost*, are in Prof. Tufte's possession.

14. Balston, *English Wood Engraving*, p. 13.

15. This description of the differences between woodcuts and wood engravings is condensed from Dorothea Braby, *The Way of Wood-Engraving* (London, 1953), pp. 14–16, 92.

16. Albert Garrett, *A History of British Wood Engraving* (Tunbridge Wells, Kent, 1978), p. 165.

17. Brett, "Wood-Engraving Then and Now," *Matrix* 8:104.

18. Balston, *English Wood Engraving*, p. 12.

19. All three can be seen in the collection of modern fine printing at the William Andrews Clark Library, Los Angeles.

20. See Howard Simon, *500 Years of Art in Illustration: From Albrecht Dürer to Rockwell Kent* (Garden City, N.Y., 1949), p. 219.

21. Sarah Manson suggests this in a letter to Virginia Tufte, 2 June 1989.

22. Lettice Sandford letter to Virginia Tufte, 19 June 1989.

23. According to the list supplied to Simon Brett By Hilary Paynter, Groom exhibited the following at the Sixteenth Exhibition of the Society of Wood Engravers: *Nectarine Fruits; Hail Holy Light; Now Morn Her Rosy Steps; Eve Tempting Adam;* and *High on a Throne of Royal State.*

24. From the file set of press cuttings from the Golden Cockerel Press—owned, and graciously shared, by Professor Roderick Cave of the Victoria University of Wellington, New Zealand.

25. Groom's illustrations are included but not discussed in Joseph Wittreich's very helpful catalogue of Milton illustrations in the *Milton Encyclopedia*, ed. William B. Hunter, Jr., et al. (Lewisburg, Pa., 1978), vol. 4, p. 77; too typical is Dixon Hunt's rather dismissive comment that the "interpretive nature of the best visual criticism of Milton seems to have been lost in the twentieth century and displaced by a merely decorative sense of 'illustration' " (John Broadbent, ed. *Introductions* [Cambridge, 1963], p. 217). Somewhat more attention, indicated by citations in note 9 above, has been paid to the more conventionally patriarchal illustrations of Carlotta Petrina, perhaps because until very recently they have better matched most verbal criticism of the epic.

26. This discussion owes much to Virginia Tufte, as does much of the interpretation that follows. Working on our book on Milton illustrators, we have discussed all Mary Groom's engravings together at length. We have also enjoyed the shared benefit of consultation with our art historian colleague, Eunice Howe.

27. Leo van Puyvelde, *The Flemish Primitives*, trans. D. I. Wilton (Brussels, 1948), p. 13.

28. Thomas Balston, "Introduction," *The Wood Engravings of Robert Gibbings*, ed. Patience Empson (London, 1959), p. 35.

29. I am grateful for this identification to my colleague Eunice Howe.

30. For the study of this important iconographic type, see Millard Meiss, *Painting in Florence and Siena After the Black Death* (1951; rpt. New York, 1964), pp. 132–56.

31. All three of the engravings mentioned in this paragraph are reproduced in Robert Garrett, *A History of English Wood Engraving* (Turnbridge Wells, Kent, 1978): Underwood, p. 134; Hughes-Stanton, p. 157; and Hermes, p. 162.

32. For a fine recent analysis of Satan's scoptophilia, see Regina M. Schwartz, *Remembering and Repeating: Biblical Creation in "Paradise Lost"* (New York, 1989), chapter 3.

33. The connection is more than fanciful. For the Ovidian halcyons in the earlier poem tie together the creation, the classical golden age, and the recreation—and new golden age—to be recovered by Christ's Incarnation and self-giving love. That Groom herself made the connection is evidenced by the fact that a wood engraving she did of the myth of Halcyon shows identical birds. And more than once, she illustrated Milton's Nativity ode.

34. Will Grohmann, *The Art of Henry Moore* (New York, n.d.), pp. 43–44.

35. In Blake's illustrations, for instance (both 1807 and 1808), she rises out of Adam's side like a spectre, drawn up marionettelike by the mere hovering hand of the Son.

36. Once one begins to read Satan's attack as a rape, a number of classical analogues— all no doubt as familiar to Groom as to Milton—begin to present themselves. Philomela is one. Another, explored in some depth by Davies, is Ceres and Proserpina (*The Feminine Reclaimed*, pp. 231–47).

37. Thanks are due to William Shullenberger for this helpful observation, one of many he made in response to an earlier version of this essay.

38. "I Sing of a Maiden," in *Religious Lyrics of the Fifteenth Century*, ed. Carlton Brown (Oxford, 1939), no. 81.

39. Blake, for instance, goes back to Michelangelo in portraying one cataclysmic and composite Fall; and indeed visual portrayals of two separate Falls—before *Paradise Lost* as well as after—were rare. One of the exceptions in Renaissance visual tradition—and Milton may well have known it—was the Medici Tapestries in Florence (now in the Academia; reproduced in Frye [figure 152]).

40. Henry A. Kelly, "The Metamorphosis of the Eden Serpent During the Middle Ages and the Renaissance" *Viator* 2 (1971), 301–27. Also see Frye, *Milton's Imagery*, chapter 16 and McColley, *Milton's Eve*, pp. 7–8.

41. He is also not without visual analogues—but they seem to come from a different direction than most illustrations. Groom's serpent, especially as portrayed in Adam's fall, greatly resembles a snake sculpted by Henry Moore in 1924. See Robert Melville, *Henry Moore: Sculpture and Drawing, 1921–69* (London, 1970), figure 5. For both Groom and Moore this pythonlike creature seems to be connected with ancient phallic rites and serpent worship—another example of their conscious "primitivism" and synthesis of mythic materials.

42. Eve's response to the phenomenon of a talking snake (IX, 553), shows that Groom's reading of the Annunciation into her encounter with Satan comes from a fairly good set of Miltonic cues: Milton's Eve asks, "What may this mean?"—clearly echoing the Virgin's response to Gabriel's promise of another prodigy: her virginal conception of Christ.

43. Georgia Christopher denies that Eve's ministrations have a pivotal role in Adam's discovery of the road to divine redemption (*Milton and the Science of the Saints* [Princeton, 1982], pp. 164–71). Joseph H. Summers, on the other hand, not only sees her role as pivotal, but focuses on the clear analogues between her posture and language and that of the Son (See *The Muse's Method: An Introduction to "Paradise Lost"* [Cambridge, Mass., 1970], chapter 7). For Philip Gallagher's recent contribution to the debate, see page 120, where he calls Eve "Adam's first human mediatrix."

44. Matthew Fox, *The Coming of the Cosmic Christ* (San Francisco, 1988).

45. This violence is vividly pictured in Groom's next illustration, where a lamb lies killed before the kneeling form of Eve and a martenlike creature gnaws on the neck of a fox, as Count Ugolino gnaws on Ruggiero's neck in Canto XXXIII of Dante's *Inferno*.

46. See my *Coranto* article, in which some of my discussion of Groom's Expulsion also appears in another context.

SORTING THE SEEDS:
THE REGENERATION OF
LOVE IN *PARADISE LOST*

William Shullenberger

HOW QUIETLY Adam regards the prospect of his own dissolution when he relaxes from the first rush of self-conscious existence and the first vigorous exercise of all his faculties:

> Pensive I sat me down; there gentle sleep
> First found me, and with soft oppression seiz'd
> My drowsed sense, untroubl'd, though I thought
> I then was passing to my former state
> Insensible, and forthwith to dissolve.   (*PL* VIII, 287–91)[1]

Never again will the thought of his own nonbeing be untroubled. Death emerges as both an anxiety and a goal only after the Fall, when our first parents feel their severance from the divinely nurtured totality which structured their individuality and assured its place in the order of being. With the Fall, death insinuates itself into the erotic life of Adam and Eve; indeed, the gamble with death becomes part of the erotic charge: "if Death / Consort with thee, Death is to mee as Life" (IX, 953–54). The first experience of intercourse after the Fall is as much a marker of their mutual love affair with death as of their desire for one another.[2] Eve expresses in her love for Adam a longing for intellectual power over him and an anxiety about her own death, which she eagerly soothes by displacing it on him; her love becomes bound up with a longing to destroy the beloved. For his part, Adam counterpoints Eve's aggressive desire by scripting a suicide pact. Seeing her fallen, he resolves without hesitation to die with her as an expression of his love. His eloquent romantic love lament, ironically spoken to himself in the mode of soliloquy characteristic of Satan throughout the poem, reiterates the erotic ejaculation of Genesis: "Flesh of Flesh, / Bone of my Bone thou art, and from thy State / Mine never shall be parted, bliss or woe" (IX, 914–16).[3] There are many levels to his feeling here: the desperate longing of the husband for his wife; his grief at the apparently remediless loss of one to whom he is bound not just as a father but as a mother is bound to a child; the reopening of the narcissistic wound, the wound to self-love which is the cost of substantial mutuality in love.⁴

Even as Eve's fallenness recalls Adam to the birth trauma of that mutuality, it tempts him to affirm both the mutuality and the narcissistic desire invested in her through the choice of a death *with* her rather than *for* her; for in the one there is erotic fulfillment, and in the other only the absurd risk of faith.⁵ With Adam's choice, the problem of death becomes bound up with the promise of love. Sexuality becomes a means to placate the death instinct through aggressive mastery of the other and the momentary release of tensions in orgasm's brief counterfeit of nonbeing. Aggression becomes so mingled with desire that fallen human love will seem inconceivable without some element of destructiveness directed either outward toward the beloved, or inward toward the self;⁶ and death itself will cast the shadow of dread over the prospect of procreation:

> All that I eat or drink, or shall beget,
> Is propagated curse. O voice once heard
> Delightfully, *Increase and multiply*,
> Now death to hear! for what can I increase
> Or multiply, but curses on my head?   (X, 728–32)

"So near grows Death to Life" (IV, 425): Freud investigates this dilemma in *Beyond the Pleasure Principle* and considers its cultural consequences in *Civilization and Its Discontents*. Speculating like Milton about the outrage death presents to human consciousness, Freud traced the threads of motivation for repetition compulsion back to the scarcely discernible yet secretly powerful instinct he called Thanatos, the death instinct, the longing to cancel all the tensions of organic and conscious existence by the return to an inanimate state. Freud opposes the death instinct to the power of Eros, the life instinct which manifests itself in the urge toward pleasure, toward renewal of life, and toward the combination of "single human individuals, and after that families, then races, peoples and nations, into one great unity, the unity of mankind."⁷ Of the death instinct, Freud writes,

It must be confessed that we have much greater difficulty in grasping that instinct; we can only suspect it, as it were, as something in the background behind Eros, and it escapes detection unless its presence is betrayed by its being alloyed with Eros. It is in sadism, where the death instinct twists the erotic aim in its own sense and yet at the same time fully satisfies the erotic urge, that we succeed in obtaining the clearest insight into its nature and its relation to Eros. But even where it emerges without any sexual purpose, in the blindest fury of destructiveness, we cannot fail to recognize that the satisfaction of the instinct is accompanied by an extraordinarily high degree of narcissistic enjoyment, owing to its presenting the ego with a fulfillment of the latter's old wishes for omnipotence. (*CID*, p. 68)

The pertinence of Freud's suggestion to the motions of desire and aggression in Milton's epic may be most evident in its application to Satan, whose potential for love has been so dispossessed by the death instinct as to make him a virtual embodiment of Thanatos. It would be hard to imagine a more succinct and exact account of Satan's motivation than Freud achieves in the above passage. The degenerative consequence of Satan's drive toward absolute self-sufficiency is his baby boy, Death, in whose shapeless body of incoherent drives—a hunger which destroys and an aggression against that which gives him life—we read the sign of Satan's own monstrous infantilism and his hapless dependency on that which he seeks to destroy.

From the moment of Eve's chilling question, "But to Adam in what sort / Shall I appear?" (IX, 816–17), the interinanimation of Eros and Thanatos in human loving observes the more subtle forms of disguise and distortion described by Freud. As Regina Schwartz writes, "the distinctions between those two principles [death and life instincts] may not be so neat . . . [they are] as mutually constituting as they are contradictory."[8] Freud's Eros and Thanatos are implicated in one another like the knowledge of good and evil, as Milton describes them in *Areopagitica* and dramatizes them in *Paradise Lost*: "as two twins cleaving together," the knowledge of good and of evil are so deeply interwoven at every level of existence, "and in so many cunning resemblances hardly to be discerned, that those confused seeds which were imposed on Psyche as an incessant labor to cull out and sort asunder, were not more intermixed" (Hughes, p. 728). Milton likens Psyche's incessant labor of sorting the seeds to Adam's doom of knowing good by evil. Like the project of Freud's analysis, the sorting of good from evil knowledge involves culling out Eros from Thanatos, sorting the confusion between Eros and the death drive precipitated by the Fall.

Several elements in the Psyche fable as Milton employs it in *Areopagitica* suggest that the confused seeds stand for the disordering of Eros, and that the labor is directed to the regeneration of love. First is the reproductive potentiality of the confused seed imagery itself, which Erich Neumann interprets as signifying both "the uroboric mixture of masculine promiscuity" and "the disordered welter of fruitful predispositions and potentialities that are present in the feminine nature."[9] Second, Psyche's quest in Apuleius's tale, like Eve and Adam's in *Paradise Lost*, involves a fall: Psyche in her love falls from innocence into a condition of wandering and painful labors, under divine scrutiny and the never remote threat of retribution. The object of her love is reconciliation with her beloved. But the erotic quest is also a religious pilgrimage. Since her beloved is the mighty God of love himself, she seeks more than the happily-ever-after ending of a worldly marriage: she seeks erotic atonement with the divine. Renaissance poets and mythographers read her story as a pagan narration of the longing of the rational human soul for divine love. Its biblical analogy is the Song of Songs, whose anagogical meaning is the mystic marriage of the soul to Christ. Thus the tale of Psyche intimates for Milton the motion of human desire, which finds its terrestrial happiness in the sometimes laborious cultivation of marital companionship and its ultimate fulfillment in God's love. [10]

Third, Milton strengthens the erotic correlation of Psyche's fate with that of our primal parents by his conceit of the Fall as a catastrophic birth: "It was from out the rind of one apple tasted, that the knowledge of good and evil, as two twins cleaving together, leaped forth into the world. And perhaps this is that doom which Adam fell into of knowing good and evil, that is to say, of knowing good by evil" (Hughes, p. 728). The uncanny twinship of good and evil knowledge, implicated erotically—"cleaving together"—in each other even at the moment of their origin, and "in so many cunning resemblances hardly to be discerned," suggests that Adam's doom is complicated by the likeness of these forms of knowledge. For if the knowledge of good and the knowledge of evil, the one leading to the renewal of life and the other leading to the violent termination of death, are so intimately involved and interwoven, how is the one to be discerned and chosen without the instinct of the other being satisfied? Like Psyche, the human soul in love, Eve and Adam in the final books of the epic begin the incessant labor of sorting asunder the confused seeds of Eros and Thanatos.

God the Father, in announcing Adam and Eve's saving difference from Satan, gives a hermeneutic key to the cause and the path of their regeneration:

> The first sort by thir own suggestion fell,
> Self-tempted, self-deprav'd: Man falls deceiv'd
> By th' other first; Man therefore shall find grace,
> The other none.   (III, 129–32)

Imagining himself "self-begot, self-rais'd" (V, 860), Satan has been tempted by the fiction of autonomous self-hood to twist his potential for love so severely in upon himself as to make genuine dialogue impossible for him, and to make his entire project of existence the attempted cancellation of all otherness, in order to spite the ultimate and ineradicable Other, God. Adam and Eve's fall, as God predicts it in Book III and as they enact it in Book IX, "is not the exploitation of weakness but the perversion of virtue" (McColley, p. 208), the particular virtue of identifying receptiveness, openness to "th'other." Even in their falling, Adam and Eve fall together, and it is in their disposition toward the other as an embodiment of the self that leads the self beyond itself that they discover the possibility of grace. Their regeneration involves the survival and reactivation of their capacity to love through the recognition of the other. The motif of the "Image" in the poem implies that identity is a metaphoric structure in which one discovers who one is when one's life is offered as an image of an other. [11] In Book IX, Satan with his charlatan's chatter displaces Adam as the other whom Eve images forth; and Eve displaces God in Adam's eyes as the center, the source, and the end of his being. Redemption, as Michael Lieb has said, involves "the reorientation of the primal image." [12] The Son initiates this work of reorientation by the prevenient grace which makes possible Eve and Adam's renewal of dialogue and their repentant turn toward the Father. In the extraordinary dialogue which leads out of the chaos of Book X, they work their way out of near despair by recovering the capacity to image forth, amplify, and transform the saving Word that is latent and unrecognized in each other's intuition. In doing so they begin the process of separating out Thanatos from Eros in the act of sexual generation which has become, with the Fall, the most terrifying aspect of existence. In renouncing suicide and celibacy as possible responses to the "propagated curse" (X, 729), they clarify and loosen the hold of the death instinct on the erotic life, making sexual generativity the basis for the propagation not only of a curse but ultimately of a promise.

   The curse on the serpent contains the seed of the promise: "Between Thee and the Woman I will put / Enmity, and between thine and her Seed; / Her Seed shall bruise thy head, thou bruise his heel" (X, 179–81). This divine utterance, to Christian interpreters the *protevangelium* or first prophecy of Christ, is both the promise and the fulfillment in time of the promise. Because the passage is theologically overdetermined, it is easy to underestimate the implications of its image base. Milton's use of the Seed image, from I, 8 on through the poem, suggests that for him, biology is not destiny; biology is eschatology. The *protevangelium* makes of the Seed a metonymy for Christ, but what is a seed? We understand it as a genetic message to the future. Milton deploys it as a spiritual message from the future. A seed is the truth of an organism, of a species, packaged to survive winter, the season of death, to survive many winters if need be. It can enter the burial ground for the sake of the future because everything about it that is mortal is stripped away. In its resilient shell it bears impenetrably and enigmatically the possibility of a form it resembles not in the least. It is released when the plant in which it forms is deflowered and given over to death. It is little; it is out of all proportion to the scale of the being whose future life it carries. It completes and implicitly originates the organic dynamism of the created order which Raphael has epitomized in the image of a plant:

> So from the root
> Springs lighter the green stalk, from thence the leaves
> More aery, last the bright consummate flow'r
> Spirits odorous breathes.   (V, 479–82)

As gardeners, Adam and Eve will gradually come to understand the saving implication of this enigma of the Seed, and their struggle to make sense of it initiates the regeneration of their love and of their hope.[13] Georgia Christopher borrows a term from the Quakers to describe this moment as an "opening," "a moment when the promise in a passage of scripture that has hitherto seemed dark, puzzling, or merely irrelevant, takes on clarity, certitude—and more important—a liberating application to one's immediate life situation" (Christopher, pp. 170, 172). In the reversal from despair to the renewal of hope which the recollection of the *protevangelium* initiates, we can see an instance of how grace operates through the Word in the Protestant dispensation. Although the Oracle is to be "verifi'd / When *Jesus* son of *Mary* second *Eve*, / Saw Satan fall like Lightning down from Heav'n" (X, 182–84), it becomes active once it is spoken, making the future now. The present Word foretells and initiates what it will finally accomplish: the final driving out of the demonic from the life of human desire in a climactic dance of death. The Son, "the Woman's Seed," incarnating without fault the promise of immortality implicit in human generative life, will decisively root out and destroy the serpent of the human love affair with death, and thus regenerate the generative life itself. But Adam and Eve do not need to wait for the Second Coming for the regenerative process to begin; it begins with the planting of the Seed of the Word by the one who is both living Oracle (*PR* I, 460) and Woman's Seed.

Sorting the seeds involves the first significant differentiation of gender tasks after the Fall. Feminist and new historicist readings of the poem stress Milton's prescriptive bourgeois conventionality in representing woman as childbearer, reproductive unit, man as increasingly alienated laborer for the great taskmaster of history.[14] From this perspective, as Eve has bowed out of Raphael's astronomy lesson, she is now excused for postlapsarian nap time while the gentlemen take up the tragic curriculum of history. History is man's business; to woman is reserved the bourgeois drawing room of private sensibility and the dream world of novelistic fiction. Perhaps the dream she recounts upon waking at the end of the poem in calm of mind, "all her spirits compos'd / To meek submission" (XII, 596– 97), could be seen in this perspective as the prototype of romantic melodrama, which provides the lonely housewife with its great compensatory themes of romantic love and deliverance from danger, loss, and longing.

But Freud may help us to understand the symbolic economy of consciousness, the distribution of different psychic tasks to Adam and Eve in the poem's closing books, in a way more consonant with Milton's theology and metapsychology than a historicist approach can allow for. Milton seems to anticipate Freud's speculation about the way that species respond to the outrage of death by the internal division of cell types between *soma*—the mortal body of the organism—and germ plasm, *seed*, which carries a potential immortality:

We might attempt to apply the libido theory which has been arrived at in psychoanalysis to the mutual relationship of cells. We might suppose that the life instincts or sexual instincts which are active in each cell take the other cells as their object, that they partly neutralize the death instincts (that is, the processes set up by them) in those cells and thus preserve their life; while the other cells do the same for them, and still others sacrifice themselves in the performance of this libidinal function. The germ-cells themselves would behave in a completely "narcissistic" fashion—to use the phrase that we are accustomed to use in the theory of the neuroses to describe a whole individual who retains his libido in his ego and pays none of it out in object-cathexes. The germ-cells require their libido, the activity of their life instincts, for themselves, as a reserve against their later momentous constructive activity. [15]

The personification of cells in their distribution of social roles for the sake of self-preservation seems an especially odd vestige of Freud's desire to model psychology on the organicism of the natural sciences which influenced his early career. [16] But if we keep in mind that he is trying to articulate an insight which is both biological and mythic, we can see his resort to figuration as an imaginative gesture toward the truth which is analogous to Milton's reception and development of the saving trope which represents Christ as "woman's Seed." Anticipating Freud's division of cellular labor as a figure for the division of psychic labor, Milton represents Adam assuming the sacrificially protective burden of the *soma*, the experience of the mortal body, as Eve embodies the preservative libidinal withdrawal which Freud assigns to the germ cell, "as a reserve against [her] later momentous constructive activity" (*BPP*, p. 44).

Thus, in the final books of *Paradise Lost,* under the shadow of death, the primal parents observe a distribution of roles wherein biology and eschatology are linked by the figure of the Seed. Eve is the seed-bearer, whose prelapsarian fruitfulness as "Mother of Mankind" (V, 389) has been honored as a terrestrial blessing in Raphael's greeting, and repeated and amplified typologically in Adam's recognition of her centrality in salvation history (Peczenik, p. 265):

> peace return'd
> Home to my Breast, and to my memory
> His promise, that thy Seed shall bruise our Foe;
> Which then not minded in dismay, yet now
> Assures me that the bitterness of death
> Is past, and we shall live. Whence Hail to thee,
> *Eve* rightly call'd, Mother of all Mankind,
> Mother of all things living, since by thee
> Man is to live, and all things live for Man.   (XI, 153–61)

Eve withdraws from the agon of history into the eternal now of the Incarnation. She is preserved intact from history so as to enjoy an indeterminate intimacy with God, who is also in sleep (XII, 611). In her dreaming, the typological distance between her and the second Eve virtually dissolves, so that she wakes, acknowledging that "all by me is lost," yet filled with a virtual and immediate knowledge of the prophesied Seed as if he were her own Son. Freud might account for this powerful centripetal motion of the imagination as a necessarily narcissistic withdrawal of libido from all external objects and concentration of it in the seed-carrying and transmitting process itself. In any case, although Eve's final words are brief, they signal her acceptance of biological function as eschatological privilege, with as clear-eyed, regenerate, and prepared an imagination as Adam shows in his more copious recitation of the ways in which he has been greatly instructed (XII, 553–73). Although it would be easy to trivialize her words, the trivialization would be more a mark of the reader's need to suppress Eve's experience than of Milton's.

Several features of the speech bear our attention. First, although Michael has led Adam to believe that it will be his patriarchal task to "Let her with thee partake what thou hast heard, / Chiefly what may concern her Faith to know" (XII, 598–99), Eve's greeting indicates that the knowledge conveyed by the divine dream may outrun his own:

> Whence thou return'st, and whither went'st, I know;
> For God is also in sleep, and Dreams advise,
> Which he hath sent propitious, some great good
> Presaging.   (XII, 610–13)

This greeting is gently and unintentionally ironic, and might indeed take some of the wind out of his newly inspired sails, for she indicates that she knows where he has been, but he can't yet say the same for her.

Second, the intimacy and immediacy of the relationship to God implied in her sleep suspends or subverts the hierarchical mediation structure by which Adam is for God only, and knows God through the manifestation of his angelic instructors, and she is in turn for God in Adam. This intimate relation to God is more intuitive than discursive, thus timeless and boundless, and it observes something of the erotic decorum and the prophetic ardor of Mary, second Eve: "Such favor I unworthy am voutsaf't, / By mee the Promis'd Seed shall all restore" (XII, 622–23). The earlier *Ave*'s addressed to Eve receive their answers in these lines, which echo the Lucan narrative of the Annunciation and prophetic lyric of the Magnificat, with their theme of divine favor bestowed upon and expressed through the lowly and unworthy handmaid (Luke i, 38, 46–56). Eve becomes one with Mary as *theotokos*, God-bearer, and speaks, as Mary does, as a prophet.[17]

Finally, in part because of the typological pressure, the textual resonances, and the sense of divine presence carried in these lines, I believe that something new begins to happen with poetic language in Eve's speech. Barbara Lewalski indicates that the speech redeems the love lyric from Satan's Petrarchan perversion of it, repeating in postlapsarian simplicity the theme of centeredness in Adam which was the burden of "Sweet is the breath of morn" lyric in Book IV.[18] Lewalski also hears the echo of Ruth's faithful pledge to Naomi: "where you go, I will go, and where you lodge, I will lodge; your people shall be my people, and your God my God" (Ruth i, 16; Lewalski, p. 277). Joseph Wittreich stresses both the prophetic significance of Eve's final utterance—"an extraordinary moment in the history of epic poetry, where the last speech is always assigned to one of the gods or to the hero or a stand-in for him who has privilege of place"—and its "unencumbered" innovation within the sonnet form.[19]

Freely transforming her pre-texts, Eve directs imaginative attention inward here, away from the register of the senses toward scarcely communicable intuition. Her repetition of the key word "all"—"thou to mee / Art all things under Heav'n, all places thou, . . . though all by mee is lost, / Such favor I unworthy am voutsaf't, / By mee the Promis'd Seed shall all restore" (XII, 617–23)—sets her utterance in sublime consonance with the sense of "allness" which reverberates throughout Adam's final confession of faith, the final instruction of Michael that precedes her waking (XII, 553–605), and with the quiet fullness of the narrative which closes the epic in the prospect of a world that lies "all before them."[20]

In this poem where everything experienced can be spoken, where even God's incommunicability condescends to the codes of dramatic and dogmatic speech, what are we to make of the reserve, the reticence of Eve's account of her dream? McColley finely hints at the motivation for this reticence when she describes Eve's dream as "one of those passages that the poet leaves open for the progression of truth within the reader" (McColley, p. 214). I can't read these words without hearing Rilke, and sensing some newly and scarcely articulate opening into an inwardness whose incommunicable depth and fullness can only be suggested—and yet the suggestion has the weight of truth because of the calm excitement and pregnant sureness of words which have just barely recovered from wonder.[21]

A political reading might characterize this inward motion as the emerging interiority of the recently constituted bourgeois subject, typically female, at its very origin romanticizing its subjection to the mobile authority of masculine power:

> but now lead on;
> In mee is no delay; with thee to go,
> Is to stay here; without thee here to stay,
> Is to go hence unwilling; thou to mee
> Art all things under Heav'n, all places thou,
> Who for my wilful crime art banisht hence.   (XII, 614–19)

From this perspective, the speech serves to mystify that power while absorbing its guilt.[22] But the firmness of Eve's final declaration—"By mee the Promis'd Seed shall all restore" (623)—suggests something radically different. If the sequestering of women from history is a component of the story of patriarchal power, Michael's instruction has made clear that that history is nothing to celebrate, but rather something to mourn and to judge. Eve counters the perverting dynamic of patriarchal authority here with a highly concentrated statement of matrilineal authority of her own, in which the divine promise for the redemption of history through love is fully planted. The promise of the Seed has been spoken before, in reference to Eve, and to Eve. In speaking the promise herself, in the last dramatic statement of the poem, Eve claims it, embodies it, and speaks it as if from the vantage of that future moment which Adam has learned to anticipate by faith: "in the last words we hear in Eden, Eve rises above lyric and moves beyond her role as protagonist in the tragedy of the Fall, to embrace her divinely appointed, central role in the epic of Redemption. Illumined by her prophetic dream, she articulates her own version of the new Christian heroism" (Lewalski, p. 277).

As the prophetic motion of her dream delivers Eve to the future intact, Adam embodies the function which Freud ascribes to *soma:* the body knowledge of human life which is destined for suffering and death. Whereas Milton stresses the Lucan prophecies to underwrite the typological connection of Eve to Mary, Paul's epistles provide him the typological antithesis between the "old man," Adam, in whom we are enslaved to the flesh, and Christ, the second Adam, through whose obedience unto death the righteous are delivered from that enslavement. "Oh wretched man that I am!" Paul exclaims in the Epistle to the Romans, "Who will deliver me from this body of death?" (Rom. vii, 24). What Paul calls here the "body of death" and elsewhere the "body of sin" (Rom. vi, 16), corrupted by Thanatos and given over, like Freud's *soma,* to death, is the inheritance of Adam, "through whom sin entered the world, and death through sin" (Rom. v, 12). Milton dramatizes in Adam's purgatorial education the transformation of the Pauline body of sin by the Word of grace.

Adam learns to think of death not as a private and material event, the death of the body, but as the outcome of a drive toward nonbeing activated by the sense of an existence at odds with the ground of its being and hating both itself and others for that. William Kerrigan describes death as the "biological repetition compulsion of our primal sin,"[23] and Adam's vision of fallen history discloses history as a pattern of repetition compulsion writ large in the distorted drives of politics and culture. History coils in on itself in a collective love affair with death, tending "from bad to worse," "To good malignant, to bad men benign, / Under her own weight groaning" (XII, 106, 538–39), dominated by an urge to power which has disclosed itself in Satan as a thwarted death wish. In each generation "one just man" resists that drive, and gains freedom from it. Yet as long as the response of love is resistance to the death drive, the historical and spiritual deadlock sustains itself; history, as Freud puts it, "must present the struggle between Eros and Death, between the instinct of life and the instinct of destruction, as it works itself out in the human species" (*CID,* p. 69).

This is the outer limit of Freud's criticism of history, deadlocked by his dualism. The deadlock is broken in *Paradise Lost* by the paradox of Christ's loving obedience unto death. By yielding himself up to death, assuming the Adamic body of sin, Christ, the woman's Seed, reverses the pattern of domination whereby, as Freud puts it, Thanatos twists Eros to its own purposes. Now love claims death for its purposes, disclosing it as a threshold where faith begins its regeneration of human bodily and imaginative life: "To the faithful," Adam proclaims as he epitomizes his regenerate insight, "Death [is] the Gate of Life" (XII, 571). Adam's growth toward insight into this paradox permits him, as Regina Schwartz writes, "to reject the trap of Satanic repetition":

Adam takes up the task enjoined him at his birth: to be the creator of something new. His example teaches that the compelled repeater is fundamentally afflicted with a dire lack of imagination. Satan can only conceive of doing what has been done. Repentance is innovative; to refuse to repeat constitutes a genuine act of the will. Indeed this is Augustine's understanding of the will: " '*initium ut esset homo creatus est*,' man's capacity for beginning because he himself is a beginning." (Schwartz, p. 104)

But this beginning, this preparation of the will to act freely toward the future rather than to reenact compulsively the past, requires a disposition toward the future as a sort of proleptic memory. Indeed, faith, as it becomes "instructed" (I, 18) in *Paradise Lost*, might be considered the freeing of the will for obedience by the paradoxical memory of a future which causes and constitutes that obedience. Adam and Eve obscurely glimpse enough of that future in the *protevangelium* to direct themselves toward it at the conclusion of Book X. Yet faith will involve, as God knows well, not only good intentions but staying power, patience; and patience is to be grounded in both hope and a tough-minded recognition of its basis in suffering. Adam's instruction in faith in the final books of the poem is thus both a blessing and a *blessure*, a wounding. On the visionary mount, he learns to bear the agony of a foreknowledge not unlike God's. He will henceforth endure as a personal memory the tragic history of all his children; there is no sin, finally, which he cannot acknowledge as his own, and no suffering which he is not to share.[24]

The climax of this process of purgatorial identification occurs with his vision of the Flood:

> How didst thou grieve then, *Adam*, to behold
> The end of all thy Offspring, end so sad,
> Depopulation; thee another Flood,
> Of tears and sorrow a Flood thee also drown'd,
> And sunk thee as thy Sons; till gently rear'd
> By th'Angel, on thy feet thou stood'st at last,
> Though comfortless, as when a Father mourns
> His Children, all in view destroy'd at once.   (XI, 754–61)

Although this is as close as Adam comes to despair, it is not the self-involved, self-pitying despair which motivated him immediately after the Fall, but an expression of mourning, of his paternal responsibility and concern. Milton redoubles the motion of sympathy and its potential for healing here, by identifying Adam's tears with those of the Flood—

evoking the redemptive possibilities of weeping in the flood-haunted lines of *Lycidas*—and by standing on the same tragic ground with Adam, signaling his own sympathy through the shift to direct address—"How didst thou grieve then, *Adam*."²⁵ Even in Adam's complaint against the prophetic foreknowledge which he must henceforth carry, we can hear echoes of the suffering foreknowledge of God expressed in Book III:

> Let no man seek
> Henceforth to be foretold what shall befall
> Him or his Children, evil he may be sure,
> Which neither his foreknowing can prevent,
> And hee the future evil shall no less
> In apprehension than in substance feel
> Grievous to bear.   (XI, 770–76)²⁶

Adam's typological relation to the promised Seed of Christ is thus double. Even as the desolation of the history he has inaugurated amplifies the distance between him and his antitype, the growth of his imaginative capability to embrace and to evaluate that history in a single action of compassionate yet ethically scrupulous understanding prefaces the Son's perfect submission to history that is also the occasion of a judgment which will transform death itself into life. Adam's compassionate moral discernment is also motivated by the Son's submission. As Michael instructs him how fully to interpret the enigma of the Seed, Adam grounds his faith in the apocalyptic Word, which makes present to his imagination that which is yet to be, simultaneously directing his pity outward from the self-enclosure of personal despair, and disciplining that pity for the painful intellectual and political labor of interpretation in a corrupted and deceptive world, sorting asunder the seeds of authentic life from the cunning resemblances intermixed with them by the death instinct.²⁷

The history of Milton apologetics has never been finer than in recent interpretation of the final two books of *Paradise Lost* as Adam's *bildungsroman*. Adam becomes the first student of Protestant poetics. He learns to demystify forms of temporal and spiritual authority; to sort asunder the confused seeds of good and evil through his sharpened recognition of fallen ambiguities and appearances; to preserve hope through learning to read providential signs typologically across the screen of history; thus to interiorize the process of regeneration, to cultivate the paradise within (XII, 587). Adam's memory, understanding, and will are progressively renovated as Michael instructs him in a way of reading temporally the broken signs of the fallen world in light of the paradoxical promise of the *protevangelium*. He learns how to think metaphorically and thus to follow the transmission of the Seed through a faith in God's Word which refuses to let history keep it buried. The *protevangelium* which organizes and directs that salvation history ultimately reveals the saving event not as a historical, physical duel but as a moral and imaginative apocalypse, by which death itself is transvalued (XII, 391–435).[28]

But despite Adam's stunning progress as a student of Protestant poetics and his own concluding three cheers for the Messiah, there remains in the final books some kind of harshness, an undertow in the presentation of history, a lump of that futurity that remains untransmutable by even the recuperative and apologetic efforts of Milton's best recent critics,[29] and this continues to make the episode of Adam's visionary and auditory instruction easier to read about than to read. There is indeed a different poetic at work here than in the prelapsarian books of the poem—call it Protestant moral and typological training, or call it, as Balachandra Rajan does, the Osiris principle, gathering and re-membering the broken pieces of the truth[30]—but there is also something at work in the poetry which resists the recuperative and apologetic power of this poetic and continues to express itself through readers' complaints.[31] A residue of Milton's own experience of the defeat of the Good Old Cause, it is implicit in the weight of the historic content of Adam's instruction, which is so laden with human sorrow and human failure that it demasks any wish we might have for a vision of progress. We want history to be progressive, but Milton disappoints us in his account of repetition-compulsion which is the evidence of the human love affair with death. "For now I see / Peace to corrupt no less than War to waste" (XI, 783–84) is a formula for the collective human incapacity to live at peace with one another and with God, to participate in the civilizing arts of Eros, which would be, as Freud says, "to combine single human individuals, and after that families, then races, peoples and nations, into one great unity, the unity of mankind" (*CID*, p. 69).[32] Perhaps we need to think through the presentation of historical content in the final books of the poem in terms of what Brecht called the alienation effect. As Brecht described the alienation effect in theatre, its deliberate and strident disturbance of the complacencies and illusions of bourgeois naturalism prevented audience complicity in the narcotic illusion of conventional art, and made possible the recognition that history, like the drama that represents it, is man-made, the consequence of self-mystifying alignments of power.[33] In the concluding books of *Paradise Lost*, we can detect something of Brecht's strategies in Milton's deliberate jarring of the desire for spiritual complacency that keeps the question of the justification of the ways of God to man perpetually open. Milton uses the alienation effect to the purpose not of theological apology, but to make complacent apology impossible. He does not reveal God at work in history so much as God at work in spite of or against history; the work of salvation history runs athwart the history of power in the world—summed up by Michael as "so shall the World go on, / To good malignant, to bad men benign, / Under her own weight groaning, till the day / Appear of respiration to the just, / And vengeance to the wicked" (XII, 537–41). That day is indefinitely deferred, although always possible at any moment; and the harshness of history in the interim is a challenge to Adam, to Milton, to Milton's readers: to believe that God is God, omnipotent and providential, in spite of the burdensome evidence to the contrary.

This tension makes of faith in the midst of history something absurd and something terrifying. Luther knew this, as did Kierkegaard. Indeed, in "The Bondage of the Will," Luther seems to take polemical delight in arguing that the appearance of divine injustice must be the very basis of faith:

But here God must be reverenced and held in awe, as being most merciful to those whom He justifies and saves in their own utter unworthiness; and we must show some measure of deference to His Divine wisdom by believing Him just when to us He seems unjust. If His justice were such as could be adjudged just by human reckoning, it clearly would not be Divine; it would in no way differ from human justice. But inasmuch as He is one true God, wholly incomprehensible and inaccessible to man's understanding, it is reasonable, indeed inevitable, that His justice also should be incomprehensible.[34]

In anthropomorphizing and rationalizing God, Milton renders him more permeable to history than the terrifying Sovereign whose enigmatic justice Luther celebrates; but the radical point about faith is preserved, even, in some ways, amplified. The material horror of the history of power, and the knowledge that the righteous from Abel to Christ and his true disciples are likely to suffer persecution and possible murder, make faith of the sort that Adam learns to cultivate a condition of absurd joy, the joy of those who are bereft of everything but the Word of a God who claims to suffer history with them, and to judge and transform history through his suffering. This Word redeems the possibility of human love, yet sets that love on the way to regeneration in a setting utterly inhospitable to it: "Adam will finally leave the Garden to procreate new life that he knows will end in family murder, intertribal marriage, and the general decay of his people; but his faith, or *recta ratio*, submits to God's speech, rather than to the logic of circumstance" (Christopher, p. 99).

"After the final no there comes a yes / And on that yes the future world depends."[35] The negatives of history solicit Adam's powerful affirmation of the Word's eventual power to make all things new. Like the implied spectator of Brechtian theatre, Adam can recite the ways of an instruction which has oriented him toward a human future with the personal discipline that stands continually to demystify history. Adam's affirmation is in turn enfolded in Eve's deeply loving disposition toward him and toward the future Seed who is both cause and ultimate consequence of the regeneration of their love. In necessarily distinctive and complementary ways, the riddle of the *protevangelium* initiates Eve and Adam into the task of sorting the seeds of love and death intermixed by the Fall. Their psychic labor in the final books of the epic disentangles the death drive from the divinely sanctioned Eros that draws them toward the promise of renewal of life in and through their mortal bodies. In Eve's dream work Milton imagines the regeneration of what Freud calls the primary process, the field of the intuitive in Raphael's parlance, and the regeneration of the secondary process, or discursive reason (V, 486–90) in Adam's hermeneutic and ethical training.[36] Their relationship becomes the repository of an idealized Eros whose motivation and teleology, the promised Seed, frees it from perversion by the death instinct. But if the extended drive of Eros is, as Freud puts it, to unite "separate individuals into a community bound together by libidinal ties" (*CID*, p. 88), Milton's survey of postlapsarian history yields little hope for the possibility of such projects. "What is astonishing about *Paradise Lost*," Fredric Jameson writes, "is the utter silence and absence of all the great themes of church and collectivity. The narrative moves at once from the family—with its great evocation of married love and sexuality—to the fallen privatized world of individual belief and individual salvation."[37] This division of spiritual labor between Adam and Eve seems then to offer hope for the regeneration of private and personal relationships but not for larger public commitments. Adam and Eve constitute the prototypical community of faith, yet at the same time they represent, as historicist critics have reminded us, the inaugural bourgeois family; thus they carry a terrible cultural burden.

The lesson for Protestant warfaring Christians is to resist evil, yet to do so paradoxically by disengaging from hope for the world, and waiting on God. The social counterpart of a marriage redeemed by the purging of the death instinct from it is the subjection of the extensive network of human relations beyond the family to Satan's usurpation, that is, to a death instinct displaced from the private to the public sphere. A political reading of *Paradise Lost* would account for this displacement as a consequence of the ideological constraints imposed by the doctrines of personal salvation and of romantic marital love.[38] In keeping with the Freudian analogies of this essay, I take this displacement as evidence for the inevitability, the ineradicability of the death instinct in a fallen world. Hence history appears cyclical, repetitive, coiled like the serpent's coils. Even post-Resurrection history takes the shape of repetition-compulsion, the unquenchable collective longing of Thanatos for the impossible quietude of nonbeing, which paradoxically can express itself only through compulsive aggression, the will to power. And the only resolution to this collective human love affair with death, "Satan with his perverted world" (*PL* XII, 547), will be the apocalyptic return of what has been repressed from history—a love which is also vengeance, a reversal of the paradigm of Freud's cultural meditation, in which Eros at last twists Thanatos to its own purposes—an ethical vengeance which satisfies the death instinct through an apocalypse of love.[39]

Thus the word "solitary" rings very loud in the final line, and it is not surprising that Bentley wanted to quiet the anxiety it produces by replacing it with the word "social."[40] As far as what the future has to offer, it is Eve and Adam's fate to remain forever solitary, and even as they leave it, the Garden is becoming scorched earth, the subjected plain of Eden before them already, in Adam's memory of the future, scarred by battle, soaked with blood. Their solitude is not just the numinous consolation that comes with their newly discovered inwardness, and its potential fruitfulness, but the loneliness of fallen existence, the loneliness of history, the political loneliness of Milton's old age, the loneliness of a spiritual individualism that has reached the historical understanding that "there is no legitimate church on earth. There are only individual souls, who may help one another but should not combine organizationally."[41] Suspicious of collectivities as an understandable consequence of his historical experience, Milton cannot in this poem embody in good faith a community of forgiveness and of love larger than the romantic Christian marriage, and so the extraordinary beauty and preternatural hope of the poem's closure need to be set in relation to the enormous devastation of the world which lies all before our first parents. The dark lights of Adam's vision of that world remain, not dispelled but blended into the sublime *chiaroscuro* of the concluding movement of the poem, deepening the wonder even as they sober the silent prospect of the way ahead. Perhaps by acknowledging both the hope embedded in Eve's dream and the mortal horror of Adam's instruction in faith, we can share something of the double-mindedness and the tough-mindedness of our first parents, not disconsolate, although there is much to afflict them; sorrowing, yet in peace (XI, 113, 117). For this is part of how the poem instructs us to keep the hope implicit in love alive, and to search in patience for the more extensive ties of love for which Milton is too honest to offer much promise.

Sarah Lawrence College

NOTES

1. *John Milton: Complete Poems and Major Prose*, ed. Merritt Y. Hughes (Indianapolis, 1957). All references to Milton's poetry and prose are to this edition and will be cited parenthetically in the text.

2. On Adam and Eve's "love-triangle with death," see Diane Kelsey McColley, *Milton's Eve* (Urbana, Ill., 1983), p. 208.

3. Fannie Peczenik nicely diagnoses the reduction in meaning and the closure of saving possibility in Adam's heartbreaking return to his initial lyric celebration of Eve's formation from his rib. See Peczenik, "Milton on the Creation of Eve: Adam's Dream and the Hieroglyphic of the Rib," in *A Fine Tuning: Studies of the Religious Poetry of Herbert and Milton*, ed. Mary A. Maleski (Binghamton, N.Y., 1989), pp. 262–63.

4. On the element of Adam's narcissistic investment in the creation of Eve, see Marshall Grossman, "Servile / Sterile / Style: Milton and the Question of Woman," in *Milton and the Idea of Woman*, ed. Julia M. Walker (Urbana, Ill., 1988), pp. 149–50.

5. I use "absurd" in the sense cultivated by Kierkegaard in, for instance, *Fear and Trembling:* "a humble courage is required to grasp the whole of the temporal by virtue of the absurd, and this is the courage of faith." Soren Kierkegaard, *Fear and Trembling*, in *A Kierkegaard Anthology*, ed. Robert Bretall (New York, 1974), pp. 128–29.

6. As Ilona Bell explains it in her essay, "Milton's Dialogue with Petrarch" in this volume, the motifs of narcissism and aggression in love account for the dilemma and the dynamic of Petrarchism.

7. Sigmund Freud, *Civilization and Its Discontents*, trans. James Strachey (New York, 1961), p. 69. Subsequent references to this book will be cited parenthetically in my text, with the abbreviation *CID*.

8. Regina M. Schwartz, *Remembering and Repeating: Biblical Creation in "Paradise Lost"* (Cambridge, 1988), p. 94.

9. Erich Neumann, *Amor and Psyche: The Psychic Development of the Feminine. A Commentary on the Tale by Apuleius*, trans. Ralph Mannheim (Princeton, 1971), pp. 95–96.

10. A suggestive essay on the implications of the Psyche myth in *Paradise Lost* is Ann Ashworth's "Psyche and Eve: Milton's Goddess without a Temple," *MQ* 18, no. 2 (May 1984), 52–58. Thomas Roche discusses the Renaissance allegorization of Cupid and Psyche as a fable about Love and the Rational Soul in his treatment of Spenser, *The Kindly Flame: A Study of the Third and Fourth Books of Spenser's "Faerie Queene"* (Princeton, 1964), pp. 125–26. Milton explicitly alludes to this allegorized fable as the climax of the Attendant Spirit's epilogue to *Comus* (1003–1011). For a review of critical interpretations of this allusion, its grounding in Boccaccio's mythography and its precedent in Spenser's Garden of Adonis, see *A Variorum Commentary on The Poems of John Milton*, vol. II of *The Minor English Poems*, ed. A.S.P. Woodhouse and Douglas Bush (New York, 1972), pp. 985–87.

11. For a more extended adaptation of Lacan to the Christian sense of selfhood in the poem, see my essay, "Wrestling with the Angel: *Paradise Lost* and Feminist Criticism," *MQ* 20, no. 3 (October 1986), 69–85. For a more thoroughgoing deconstructive approach to gender and identity in the poem, see Grossman, "Servile / Sterile / Style." From a feminist and new historicist perspective, Janet Halley reviews a range of previous studies in exploring the possibility of "autonomous female subjectivity" in Milton's literary career; see "Female Autonomy in Milton's Sexual Poetics," in *Milton and the Idea of Woman*, pp. 230–53.

12. Michael Lieb, *The Dialectics of Creation: Patterns of Birth and Regeneration in "Paradise Lost"* (Amherst, 1970), p. 205.

13. On the structural relation of the vegetation imagery to prelapsarian and postlapsarian existence, see Kathleen M. Swaim, "Flower, Fruit, and Seed: A Reading of *Paradise Lost*," in *Milton Studies* V, ed. James D. Simmonds (Pittsburgh, 1972), pp. 155–76. The fullest handling of the centrality of the *protevangelium* in *Paradise Lost* is Georgia Christopher's. See Christopher, *Milton and the Science of the Saints* (Princeton, 1982), p. 169. See also John M. Steadman, "Adam and the Prophesied Redeemer (*Paradise Lost*, XII, 359–623)," *SP* 56 (1959), 214–25, and C. A. Patrides, "The 'Protevangelium' in Renaissance Theology and *Paradise Lost*," *SEL* 3 (1963), 19–30.

14. Marcia Landy lays the groundwork for these readings in "Kinship and the Role of Women in *Paradise Lost*," in *Milton Studies* IV, ed. James D. Simmonds (Pittsburgh, 1972), pp. 3–18. Other essays on the bourgeois construction of gender in the poem include Jackie Di Salvo, "Blake Encountering Milton: Politics and the Family in *Paradise Lost* and *The Four Zoas*," in *Milton and the Line of Vision*, ed. Joseph Anthony Wittreich, Jr. (Madison, 1975), pp. 143–84; Janet Halley, "Female Autonomy and Milton's Sexual Poetics," cited in note 11; Mary Nyquist, "The genesis of gendered subjectivity in the divorce tracts and in *Paradise Lost*," in *Re-Membering Milton: Essays on the Texts and Traditions*, ed. Mary Nyquist and Margaret W. Ferguson (New York, 1988), pp. 99–127; Maureen Quilligan, *Milton's Spenser: The Politics of Reading* (Ithaca, 1983).

15. Sigmund Freud, *Beyond the Pleasure Principle*, trans. and ed. James Strachey (New York, 1961), p. 40. Subsequent references to this book will be cited parenthetically in my text, with the abbreviation *BPP*.

16. See Peter Gay, *Freud: A Life for Our Time* (New York, 1988).

17. For the typological relation of Eve to Mary, see Mother Mary Christopher Pecheux, "The Concept of the Second Eve in *Paradise Lost*," *PMLA* 75 (1960), 359–66. See also Dayton Haskin, "Matthew, Mary, Luke, and John: The Mother of the Word in Milton's Poetry," *Proceedings of the PMR Conference*, 11 (1986), 75–86.

18. Barbara Lewalski, *Paradise Lost and the Rhetoric of Literary Forms* (Princeton, 1985), p. 277.

19. Joseph Wittreich, *Feminist Milton* (Ithaca, 1987), pp. 105, 107.

20. The word "all" occurs eighteen times in the last ninety-seven lines of the poem. Although Eve's speech is the briefest of the final speeches, she employs the word four times, in highly concentrated syntactic figures which stress the terrestrial completeness and consummation she finds in Adam, and the eschatologic antithesis between the "all" that her crime has lost and the "all" that her seed will restore. Isabel MacCaffrey notes that this postlapsarian love lyric concentrates in its brevity the theme of Eve's magnificent prelapsarian descant on the sweetness of Eden (*PL* IV, 641–56); see *"Paradise Lost" as Myth* (Cambridge, Mass., 1959), p. 77.

21. See, for instance, Rilke's description of Eurydice: "She was deep within herself, like a woman heavy / with child, and did not see the man in front or the / path ascending

steeply into life. Deep within / herself." "Orpheus. Eurydice. Hermes." *The Selected Poetry of Rainer Maria Rilke*, ed. and trans. Stephen Mitchell (New York, 1989), pp. 51–53.

22. The works previously cited by Grossman, Halley, Di Salvo, Nyquist, and Quilligan explicitly or implicitly support such a reading. See also Christine Froula, "When Eve Reads Milton: Undoing the Canonical Economy" *Critical Inquiry* 10 (1983), 321–47, and Francis Barker, *The Tremulous Private Body: Essays in Subjection* (London, 1985).

23. William Kerrigan, *The Sacred Complex: On the Psychogenesis of "Paradise Lost"* (Cambridge, Mass., 1983), p. 252.

24. The only other epiphany in English language literature which I can think of which quite approaches the tone of Adam's discovery of conviction, compassion, repentance, agony, and redemptive joy occurs at the end of Flannery O'Connor's "The Artificial Nigger":

> [Mr. Head] realized that he was forgiven for sins from the beginning of time, when he had conceived in his own heart the sin of Adam, until the present, when he had denied poor Nelson. He saw that no sin was too monstrous for him to claim as his own, and since God loved in proportion as He forgave, he felt ready at that instant to enter Paradise.

Flannery O'Connor, *The Complete Stories* (New York, 1982), pp. 269–70.

25. Christopher Grose has suggested to me that there is a virtually liturgical element to the narrator's choral entry into the action of his poem at this point. Perhaps this is analogous to his merger with the angelic chorus in the hymn of praise which ends the first colloquy in Heaven (*PL* III, 412–15).

26. Compare God's first speech in *PL* III, 86–134. What Adam makes explicit here is the grief, and the burden of a compassionate foreknowledge, which create the undertone of the Father's angry doctrinal self-justification. The best account so far of the tone of the Father's speech appears in Michael Lieb's essay, "Milton's 'Dramatick Constitution': The Celestial Dialogue in *Paradise Lost*, Book III," in *Milton Studies* XXIII, ed. James D. Simmonds (Pittsburgh, 1987), p. 225.

27. Kathleen Swaim describes Adam's instruction by Michael as a reorientation of the memory "from a memory for things to a memory for words, specifically the Word of Christian redemption, which is also a redemption of the imagination. . . . For the fallen, theological as well as psychological memory is the medium of one's relationship with the deity, and Christ is the mediator of the Word and the promises; he is the final cause and the energy and process through which man attains his end and his perfection, logically, psychologically, and theologically." *Before and After the Fall: Contrasting Modes in "Paradise Lost"* (Amherst, 1986), p. 236.

28. For exemplary works on the themes and tactics of Protestant poetics in *Paradise Lost*, see especially the works by Lewalski, Christopher, and Swaim which I have previously cited, as well as Robert L. Entzminger, *Divine Word: Milton and the Redemption of Language* (Pittsburgh, 1985); Lewalski, "Structure and Symbolism of Vision in Michael's Prophecy, *Paradise Lost*, Books XI–XII," *PQ* 42 (1963), 25–35; Mary Ann Radzinowicz, " 'Man as a Probationer of Immortality': *Paradise Lost* XI–XII," in *Approaches to "Paradise Lost": The Tercentenary Lectures*, ed. C. A. Patrides (Toronto, 1968), pp. 31–51; Raymond Waddington, "The Death of Adam: Vision and Voice in Books XI and XII of *Paradise Lost*," *MP* 70 (1972), 9–21. Stanley Fish reviews critical treatments of Books XI and XII in his discussion of the history and ideology in critical practice; see "Transmuting the Lump: *Paradise Lost*, 1942–79," in *Doing What Comes Naturally: Change, Rhetoric, and the Practice of Theory in Literary and Legal Studies* (Durham, N.C., 1989), pp. 247–93.

29. We have C. S. Lewis to thank for the immortal description of Books XI and XII

as "an untransmuted lump of futurity." *A Preface to "Paradise Lost"* (London, 1942), pp. 129–30.

30. B. Rajan, "Osiris and Urania," in *Milton Studies* XIII, ed. James D. Simmonds (Pittsburgh, 1979), pp. 221–35. Kathleen Swaim's *Before and After the Fall* is our most ample and subtle treatment of the differences between prelapsarian and postlapsarian poetic and logical conditions and strategies.

31. Georgia Christopher accounts for this harshness through her diagnosis of "the irreconcilable cleavage between the way of the world and the way of the Word" which discloses "how the surface of history stands in ironic relation to divine activity" (pp. 187, 191).

32. On Milton's early humanist formulation of a poetic and cultural theory resembling the erotic organization suggested by Freud, see Christopher Grose, *Milton and the Sense of Tradition* (New Haven, 1988).

33. See especially "A Short Organum for the Theatre," in *Brecht on Theatre: The Development of an Aesthetic*, ed. and trans. John Willett (New York, 1964), pp. 179–281. Brecht's remarks about the structure of epic theatre are especially pertinent to Michael's strategy of educating Adam through alienation effect: "[T]he individual episodes have to be knotted together in such a way that the knots are easily noticed. The episodes must not succeed one another indistinguishably but must give us a chance to interpose our judgment" (p. 201).

34. "The Bondage of the Will," in *Martin Luther: Selections From His Writings*, ed. John Dillenberger (Garden City, 1961), p. 200.

35. Wallace Stevens, "The Well Dressed Man with a Beard," *The Collected Poems of Wallace Stevens* (New York, 1969), p. 247.

36. Freud characterized the primary process as the spontaneous wish-fulfilling activity of the unconscious, allowing psychic energy to flow freely in the expression of unconscious wishes through the mechanisms of condensation and displacement; and the secondary process as the deliberative work of the conscious mental system, which adjusts wishes to realities external to the person in order to allow a degree of satisfaction, sometimes delayed. See J. Laplanche and J. B. Pontalis, *The Language of Psycho-Analysis*, trans. Donald A. Nicholson-Smith (New York, 1973), pp. 339–41.

37. Fredric Jameson, "Religion and Ideology: A Political Reading of *Paradise Lost*," in *Literature, Politics and Theory: Papers from the Essex Conference 1976–84*, ed. Francis Barker, Peter Hulme, Margaret Iversen, and Diana Loxley (New York, 1986), p. 54.

38. See especially David Aers and Bob Hodge, " 'Rational Burning': Milton on Sex and Marriage," in *Milton Studies* XIII, ed. James D. Simmonds (Pittsburgh, 1979), pp. 3–33.

39. The apocalypse of love will become a prominent Romantic theme. In his splitting between Adam and Eve of the psychic ordeal of transforming death from within by love, Milton anticipates Blake's rendering of Oothoon and Milton in his epic *Milton*, and Shelley's Asia and Prometheus in *Prometheus Unbound*.

40. Bentley proposed the following more consoling conclusion: "Then hand in hand with social steps their way / Through Eden took, with heav'nly comfort chear'd." The way for this cheerful distich was prepared by Addison, who proposed that the poem would end better with a deletion of the final two lines, so that the final note sounded would be of "Providence their guide." Addison testifies to the anxiety that Milton's conclusion provokes by noting that "These two verses, though they have their beauty, fall very much below the foregoing passage, and renew in the mind of the reader that anguish which was pretty well laid by that consideration." For Addison's and Bentley's comments, with an effective scholarly examination and rebuttal of their responses, see Thomas Newton's notes in *Paradise*

Lost. A Poem in Twelve Books. 9th ed., ed. Thomas Newton, D. D. (London, 1790), vol. II, pp. 441–45.

41. Christopher Hill, *Milton and the English Revolution* (New York, 1978), p. 300. See also David Aers and Bob Hodge, whose analysis of the motif of loneliness in Milton's work is based on the "unprecedented inner loneliness" of Protestant bourgeois man as Max Weber presented it (p. 8).

THE EXPERIENCE OF DEATH AND
DIFFERENCE IN *PARADISE LOST*

William E. Engel

The continuall worke of your life, is to contrive death; you are in
death, during the time you continue in life: for, you are after death,
when you are no longer living. Or if you had rather have it so, you are
dead after life: but during life, you are still dying. . . . [C]hildren are
afraid of their friends, when they see them masked; and so are we:
The maske must as well be taken from things, as from men, which
being removed, we shall finde nothing hid under it, but the very
same death, that a seely varlet, or a simple maid-servant, did lately
suffer without amazement or feare.

> —*John Florio, Essayes of Montaigne*, I, 19

IN HIS EFFORT to "assert Eternal Providence" Milton devised a
complex and unified epic narrative. To relate his "advent'rous Song" of
"Man's First Disobedience," Milton temporally rearranged the events and
characters, and spatially resituated the instruments associated with the
origin and eventual overcoming of "Death . . . and all our woe."[1] To accomplish his design he pioneered a metric practice that rehabilitated the
timely use of caesura, and sought to free the "Heroic Poem from the
troublesome and modern bondage of Riming."[2] And yet for all its complexity, adventurousness, and daring, the matter expressed in *Paradise Lost*
both supports and gives new meanings to a conventional, linear view of
human history. This teleological view of human history, integral to Milton's epic project, encompasses the creation of man and woman; the Fall,
followed by the entrance of "Death into the World, and all our woe"; the
Son's incarnation, death, and resurrection; his second coming on the day
of judgment, the final victory over Death and hell, and the establishment
of a New Jerusalem. As a process and as a character in this divine narrative, Death exists at personal, historical, and cosmic levels. The problem
of how to represent and thus acknowledge all of these aspects of Death at
once, while still trying to recognize salient differences, is one that Milton
meets head-on.

This problem forms the basis of my inquiry, and in what follows I will isolate and examine some of the key assumptions underlying Milton's method for depicting the troublesome figure of Death. I say troublesome because it is a figure which stands over and against human life; as such it threatens to disrupt (because it brings to its ultimate culmination) the teleological momentum of life. It is troublesome with respect to figural tradition as well, because Death's own overcoming necessarily is modeled on man's in the face of death. After all, according to the divine scheme, God the Son volunteers to redeem man from 'the eternal thralldom of Death: "Death his death's wound shall then receive, and stoop / Inglorious, of his mortal sting disarm'd" (III, 252–53).

The quibble on Death's death appears in much of the poetry of the Renaissance (most notably in Donne's "Holy Sonnet" beginning "Death be not proud"). And yet because of Death's thematic centrality in Milton's epic project, his treatment of it necessarily goes beyond mere rhetorical *reductio*. The problematic personification of Death in *Paradise Lost* has often been recognized by Miltonists, and has been analyzed with instructive results in the light of iconography and theology.[3] However, no study has treated Milton's rhetorically figured image of Death in the light of what conventional philosophy permits and excludes. This will be my task: to examine Milton's characterization of Death in the light of the Western metaphysical tradition. More particularly, and pursuing recent developments in this tradition, I take as my point of departure Jacques Derrida's attempt to extend the theory of language as a system of interrelated signs. The premise of this theory is stated succinctly in Ferdinand de Saussure's *Course in General Linguistics:* "in language there are only differences. Even more important: a difference generally implies positive terms between which the difference is set up; but in language there are only differences without positive terms."[4]

As will become more clear as this investigation proceeds, we stand to learn a great deal about Milton's use of poetic language by considering it in the light of Derrida's assessment that language in general is neither mysterious nor mystical, but simply a series of differences. And further, that no concept, in and of itself, is metaphysical; no concept can exist outside all the textual work in which it is inscribed.[5] Because Milton's conception of human history and the divine drama is based on the very transcendental referents Derrida denies, we might expect it to be readily subject to Derrida's critique of the idealism inherent in such notions of teleology. But the relationship between the two cannot be reduced to a deconstructive assault on *Paradise Lost*.[6] Herman Rapaport has argued that Milton shares with Derrida the trait of working within a philosophical and metaphysical tradition, while attempting to lay siege to and affect that tradition by developing and using a radically new and adventurous style. Further, we "cannot simply take any English poet and turn the poststructuralist critical machine loose on him or her in good faith" (Rapaport, p. 21). Milton's epic lends itself to Derridean principles of analysis primarily because in the textual system of *Paradise Lost*, Death functions in ways analogous to "diff*erance*" in the discourse of Derrida, as a kind of unrepresentable otherness which both constitutes and threatens the possibility of conceptualization.

To indicate how a Derridean approach can provide insight into Milton's poetics, I will bring together several exemplary articulations of the idea of Death. They share a tacit and self-reflexive acknowledgment that what finally is represented is something other than, and in addition to, the image of Death itself. That which is represented retains the mark of a past element that has already let itself be hollowed out by the mark of its relation to a future element. In a sense, this is what Derrida means by diff*erance*.[7]

Implying far more than if it were simply a newly coined word, diff*erance* also signifies the ongoing interplay of the one with the other once the original word has been marked by the silent and paradoxical intervention of the phoneme *a* (which does not change the pronunciation of *difference* but still implies an additional and different meaning). The sign, phonic as well as graphic, is a structure of difference; thus, for Derrida, what opens the possibility of thought is not merely the question of being, but also the never-annulled difference from "the completely other." As Gayatri Spivak has observed further in this regard: "Such is the strange 'being' of the sign: half of it always 'not there' and the other half always 'not that.' The structure of the sign is determined by the trace or track of that other which is forever absent. This other is of course never to be found in its full being."[8] Accordingly, the transformation of difference as a typological category into diff*erance*, both as a typological and a temporal category, is recognized by its differing from its previous state and also by its deferring any final and future determination of meaning. The future state is situated with respect to its past (it therefore has a history), and is realized by the intrusion of *a* into the field of signification expressed by the word *difference*. In the case of Milton's rhetorical portrait of Death, according to Christian teleology, the future element which disfigures Death is its own implied future absence.

With this in mind, I will situate several examples, fundamentally related by their treatment of death and difference, so that each can indicate about the others what none can declare about itself alone. Specifically, I will relate Milton's poetic expression of Death as the "other shape" to the lively image of Death and its place in early printing. Further, I will analyze these images in light of Derrida's notion of differance—as neither word nor concept, but embodying a silent marker, "secret, and discreet, like a tomb."⁹ With the ultimate aim of learning more about the composition of *Paradise Lost,* this essay will situate and discuss Milton's characterization of Death with respect to Derrida's suggestive statement about the role of figurative language in Western thought: "Metaphor always carries its own death within itself."¹⁰

Following the description of Sin, the first "formidable shape" guarding hell's gates, Milton describes "[t]he other shape":

> Before the Gates there sat
> On either side a formidable shape;
> The one seem'd Woman to the waist, and fair,
> But ended foul in many a scaly fold
> Voluminous and vast, a Serpent arm'd
> With mortal sting:
>   . . . .
>   The other shape,
> If shape it might be call'd that shape had none
> Distinguishable in member, joint, or limb,
> Or substance might be call'd that shadow seem'd,
> For each seem'd either; black it stood as Night,
> Fierce as ten Furies, terrible as Hell,
> And shook a dreadful Dart; what seem'd his head
> The likeness of a Kingly Crown had on.   (II, 648–73)

Milton's characterization of Death as the "other shape" is not only the "other" when compared to Sin, but also when compared to living human beings. (Moreover this image of Death as "the other" bears comparison to the strange "being" accorded to the sign by Derrida: half of it always "not there" and the other half always "not that."¹¹) There is a long, well-documented history of portraying Death as the opposite of what was considered familiar, and ascribing to Death characteristics of "the other"—the stranger, the foreigner, the alien.¹² But what assumptions about human knowledge and representation are implied in Milton's rhetorical characterization of Death as the "other shape"?

Clearly Death here is personified; and yet, at the same time, the figure is carefully distanced from what is commonly understood by the trope of personification. This image thus evokes something that resembles what is all too well known and understood: an image of man, but one undone and overcome by death. Hence it is both the image of the other and also a gruesome reflection of each of us after we have ceased to be. A depiction of death like Milton's is far more unsettling than a simple tomb effigy showing a deceased person lying serenely in state, perhaps because such a rhetorical portrait as that in Book II of *Paradise Lost* presents Death as being anything but still, quiet, and calm. Such a disjunction of stillness and movement marks almost all representations of Death in the Renaissance—as does the double standard that Death is within us at all times, and yet is visualized as the alien, as the other. Zones of tension like these will be shown to be instrumental to Milton's poetics of paradox, through which he informs the reader with a series of images, yet calls into question the means by which these same images are presented.[13] There is another, more overtly textual, reason for focusing on the "other shape." As Joseph Summers observed, "It is the other which commands all of [Satan's] attention: it is not even 'real,' it has no certain shape, and yet it wears a crown and challenges Satan to combat."[14] To look more closely at this other shape is to rediscover, by degrees, the presence of death in the divine scheme, and thus to learn more about Milton's attitude toward representing that problematic relation. Milton's use of hyperbolic similes to portray the other shape startlingly brings to prominence the conventional operations of metaphor, which when applied to the body they would translate into another sense, are found wanting.[15] And yet, for all of its imputed ambiguity of shadow and substance, "[t]he other shape / If shape it might be call'd" still conveys a figure which stands over against life: black, fierce, and terrible, this characterization of Death stands menacingly over and against, and up to Satan, the archfiend. This rhetorical figure of that which defies figuration is extraordinary (even for Milton), and stands out as an extravagantly paradoxical moment in the epic—a moment which is at once poetic and profoundly philosophical.

This intersection of poetry and philosophy sets the scene for inquiring how Milton's epic gives voice to a complex and yet sustained discourse which aims to accomplish "[t]hings unattempted yet in Prose or Rhyme." The poet aspires to "assert Eternal Providence, / And justify the ways of God to men" (I, 25–26), but something else quite significant is accomplished as well. As a by-product of enunciating the poem's theme and asserting Eternal Providence, *Paradise Lost* also asserts an internally consistent rhetoric, one complete with implicit rules of inclusion and exclusion, and governing proper and improper uses of tropes and figures of speech.

Any time a rhetoric defines metaphor (whether by explicit definition or, in Milton's case, as a poetic practice), a philosophy of representation is thus implied, and, as Derrida has argued, so is a conceptual network in which philosophy itself has been constituted.[16] Closer scrutiny of how the epic portrays Death (as that which overturns being) will help to make explicit Milton's implied philosophy of representation. The very heart of this philosophy is evident in moments of self-consciously poetic tension, like that exhibited through his "writing into being" a character who is neither substance nor shadow, but whose terrible power can be exercised despite its ontological indeterminacy.

Such a portrait of Death is disturbingly similar in kind, though different in degree, from oxymorons which likewise play off the tension between light and dark—for example "darkness visible"; "ever-burning Sulphur unconsum'd"; and "veins of liquid fire" (I, 63, 69, 701). Milton's favoring of antithetical elements within a parallel structure indicates (and reiterates) his plan for a philosophy of representation; furthermore, it can be seen at work in other sections of *Paradise Lost* as clusters of images that address the coming to knowledge of one's implied future passing. Not only is this implied future passage the fate of Adam and Eve, and (by extension) of all readers, but it is also the destiny of metaphor itself in *Paradise Lost*. Death too is inscribed in this destiny as a monstrous entity (if entity it might be called), and is represented through similes whose images dematerialize even as they are put in language.

Although Death is accorded his traditional and identifying props of the "deadly Dart," a crown, and later his "Mace petrific" (X, 294)—which is both a tool for building the highway to Earth and a symbol of his dominion—these conventional attributes are deliberately set at odds with the rest of Milton's description of Death. Milton selected from among the available iconographic traditions—especially the earlier Renaissance theme of Death as king, which he conflated with ever-hungry Death, the destroyer. As Albert Labriola noted, Milton's rhetorical image of Death is a "personified description" of death which "incorporates the biblical Angel of Death and the skeleton in the Dance of Death and the Renaissance Triumphs of Death."[17] I also concur with Roland Mushat Frye (p. 115) that Holbein's classic woodcuts of the Dance of Death are not Milton's exclusive model (there is no trace of organic imagery associated with Death in *Paradise Lost:* no shreds of bone or flesh, no worm-eaten maw, no vermin slithering in and out of eye-sockets). But I would suggest further that Milton's complicated allegorical image elicits the same sort of jarring reaction that is evoked by the animated cadavers in the Dance of Death; there is a sympathy between the two strategies for representing the unrepresentable. The fusion of potentially discordant iconographic traditions indicates the insufficiency, for Milton, of any one of them to suit his larger poetic and polemical design. For Milton no simple use of the Protestant doctrine of accommodation (allowing for aspects of God and his plan to be "accommodated" to human understanding through metaphors and analogies) was a completely satisfactory solution to the problem of describing faithfully those notions which implied an entire structure of belief—notions such as death, god, and grace.[18]

Milton's solution to the problem, posed by the limits of conventional iconography, was to fuse into one allegorical body these various figural traditions. We may well ask: What is the epistemological premise of such a portrait, a principal part of which is its very denial of being able to portray the object of its scrutiny? How does the image of man's mortal foe go beyond being a commonplace device and, as a result of the compounding of several figural traditions, become a lively character capable of eroding the conventions of expression upon which its very presence depends? We can move toward answering these related questions by turning to the earliest known representation of the printing press. It is at a very particular and telling moment—when printing represents the image of its own operations in conjunction with the image of man's yielding to the grip of Death—that we can see operating most clearly the figurative mechanisms used to present what defies representation.

On a page from *La Grāt Danse Macabre* (see fig. 1), the pressman is shown as being subjected to the very process he strives to allegorize, namely death. On the left, a lively cadaver stops the arm of the compositor. In an adjoining room, crudely signaled by a column recessed from the rest of the print shop, another cadaver halts the bookbinder. These men are the subject of a printed image that is designed to circulate even as they, in the implied future moment of their own deaths, remain immobile. Thus the men responsible for the printed image of Death are able to arrest their own images by carrying out their trades, even as they create multiple copies of the product of their collective ingenuity. The printed image of Death, seen in this light, does to the image of man what Death in fact does to men. Like Death, this image is shown halting men, in midsentence and midgesture; the mottoes and verse-dialogue for each section of the picture collectively evoke Death in its function, because they halt the range of possible meanings. In this sense, the very process of devising and executing such a *memento mori* emblem is recalled in man's figurative passage to death.

This engraving, which portrays one episode in man's journey through life, constitutes a single frame in a *danse macabre;* it is one of a series of similar illustrations of skeletons encountering men and women of all social stations. Because its message, in general, duplicates that of every other page in the volume, metonymically it stands in for any other episode. Like the other episodes in the book, the visit of the dead men to the print shop represents the journey of man as the progression to death. But unlike the

1499. LYONS

Figure 1. *La Grãt Danse Macabre* (Lyons, 1499). Falconer Madan, "Early Representations of the Printing-Press," *Bibliographia* 1 (London, 1895), 223–48, 225; and reproduced from A. W. Pollard, *Early Illustrated Books* (London, 1893).

other episodes, paradoxically, it represents Death's "progress" as a halting of the process that has made its depiction possible.

A similar example, showing the complex interplay of images of death and printing, occurs in the *Booke of Christian Prayers* (the standard Anglican prayer book instituted for home use during the reign of Queen Elizabeth [see fig. 2]). In the top-left border a compositor is summoned by a skeleton holding an hourglass aloft; the subscripted verse-motto reads: "Leave setting thy page: spent is thine age." Beneath this, a caped skeleton interrupts the activities of both pressman and inker. Above them, stylized arrows point out Death's quarry; the motto reads, "Let printing stay: and come away." The skeleton on a tomb at the foot of the page, like a "transi" carving, shows what the corpse enclosed underneath it certainly will become. Above it, reminiscent of an abbey tomb inscription, is the motto both to this image and, more comprehensively, to the several emblems bordering the page: "We Printers wrote with wisdomes pen / She liues for aye, we dye as men."

Printing assured extensive repetitions of this already popular theme, and yet, unlike the earlier Dance of Death murals and relief paintings from which these macabre images were drawn,[19] the mechanical reproduction of words and pictures of Death assured a steady flow of identical copies—none of which merited special status over another. Despite its wide circulation, each printed image implied a range of meanings that went beyond that connoted by itself alone; the fact that it had innumerable copies, or doubles, undermined the idealized conception of a unique or authentic image with priority or authority over and above the others.

The invention of the woodcut struck at the root of the quality of authenticity even before its late flowering.[20] The printed copies of such a design—like one's reflection, which accompanies everyone—provide a glimpse of oneself both as self and as the other, as one's own mortal double. Seen in this way, as a mirror image of oneself, the printed image of death is a reminder of one's inevitable future passing. During the seventeenth century, the images of Death coming from the outside to lead people away from life were replaced by those which presented a penetrating reflection of men and women carrying their own deaths within themselves (see fig. 3). Images like the *Mirror of Life and Death* and those in Holbein's Dance of Death, all declare that every individual dies according to his or her own condition. Death (like its various figural representations) may take on many forms, but all lead to the same end. As John Webster's *Duchess of Malfi* stoically observes: "death hath ten-thousand several doors / For men to take their exits, and 'tis found / They go on such strange geometrical hinges, / You may open them both ways" (IV, ii, 208–211).

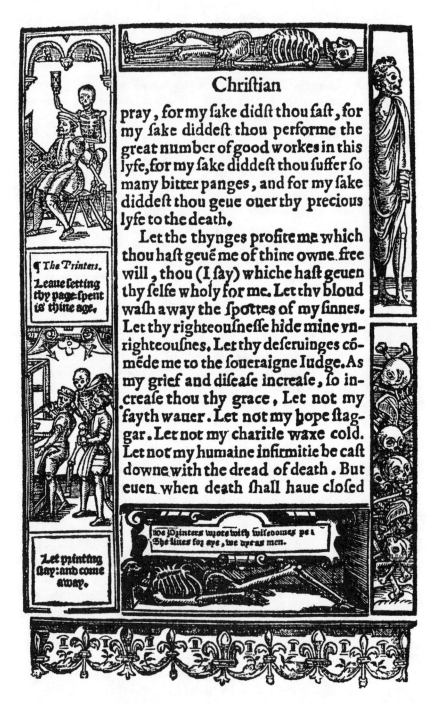

Christian

pray, for my fake didft thou faft, for
my fake diddeft thou performe the
great number of good workes in this
lyfe, for my fake diddeft thou fuffer fo
many bitter panges, and for my fake
diddeft thou geue ouer thy precious
lyfe to the death.

Let the thynges profite me which
thou haft geué me of thine owne free
will, thou (I fay) whiche haft geuen
thy felfe wholy for me. Let thv bloud
wafh away the fpottes of my finnes.
Let thy righteoufnefle hide mine yn-
righteoufnes. Let thy deferuinges có-
méde me to the foueraigne Iudge. As
my grief and difeafe increafe, fo increafe thou thy grace, Let not my
fayth wauer. Let not my hope ftag-
gar. Let not my charitie waxe cold.
Let not my humaine infirmitie be caft
downe with the dread of death. But
euen when death fhall haue clofed

¶ The Printers.
Leaue fetting
thy page:fpent
is thine age.

Let printing
ftay:and come
away.

The Printers wrote with wifedomes pé t
She liues for aye, we vp as men.

Figure 2. *The Booke of Christian Prayers* (London, 1578), with permission of the Huntington Library, San Marino, California.

Figure 3. "Le miroir de la vie et de la mort" (Musée Caravalet, Paris); reproduced from Philip Ariès, *Images de l'homme devant la mort* (Paris: Editions de Seuil, 1983), figure 289, with permission.

But the allegorical (which is to say the personified) image of Death, represented variously in the series of seemingly identical reverse or mirror images of the print block, attested to both the material and ideological effects of the printing apparatus. Moreover, these redundant images, although powerful enough to elicit, repeatedly, an immediate response, are themselves mirrored in the process of passing away to death. The power of difference to engender unique meanings among the copies is canceled by virtue of those operations regulating the means of their own material production. So too the material effects of death provide the basis for us to produce its image, again and again, as a decaying body.

This is evident from the visual and textual expression of death in one of the most widely circulated of the Renaissance Dances of Death, *Les simulachres et historiees faces de la mort* (1538), illustrated by Hans Holbein the Younger. The preface acknowledges the limitations of human artifice, and reasons that when depicting death, which no one can report from his own experience, one must decide upon a convention to designate what defies representation. The preface continues by rationalizing that since Death cannot be seen directly (and what is invisible cannot be represented properly by what is visible), its depiction is best left to our recollections of death's trace on the body of one who is dead.[21] Accordingly Holbein, like others before him, represented bodies undergoing decay, bodies in various states of putrescence, bodies in the process of "becoming nothing." As was the case with the earlier Renaissance portraits of "Death as King," Holbein's "*simulachres*" reminded the viewers that they were both subject to decay, and the subject of this visual text on decay. This double message is conveyed through nightmarish visions of skeletons beating drums, wielding lances, and playing wind instruments—to name but three of the activities of Holbein's "*simulachres.*" Equally disturbing is the vision of "Death as King," where a lively corpse wears a crown. The crown, like the knight's lance, is a familiar symbol denoting one's station—though a station which, in the face of Death, gives over its customary meaning.[22] Paradoxically these "*simulachres . . . de la mort*" in the *danse macabre*, through which the artist presents a "concrete embodiment of what is really an abstraction,"[23] take on a symbolic life of their own. This point is central to Milton's choice to bend and blur a series of traditions to render an image of Death that differs from the iconological principles of the standard "Dance of the Dead"; yet Milton's practice also implies that he deferred breaking away from the figural traditions which show "crowned" death as man's ghastly mirror image. Milton's rhetorical portrait of Death remains a hyperbolic expression of man at his most prideful and greedy; he is an insatiable and ruthless sovereign.

One final irony is implied in the conventional depiction of Death mirroring men and women. Just as manufactured images or replicas of the human form all might look the same, men and women (made in God's image) all look the same to the eyes of Death. George Strode summarized this commonplace view in *Anatomie of Mortalitie* by comparing men to chess pieces:

For while the play indureth there is great difference in the men, greater respect had to some then to others; but when the Check-mate is giuen, & play ended, then the men are tumbled together, and put into the bag, from whence they were taken out, & the lesser men uppermost many times there being no difference. And so it is in the world. There is great difference in men, & greater respect had to some then to others (as it is meet to be) but when death commeth (as surely it will come to all sorts) then there will be no such difference in the graue, neither doth Death know any such difference for he spareth none.[24]

And yet, within Dances of Death, Death's effacement of difference often involves a mirroring, or mocking, of people according to their particular stations. Clearly, then, differing positions are important, especially where depictions of Death's disregard for them are concerned. This tension is played out with a telling trace of self-parody in the illustrations of Death and the process of printing, the jarring implications of which were high-lighted by the commonplace mottoes and verses.

This way of reading—which necessitates a simultaneous crossing and merging of how we think about images and text—also exemplifies a method for apprehending emblematic conceits that was well within the range of everyday experience. As John Sparrow has observed: "The Renais-sance spectator . . . found no difficulty, whether he was confronted by a building or by a picture, in looking, as it were, with one eye while he read with the other, and the artists of the time ministered to that double vision."[25] But when the thing being regarded is oblivion, or a shape "that shape had none, / Distinguishable in member, joint, or limb," how can this principle of double vision be applied? The answer lies in the future anterior, in the tense which allows us to project ourselves into a moment yet to come when we can say that something (such as ourselves) has already been. This projection of ourselves in the Christian teleological scheme is contingent on a prior consideration of our passage from this life, a movement facilitated by the image of our own corporeal ruin. As such, this image functions as a monumental, although decaying, remembrancer of what once was—and a shadow of what will be.

The frisson elicited by such an image—as well as by yoking together words and images of perpetuity and transience, of the permanence of wisdom and the impermanence of men, of printing and stopping the presses—recalls Milton's special application of the common Renaissance understanding of *concordia discors*.[26] We must bear in mind, however, that Milton's characterization of Death is more complex than the resolution or reconciliation of apparently opposing perspectives or habits of thinking. Rosalie Colie has observed that during the Renaissance paradoxes generated self-referential activity—"operating at the limits of discourse, redirecting thoughtful attention to the faulty or limited structures of thought"—and that "paradoxes play back and forth across terminal and categorical boundaries" (p. 7). Literary paradoxes therefore use, and at the same time call attention to, the conventions governing their composition. The observer is made aware of both the content expressed and the mechanisms of thought which enable him to fathom it. As with the Dance of Death illustrations and verse-commentaries, Milton's poetic portrait of Death evokes a series of seemingly incompatible images which turn back on themselves and, through a paradoxical twist, turn the reader back on himself and his mortality. Milton recognizes and articulates a single image to call to mind the constitutive elements of an entire metaphysical scheme predicated on transgression and salvation. He focuses on a particular image, in this case Death, and describes it from a series of figural perspectives, so as to confound the imagination. Thus in the absence of conventional reason, in a moment of recognizing one's ability to grasp the whole in an instant, the reader appreciates and bears witness to God the Father's scheme for salvation, and God the Son's selfless love and charity, which is tantamount to God the Holy Spirit's special wisdom. Milton acknowledges God's wisdom as being beyond the scope of human reason and mortal vision. It is according to this design that he frames his response to his readers regarding the ways of God.

By confronting us with tokens of mortality, Milton provides the means for our recognizing the transhistorical and cosmic sweep of God's gaze and of God's plan. And in so doing, implicitly he acknowledges his recognition of the limits of his own discourse. The subtext in both cases— the "other shape" in *Paradise Lost* and the lively character of Death leading the Dance—is "memento mori" ["remember you too must die"]. Further, Milton's application of the language of paradox, translated into evanescent figures, accords with the emblematist's endeavor to call to mind an image that is virtually inexhaustible in its significations and which, as Ernst Gombrich has said of this effect, "shows us so much 'in a flash' that we return from its contemplation as from a dream we can no longer quite recount or explain."[27]

To enhance the impact of his paradoxical figure of Death, Milton positions a triplet of similes which engenders another kind of disorienting experience. He supplies the reader with a way to realize the transference of language (from thought-image to linguistic sign) by giving referents that at first glance appear to delimit the range of meanings because they are accommodated to mortal vision: "Black . . . as Night, / Fierce as ten Furies, Terrible as Hell." Upon reflection, we ask ourselves, by what standard we are to judge, without scale or degrees, just how black is night, how fierce are the pagan avatars of vengeful justice, how terrible is hell? But rhetorical flourish cannot be reduced to simple operatic parody; these three similes are also topical antitheses to the characteristics of the Son (light, gentle, and loving) who, as a man, will be overcome by death, but ultimately will win the victory of victories over Death. Milton's goal in this is reminiscent of that of the emblematist: exploiting the tension between clarity and obscurity, he confronts the viewer with a compounded image which at first seems easily discernible; but, upon further consideration, each component acquires new and complex meanings with respect to the others. For example, by naming Night, the Furies, and Hell as things Death is said to be like, the reader is given a sense (or so she thinks) of what an aspect of Death is said to be like. Milton here subverts the biblical tradition which asserts that naming is an act of power, which verbalizes (and thus realizes) the essence of the thing named. What Milton shows, in fact, is that to name the attributes of Death does not provide any substantial knowledge about the subject. Thus, in the case of Death, frustration awaits those who would believe that naming is synonymous with knowing.

Yet this strategy is carried to the other extreme by Milton's withholding the name of "Death" for 121 lines after his shape is introduced into the text (II, 666). Because of his allusions to the conventional tropes associated with the figure of Death, we are not in doubt about the identity of the figure even though we may lack a nominal sign to situate it unequivocally. But when Death finally is named within Milton's epic, the impact of its dramatic power is intensified by its context: Sin's recollection of Death's horrible, painful, and violent birth. To accentuate and augment the import of this primal linguistic moment of Death's origin, of Death's intrusive appearance on the world's stage, the name of the "other shape" is made to echo. The very word "Death" lingers and reverberates—not only within the imaginary space of Sin's dismal refuge, but also within the theaters of our own minds:

> but he my inbred enemy
> Forth issu'd, brandishing his fatal Dart

Made to destroy: I fled and cri'd out *"Death"*;
Hell trembl'd at the hideous Name, and sigh'd
From all her Caves, and back resounded *"Death."*   (II, 785–89)

The repetition of the word whose very name spells the implied future cancellation of human life, along with the rhetorical play of the echo, can be understood as a verbal equivalent to the self-reflexive image of Death as a gruesome reflection of man after his own death. But something else is implied in Milton's use of this fairly conventional poetic device associated with the echo. Sin's original naming of Death is analogous to Holbein's woodblock used to print the image of Death, insofar as both bring into being an original from which later, secondary likenesses are produced; the echo is like the printed image in the Dance of Death. After all, both the echo and the printed page are shadows of that which brought them into being: both bear the trace of the original which has since been worn out or is no longer in close proximity to the reproduction. The same may be said of Milton's portrait of Death as the awful offspring of Sin, and of Sin which is a perverted replication of Satan. Each element in this chain calls to mind the image (if not the presence) of the others. Death, in the Christian scheme, is unthinkable without Sin and Satan; just as an echo is unthinkable on its own, unconnected to a voice, without a point of origin or a prior history. Further, the tropological effect of the echo is itself echoed through the doubly heard word: "Death." Even though Sin originally said the word once and it came back to her as an echo, she voiced it twice in her relation of the events to Satan—thus she mimics, she echoes, the echo of her own voice.

Therefore, within the poem, the iteration of "Death" quite literally calls to mind the mnemonic function of Milton's plan to construct Death as the embodiment (were it possible) of ontological otherness, as a trace of that which erases the trajectory of its own future movement. Death, too, elsewhere is alluded to in visual terms which conjure images of a presence that is not a presence. Such rhetorical maneuvering again highlights Milton's preoccupation, where the portrait of Death is concerned, with what might be termed an ontology of absence. For example, when the epic turns its "Notes to Tragic" (IX, 6), Death is identified as the shadow of Sin, whose own being resulted, Minerva-like, from Satan's prideful thoughts of "bold conspiracy against Heav'n's King" (II, 751–61). Misery is said to be Death's harbinger (IX, 13), and Death is the shadow of Sin; Sin, in turn, results from the idea of (and thus is herself a shadow of) the archfiend's fatal, narcissistic pride: "Thyself in me thy perfect image viewing" (II, 764).

What, then, is the substantial thing for which all of these infernal shadows serve as featureless likenesses? The simple answer, of course, is man—in all of his and her manifold, and various forms of mortality. But it is something else as well, and less. The more complex and more complete answer to this question comes into focus if we again refer to Strode:

[N]othing in all the world can inforce a man sooner to liue soberly, righteously, and godly . . . [than] the due consideration of his owne infirmities; [than] the certaine knowledge of his mortality, and the often and continuall meditation and remembrance of his last gaspe, death, and dissolution, when as a man then becommeth no man. (p. 84 [sig. G2v])

Coming to this kind of "certain knowledge" presumes a special kind of prospective memory which entails the paradoxical remembering of oneself as if one had ceased to be ("when" one "becommeth no man"). Strode's comment bears comparison to Milton's situating within his epic those conditional metaphors and figurative oxymorons which unravel from within the very notions of ontology upon which their referents depend ("If shape . . . Or substance might be call'd that shadow seem'd, / For each seem'd either"). This is also the case with Milton's hell, the "Dungeon Horrible" which "Eternal Justice had prepar'd" (I, 61, 70), described in terms of "Land that ever burn'd / With solid, as the Lake with liquid fire / And such appear'd in hue" (I, 228–30), as well as with the otherwise unthinkable face of Chaos, "the Anarch old" with his "visage incompos'd" (II, 988–89).

Descriptions like these imply an anxiety about concepts like death, hell, and anarchy—not because they are beyond the powers of description, but precisely because of the aesthetic liberties that their insistence on being represented calls forth from within the limiting structures of thought and language. Descriptions like these urge a way of thinking about figuration—and a philosophy of composition—that is at once bound to teleological restrictions, yet constantly dancing around the theological and aesthetic assumptions that govern and delimit the range of what is considered possible. Such a knowledge of the limits and liberties associated with language is fundamentally related to death. In this poem, for example, both poetic language and the figure of death are used in the service of a more encompassing scheme; both are prefigured in the future perfect as fulfilling the function for which they were called into existence—and then are discarded and, in effect, extinguished.

The affinity between language and death is expressed in other ways in *Paradise Lost*. Perhaps the most obvious case is Satan's rhetoric of temptation which results in Eve's taking and eating the forbidden fruit and subsequently coming to know death (IX, 532–779). But even before the fatal words of the archfiend penetrate the consciousness of our original mother, the idea and the possibility of death have verged perilously close to life, both in terms of syntax and also the rhetorical trope of *topographia* (or, as Puttenham calls it, "counterfeit place"). We can discern this verging in Adam's telling remark about his inability to know what experience (or "thing") is implied by the word death: "So⸱ near grows Death to Life, whate'er Death is / Some dreadful thing no doubt" (IV, 425–26). Even before Adam has transgressed and come to a new kind of knowledge of death, it exists for him, as an indistinct concept—but nonetheless as an indubitable one, revealed to him by heavenly powers. Within Milton's epic, and for us as well, Death remains inevitable although ontologically indistinct. To the immemorial quandary regarding how death, as the termination and antithesis of life, can be said to have a mode of being, Milton responds with an elaborate allegory involving an equally enigmatic personification. And yet, as Milton knew well, even though Death may exist as an allegorical figure within a fictive construction like *Paradise Lost*, its real presence cannot be denied.

When we look closer at the tautological solution to this thorny onto-theological contradiction, we can discern that Death (both as a character in Milton's epic and as a fundamental truth of the human condition) is denied the same ontological status as Adam, at least insofar as his progeny can understand being. Nevertheless Death exercises a very real power. Raphael tells Adam that unless he and Eve govern their appetites and refrain from eating of the Tree of Knowledge of Good and Evil, they might be surprised by Sin "and her black attendant Death" because "Death is the penalty impos'd" (VII, 544–47). While "black" may stand as the antithetical parallel to "holy light," the import of Death's status, although antithetical to life and light, is figured as always existing in relation to—as a potentially necessary part of, rather than as opposed to—the operation of the divine scheme.

Such a figure of Death therefore is to be known by men and women as always in passage and embodying meaning, even as it enables the passing on and the passing away of that very meaning. This helps account for Milton's need both to represent Death, and paradoxically to encode into this representation the seed which eventually will lead to its disintegration and passing away. This move is heralded at the moment when it is conceived and subsequently brought into being. In Christian theology, this finds a parallel expression in the doctrine of original sin. Philosophically, such a procedure parallels (both in method and intent) what Derrida calls putting a term "under erasure." To mark a term "*sous rature*," is to write a word, cross it out, and then print both word and deletion. This process calls forth a complex meaning for the term "under erasure," because the word is designated as being both necessary and yet inadequate to pass on a particular sense, and also bears the mark of being superseded by an implied, though absent, alternative. The same may be said of Death in *Paradise Lost*.

With this in mind, it is appropriate now to bring face to face Milton's evanescent portrait of Death and Derrida's sentence: "Metaphor, then, always carries its death within itself."[28] At the heart of Derrida's critique of philosophy's circular project is an analysis of the operations of the ways philosophy uses metaphor to present the truth of being.[29] For Derrida metaphor is a detour to truth; it is truth "outside itself" in the borrowed dwelling of metaphor, but also "itself," since metaphor points at its own truth.[30] As it applies to Milton, the process of death, contextualized as the wages of sin, is personified as a character whose aim is to depersonify all mortals, and who, because of the operation of Eternal Providence, always carries within itself the implied future presence of its own overcoming, its own death.

But what does it mean to say that Milton's rhetorical portrait of Death takes into account its implied future passing? What are the implications of having brought together Milton's image of Man's overcoming, with the same theme graphically depicted in the Dance of Death? Milton's portrait of the "other shape," fashioned out of tropes, similes, and conditional metaphors may be seen as a mirror held up to the Derridean notion of *differance*. I say mirror because Milton's idealist view of teleology, and his elastic and transcendental notion of onto-theology, is the reverse image of Derrida's materialist critique of such ideality. This is not to say that the one is the opposite of the other, but rather that the philosophical premises of each are complementary aspects of one another. Milton's poetic practice argues against any simple, idealized notion of a closed system. In fact, as the final books of *Paradise Lost* show, death is the gate to life and only seems to connote ontological closure. The rhetorical portrait of Death functions in Milton's presentation of ontology much the same way *differance* functions in Derrida's anti–idealistic critique of ontology—to stimulate and to resist the longing for the security of a closed system. As Rapaport has argued, "Milton does not accept the logocentric concept of the book, since he incorporates important resistances within his texts to prevent the word from acceding to an idolatrous notion of the Word" (p. 15). Milton destabilizes conventional notions of onto-theology through his poetry, and Derrida achieves the same in philosophy. Milton and Derrida, each according to his own ends, stimulate a sense of anxiousness in the reader that is

related in kind, if different both in ultimate purpose and in degree. Milton
addresses the threat death poses to the human imagination and the individual's effort to come to grips not only with such a concept, but also with the
prospect of his own imminent and eventual decay, of his own nonbeing—or
as Strode phrased this paradoxical state of self-knowledge, "when a man
becommeth no man." Although Derrida would have us act on our recognition that we can only think within the limits of our available discourses and
can use only the terms and concepts appropriate to them, there remains a
tacit uneasiness with this presupposition. An intellectual dizziness, a giddi-
ness attends any contemplation that our received notions about a fixed
order of conceptual relations can be displaced, and, further, that we can
project our thinking outside of the very structures of thought and language
which make such projection possible.

Milton's rhetorical portrait of the "other shape," and Derrida's characterization of the other within language itself as difference, mirror one
other in another way as well. Both are fundamentally similar as attempts
to conceptualize what defies the powers of straightforward conceptualization. Like Milton's portrait of Death, the projection of Derridean difference is that which is the ultimately untranslatable, the undefinable, the
unthinkable. Gayle Ormiston has observed, "difference cannot be thought
by any ontology, nor can it be elevated to a master word, master concept
or master key."[31] Further, Derrida's difference is a chain of textual configurations and substitutions which has no ontological closure. Milton's "other
shape" (of Death) cannot be imagined through ontological categories of
difference, but rather through a reformulated, doubled notion of onto-
theology which allows for the phenomenal projection of Death receiving
his death's wound (III, 252–53). Derrida's play of difference—like Milton's trope of the shadow of Sin constituting Death—is rhetorically inscribed, enmeshed in a chain of other concepts, other words, other textual
configurations and substitutes.[32] The existential implications are that we
can only imagine Death fully at the moment when we can realize our own
moment of passing from life to death. It is our foreknowledge of this
eventual disappearance of ourselves that makes the recognition of such a
moment possible at all—a moment made possible because of our having
seen it in others, when we see our own future selves mirrored in another's
present condition.

With such an understanding of difference, we can see in a new light
the chilling importance of Michael's words to Adam in Book XI, after
Adam has glimpsed the panorama of his progeny's tragic history. Hoping
that Cain's slaying of Abel is the extent of Death's mark, a trace that
exhausts itself and is extinguished, Adam inquires: "But have I now seen

Death?" (XI, 462). "Horrid to think" Adam exclaims; and then, moving beyond mere intellection and projecting his consciousness into the realm of genuine existential anxiety: "how horrible to feel!" (XI, 465). Michael— who is privy to God's plan for man's eventual redemption, and therefore can express things about the "end of days" in terms of the future perfect— then recounts from a prescient perspective the inevitable extension of the ongoing chain of concepts and tragic signifiers within which Death is enmeshed, with which Death is involved, and for which Death is responsible. As will become more clear in my concluding remarks, Death's place in this chain is one which, from the start, is destined to be superseded; or, to speak figuratively, it is a bridge which is passed over and then overlooked; or, to speak metaphorically (and of metaphor), Death is the ultimate vehicle, in that it transports the quick from this world to the next and then will be no more.

Michael explains that Death has many particular forms and effects, but it cannot be said to have a single and definable aspect that Adam can see—and about which he can declare, once and for all, that he has seen the extent of Death. Ultimately, Death's span, like that of man, can be evaluated only once his days are finished and all his deeds are done:

> Death thou hast seen
> In his first shape on man; but many shapes
> Of Death, and many are the ways that lead
> To his grim Cave, all dismal; yet to sense
> More terrible at th' entrance than within.
> Some, as thou saw'st, by violent stroke shall die,
> By Fire, Flood, Famine, by Intemperance more
> In Meats and Drinks, which on Earth shall bring
> Diseases dire, of which a monstrous crew
> Before thee shall appear; that thou may'st know
> What misery th' inabstinence of *Eve*
> Shall bring on men.   (XI, 466–77)

This chain of differences, which resolves into the same end, belongs to Milton's characterization of Christian teleology, culminating with the four "last things": death, judgment, heaven and hell; and this chain of events is forged by the metaphysics of "Eternal Providence." Again, as was the case with the echo effect (II, 785–89), each significant term in the chain is unthinkable without the others. Not only is death enmeshed with Sin and Satan, but also, insofar as it is a term in a brief, divine sentence, it is enmeshed within the eschatological scheme.

The doleful images of Death exercising and validating his power—as well as the image of Death himself standing over and above the horrid scene of his triumph, shaking his deadly dart "but delay'd to strike" (XI, 491–92)—are contextualized as the consequence of the absence of absti- nence. Eve's transgression is phrased not as an action, but as a refusal to "not act." Set before Adam's gaze (and that of the reader's mind's eye) is a *tableau vivant* of a memorable and pathetic house filled with "[n]umbers of all diseas'd, all maladies / Of ghastly Spasm" (XI, 480–81). The cata- logue of the afflicted is meant to summon, through language, the forms assumed by Death as well as the forms of men and women transmogrified. This was seen to be the case with the Dance of Death as well, where men and women of all social stations are summoned by Death to leave their stations and take their exits. Such then are the infinitely various faces of mortality, all of which lead to one and the same end, to one cave.

But the image does not stop here: the Cave of Death, has a mysteri- ous way out, at least for those who recognize and accept the "one greater man" who comes to vanquish death and who makes possible our glorious resurrection in life everlasting. And to return to the passage "to sense / more terrible at th'entrance than within," we can see that the Cave of Death has other representational implications for Milton as well. As with his portrait of Death drawn from several iconographic sources, the poet here brings together the conventional tropes of Death's ravenous appetite (II, 805, 843–44) and the medieval depiction of the demonic "hell-mouth." But, insofar as death is the fate of life to the faithful, is there a "within" to Death any more than there is a "within" to Derridean differance? In the case of the faithful, in the end, although death overtakes and marks every- one, it is understood as that which is ultimately deferred—because of a final trump. Like Derrida's notion of differance, Milton's figure of Death conditions and betrays the very delivery of its lineage.

The "other shape," both in its tropological and existential senses, remains just beyond our (and its own) reach. Similarly man's hope on earth to retain or regain his original form, a divine image untainted by sin and death, remains out of the question. However, he or she can project this possibility, and speak of it in the future perfect. One can imagine such a condition because, after all, he has been created as the "divine Simili- tude," the image of God in flesh, an image which is restored in the incarnate Christ. The fundamental grounding of this self-reflexive relation implied by the divine scheme is expressed concisely in Adam's questions to Michael, beginning with "Why is life giv'n / To be thus wrested from us?" (XI, 502–503):

>   Can thus
> Th' Image of God in man created once
> So goodly and erect, though faulty since,

To such unsightly sufferings be debas't
Under inhuman pains? Why should not Man,
Retaining still Divine similitude
In part, from such deformities be free,
And for his Maker's Image sake exempt?   (XI, 507–14)

It is with such questions already anticipated that Milton, unlike the emblematists who perpetuated the Dance of Death, conveys the rhetorical portrait of Death through similes that are not permitted to verge too close to resembling man. The "other shape," finally, is not even a shadow or image of anything; rather it "shadow seem'd." As such, within the circuit of Milton's use of similes—whether black, fierce, or terrible— projected across the abyss of eternity, this shadow mocks our prospective vision of our incorruptible form in the moment of an implied future passing, because, after all, this seeming shadow can cast none of its own. By virtue of the way it enables the passing on and passing away of meanings, metaphor, like Milton's figure of Death, prefigures the "End of Things"; metaphor—the rhetorical figure of translation, whether applied to bodies or words—like man and like death, always carries its death within itself.

Vanderbilt University

NOTES

This essay grew out of a paper presented at the Southwest Regional Conference of the Renaissance Conference of Southern California on 7 April 1989 at the Huntington Library. I would express here my gratitude to my colleagues, Jay Clayton and Leonard Nathanson, who read the earliest drafts; and to the editors of this collection, Wendy Furman, Christopher Grose, and William Shullenberger, who tirelessly suggested ways I could make this essay more coherent.

1. *John Milton: Complete Poems and Major Prose*, ed. Merritt Y. Hughes (Indianapolis, 1957). References to *Paradise Lost* are to this edition. The phrases just quoted appear in the opening section of the poem, 211–12.

2. See the Miltonic justification "why the Poem Rimes not" in Hughes, *Complete Poems and Major Prose*, p. 210.

3. Among the studies which have been a springboard for my own inquiry are Robert B. White, Jr., "Milton's Allegory of Sin and Death: A Commentary on Background," *MP* 70 (1972–1973), 337–41; Roland Mushat Frye, *Milton's Imagery and the Visual Arts: Iconographic Tradition in the Epic Poems* (Princeton, 1978), pp. 113–118; and Cherrell Guilfoyle " 'If Shape It Might Be Call'd That Shape Had None': Aspects of Death in Milton," *Milton Studies* XIII, ed. James D. Simmonds (Pittsburgh, 1978), pp. 35–58.

4. Ferdinand de Saussure, *Course in General Linguistics*, trans. Wade Baskin (New York, 1966), p. 120.

5. Jacques Derrida, *Positions*, trans. Alan Bass (Chicago, 1981), p. 57.

6. For a detailed investigation of this theme, which follows from the same premise but which extends the implications of such an approach beyond the scope of my more modest project, see Herman Rapaport, *Milton and the Postmodern* (Lincoln, Nebr., 1983).

7. It is hardly accidental that Derrida selected the word *difference* as the term in which he would place a pivotal sign from which future readers might participate in a reevaluation of the production of language and meaning. Difference, according to structuralist terminology, is the fundamental principle used to explain the production of meaning, understood as the positing and recognition of differences. See Saussure, *Course in General Linguistics*, esp. pp. 101–22.

8. Gayatri Chakravorty Spivak, "Translator's Preface" in Jacques Derrida, *Of Grammatology* (Baltimore, 1982), p. xvii.

9. Jacques Derrida, "Differance" in *Speech and Phenomena and Other Essays on Husserl's Theory of Signs,* trans. David B. Allison (Evanston, Ill., 1973), p. 129; and see pp. 130–60 for further clarification of differance.

10. Jacques Derrida, "The Ellipsis of the Sun: Enigmatic, Incomprehensible, Ungraspable" (from "White Mythologies") in *Margins of Philosophy*, trans. Alan Bass (Chicago, 1982), p. 271.

11. See Spivak, "Translator's Preface," *Of Grammatology*, p. xvii: "Derrida suggests that what opens the possibility of thought is not merely the question of being, but also the never-annulled difference from 'the completely other.' "

12. Henri Stegemeier, *The Dance of Death in Folksong, with an Introduction on the History of the Dance of Death* (Chicago, 1939), discusses references to Death as "Der schwarze Mann" (p. 24). He notes "Sometimes Death is referred to as a black man because he is a mummified figure. Another explanation of Death as a black man is that such a figure recalls those who died during the Black Plague" (p. 200). Further research along these lines may substantiate a link as well between this image and Renaissance conceptions of the Moor as the dangerous foreigner; and also a link between "Der schwarze Mann" and the dark, hooded figure of the wandering Jew as the cursed, tainted and contaminated alien walking among us.

13. My approach to this theme is indebted, initially, to Rosalie L. Colie, *Paradoxia Epidemica: The Renaissance Tradition of Paradox* (Princeton, 1966), esp. pp. 169–89. My project differs from Colie's in that I focus on elementary aspects of semantic and rhetorical inversions as the building blocks of Milton's epic project; Colie was concerned primarily with Milton's relation to, and his efforts to resolve (or sometimes to extend), the paradoxes inherent in Christian doctrine. See also her earlier investigation of this theme, which examines the centrality of Christian paradoxes in Milton's arrangement of his great argument: "Time and Eternity: Paradox and Structure in *Paradise Lost*," *Journal of the Warburg and Courtauld Institutes* 23 (1960), 127–38.

14. Joseph H. Summers, *The Muse's Method: An Introduction to "Paradise Lost"* (Cambridge, Mass., 1962), p. 47.

15. I am using the term *metaphor* in its Renaissance context of "an instrument of everyday language" which is "but an inversion of sense by [the figure of] transport." See George Puttenham, *The Arte of English Poesie* (1589; facsimile rpt. Kent, Ohio, 1970), III, 7, p. 166.

16. Derrida, "The Ellipsis of the Sun," p. 230. By "philosophy" Derrida means here those discursive attempts in the modern metaphysical tradition (most notably from Des-

cartes to Nietzsche) to ask questions about being and about the subject asking such questions. Derrida, following Heidegger, maintains that the language traditionally used in philosophy is comprised of and constitutes a closed circuit of meanings; thus all "valid questions" are those which are necessarily articulated with the terms generated by, and within, that system. Consequently, that which is "proved" is nothing other than what was assumed from the start. In Milton's case the presupposition is "Eternal Providence" and, not surprisingly, this is "proved" through the twelve books of *Paradise Lost.*

17. William B. Hunter, Jr., *The Milton Encyclopedia*, 2nd ed. (Lewisburg, Pa., 1978), p. 120.

18. On the doctrine of accommodation as it applies to Milton's epic poem, see Roland Mushat Frye, *God, Man, and Satan: Patterns of Christian Thought in "Paradise Lost," "Pilgrim's Progress" and the Great Theologians* (Princeton, 1960), pp. 7–13. For further clarification of this problem, one which involves both aesthetics and theology, see Sister M. Hilda Bonham, "The Anthropomorphic God of *Paradise Lost*," *Papers of the Michigan Academy of Science, Arts and Letters* 58 (1968), 329–35; and C. A. Patrides, "*Paradise Lost* and the Theory of Accommodation," in *Bright Essence* (Salt Lake City, 1971), pp. 159–63.

19. The façade at St. Innocent's in Paris provided a stable pattern and design for the printed books on the Dance of Death during the fifteenth century. See, for example, *The Paris Dance of Death (1490)*, introduction by William M. Ivins, Jr. (Washington, 1945), pp. iii–x; Francis Carco, *La Danse des Morts* (Geneva, 1944), p. 11; James M. Clark, *The Dance of Death in the Middle Ages and the Renaissance* (Glasgow, 1950), pp. 22–40.

20. See Walter Benjamin's "The Work of Art in the Age of Mechanical Reproduction," in *Illuminations*, trans. Harry Zohn, ed. Hannah Arendt (1970; rpt. Bungay, Suffolk, 1982), pp. 219–253, esp. 245.

21. See *The Dance of Death by Hans Holbein the Younger, a complete facsimile of the Original 1538 Edition of "Les simulachres & historiees faces de la mort,"* (New York, 1971), p. 5 (sig. A3). Although the gist of this passage is summarized in my text, I give the original below [printer's contractions are silently expanded]: "Icy dira vng curieux questionaire: Quelle figure de Mort peult estre par viuant representée? Ou, comment en peuuent deuiser ceulx, qui oncques ses inexorables forces n'experimenterent? Il est bien vray que l'inuisible ne se peult par chose visible proprement representer. . . . Et pourtant qu'on n'a peu trouuer chose plus approchante a la similitude de Mort, que la personne morte, on a d'icelle effigie simulachres, & faces de Mort, pour en noz pensees imprimer la memoire de Mort plus au vif, que ne pourroient toutes les rhetoriques descriptions des orateurs."

22. A typical poetic expression of this theme is the often cited passage from Shakespeare's *Richard II*, III, ii, 144–77.

23. See Werner Gundersheimer's introduction to *The Dance of Death* (New York, 1971), p. xi.

24. George Strode, *The Anatomie of Mortalitie*, 2nd ed. (London, 1632), p. 53 (Sig. E3) [printer's contractions have been expanded silently]. Cf. John Skelton's "Lines upon a Dead Man's Head," 29–32: "Our days be dated / To be checkmated / With draughtes of death / Stopping our breath."

25. John Sparrow, *Visible Words: A Study of Inscriptions in and as Books and Works of Art* (Cambridge, 1969), p. 48.

26. See Colie, *Paradoxia Epidemica*, pp. 32, 273–99.

27. See E. H. Gombrich, "Icones Symbolicae," in *Symbolic Images: Studies in the Art of the Renaissance II*, 2nd ed. (Oxford, 1978), pp. 160–61, for this characterization of the metaphysical conceit (used to duplicate Dante's poetic method and experience "on the highest level").

28. Derrida, *Margins of Philosophy*, p. 271.

29. See note 16; cf. note 15.

30. Spivak, "Translator's Preface," *Of Grammatology*, p. lxxiv.

31. Gayle L. Ormiston, "The Economy of Duplicity: Differance" in *Derrida and Differance*, ed. David Wood and Robert Bernasconi (Coventry, 1985), pp. 61–74; p. 61.

32. See Derrida, *Positions*, p. 40.

EFFICIENT CAUSALITY AND
CATASTROPHE IN *SAMSON AGONISTES*

John Steadman

—For Professor Maurice Kelley, with gratitude

THE PROBLEM OF THE causal relations between the catastrophe of *Samson Agonistes* and the preceding scenes has been a recurrent theme in Milton criticism since Samuel Johnson's notorious denial of any causal connection between the end and the middle of the drama. In responding to Johnson's strictures William Riley Parker and a wide range of other scholars emphasized the motifs of Samson's regeneration and/or moral recovery during his successive encounters with both Danites and Philistines; this interpretation long enjoyed the status of general consensus. More recently, however, revisionist criticism has challenged such interpretations—in particular denying the protagonist's regeneration, his reconciliation with God, and the role of divine providence in the plot— and has also reopened the question of the actual motivation of the catastrophe. Like Johnson before him, Stanley Fish finds no causal connections between the catastrophe and the events that have preceded it; more significantly, he casts doubt on a divine source for the hero's "rousing motions."[1] Similarly, Irene Samuel argues not only against widely held views of Samson's regeneration but specifically against the view that his destruction of the Philistines is divinely prompted.[2] In like manner Lawrence Hyman questions the "assumption that almost all readers have held, namely that in his final action, Samson expresses his submission to God's will." For Joseph Wittreich, in turn, Milton's drama is, in all probability, not about Samson's regeneration but about his second fall. These and similar interpretations challenge previously received views of plot structure, character motivation, and tragic affects in *Samson Agonistes*, but they have not succeeded in disproving them. Despite the skill with which the revisionist arguments have frequently been advanced, they have not succeeded in establishing a general consensus. In the following pages I should like to resurvey the evidence for more traditional interpretations of the catastrophe—reexamining its bearing on the problem of tragic affects, and its probable moral and theological significance.[3]

Today the text of *Samson Agonistes* seems far more problematical—and the task of interpreting it far more difficult and more complex—than at the time of William Riley Parker's important study of the drama in relation to Greek tragedy. As Joseph H. Summers, Anthony Low, and other critics have recognized, one of the problems that confronts the modern reader, as it once confronted the poet himself, is the difficulty of reconciling an Old Testament subject with a classical Greek genre and with the moral and theological values of seventeenth-century English Protestantism.[4] Another problem is the unreliability of the dramatis personae as guides for the interpretation of the dramatic situation and action. As a dramatist the poet does not speak in his own person,[5] and the closest approximations we can find to an authorial voice are to be found in the preface and in the Argument of the play. In interpreting the tragedy we are thus compelled to rely on the limited and sometimes mistaken statements of the persons and the Chorus at different stages in the development of the action. Those statements are conditioned not only by the moral character of the speaker but by rhetorical exigencies—by his or her need to make a plausible and persuasive argument in dialogues with other persons.[6] Thus, not surprisingly, one finds a tendency in recent scholarship to disintegrate the drama, to overemphasize the mistaken beliefs of the *personae* (and of the Chorus in particular),[7] and to stress the unresolved and even contradictory elements in the play—thus underestimating the importance of the identity and moral character of the speakers, and neglecting or subverting whatever clues or cues the poet has chosen to give us.

In analyzing the development of the action and the various motives and issues it involves, then, one must reconsider the problem of the reliability of the speakers and the relative authority of their statements. One factor is surely the moral character (in the fullest sense) of the dramatis personae—their personal and moral attributes, their nationality and religion—and their relationships to Samson and Samson's God. Despite considerable criticism of the reliability of the Chorus of Danites, in a drama centering on the conflict between the true God and a false god, it is reasonable to attach greater authority to the statements of the Hebrews than to those of their idolatrous enemies. Similarly, although Dalila does not lack defenders among twentieth-century critics,[8] in her dialogue with Samson, it seems logical to give greater credence to the betrayed than to the betrayer.

Again, the catastrophe of the tragedy as related by the Messenger ("what *Samson* had done to the *Philistines*, and by accident to himself") and the final statements by Manoa and the Chorus, would appear to provide a more valid basis, and a more plausible perspective, for judging and evaluating the persons and events of the drama than the previously uncertain and ambiguous responses of the Chorus and other dramatis personae. In like manner, despite the limited insights of the Chorus, their odes (or *stasima*) at the end of the various episodes frequently sum up, if only partially, the significance of the preceding scene, defining and moralizing the issues it has involved. Though these odes are not altogether normative, though they do not possess finality or a complete vision of the truth, they nevertheless possess a temporary authority—and far more validity than many revisionists have been willing to concede. Of particular authority, moreover, are the final choruses and the catastrophe itself. In the Greek tragedies, which were in Milton's view the "best rule to all who endeavor to write Tragedy," there is often a progressive movement from initial ignorance and uncertainty toward ultimate comprehension and insight. The utterances of the Chorus in these dramas, mediating between the protagonist and the audience, accordingly reflect both blindness and insight, underscoring the principal values in the dramatic action and their significance at various stages in the development of the plot. In *Samson Agonistes* much of the dramatic effect proceeds from this movement from partial ignorance toward eventual (even if incomplete) understanding; the doubt as to "What th'unsearchable dispose / Of highest wisdom brings about" culminates in the ultimate recognition that "All is best. . . . / And ever best found in the close" (1745–1748).[9]

In the light of the probable authority of the Chorus in *Samson Agonistes*, particularly in the close, let us reexamine the catastrophe of this drama (as reported by the Messenger and interpreted by Manoa and especially the Chorus) and the events and nonevents leading to it. In the passages following the Messenger's narration we have, I think, valid grounds for accepting the Chorus' final verdict on the Philistines:

> So fond are mortal men
> Fall'n into wrath divine,
> As thir own ruin on themselves to invite,
> Insensate left, or to sense reprobate,
> And with blindness internal struck.   (1682–86)

The same Semichorus makes explicit the role of Israel's God in bringing about the catastrophe:

> Among them hee a spirit of frenzy sent,
> Who hurt thir minds,
> And urg'd them on with mad desire
> To call in haste for thir destroyer.   (1675–78)

These passages represent the final insights toward which the Danites have been slowly, and often erratically, progressing; and they serve to guide the responses of Milton's reader.

The following Semichorus stresses the revival of Samson's virtue, and the final verses of Manoa and the Chorus give explicit expression to the divine favor vouchsafed Samson,

> With God not parted from him, as was fear'd,
> But favoring and assisting to the end.
> . . . .
> Oft he seems to hide his face,
> But unexpectedly returns
> And to his faithful Champion hath in place
> Bore witness gloriously.   (1719–20, 1749–52)

Manoa's final speech also places emphasis on the motif of Samson's revenge: "on his Enemies / Fully reveng'd" (1711–12). This motif has biblical authority in Samson's prayer (Judges xvi, 28) "that I may be at once avenged of the Philistines for my two eyes." Milton significantly transfers the explicit mention of revenge from Samson himself to the Chorus and Manoa.[10]

On the basis of Milton's remarks on the catastrophe in the Argument and their partial reaffirmation in the final choral odes, the reader may also accept as valid the choral vindication of the hero from the possible charge of suicide:

> Among thy slain self-kill'd
> Not willingly, but tangl'd in the fold
> Of dire necessity, whose law in death conjoin'd
> Thee with thy slaughter'd foes in number more
> Than all thy life had slain before.   (1664–68)

The Messenger emphasizes the same point: "*Samson* with these inmixt, inevitably / Pull'd down the same destruction on himself" (1657–58). In this context it is significant that Milton suppresses the biblical passage in which Samson prays that he may perish with the Philistines (Judg. xvi, 30): "And Samson said, let me die with the Philistines."[11]

The final peripeteia in *Samson Agonistes* is essentially a reversal contrary to expectation. The Philistines have "Unwittingly importun'd / Thir own destruction to come speedy upon them" (1680–81). God has "unexpectedly" returned to bear witness to Samson. The plot of the drama is accordingly a "complex" plot, in which the change of state (metabasis) or fortune not only occurs suddenly—"*Gaza* yet stands, but all her Sons are fall'n, / All in a moment overwhelm'd and fall'n" (1558–59)—but is also accompanied by a peripeteia. For the greater part of the drama, however, the external situation is comparatively static; the dramatic emphasis falls on the hero's moral struggles—as the title *Samson Agonistes* would on one level suggest—and the dramatic action is in several respects close to that of the comparatively "simple" tragedy of suffering.[12] The great change in Samson's fortune—from prosperity and glory to ignominy and bondage—has occurred before the beginning of the play. The principal developments in the succession of scenes are the visits of the hero's fellow countrymen and enemies and the series of psychological and moral crises that these visits evoke. Up to the second visit of the Philistine Officer, Milton presents a hero who suffers but does not act; he acts decisively against his enemies (and himself suffers violent death) only at the end. The final outcome—its contrasts signaled by the division of the choral ode into two complementary semichoruses—both links and differentiates the hero and his foes, bringing victory to the one and defeat to the others. Thus there are in a sense contrasting and antithetical ends for the worshippers of the true God and those of the false god; yet the poet avoids the pitfall of a "double ending" for his tragedy by involving Samson in the same catastrophic death as his enemies.[13]

The relation between the catastrophe and the preceding events involves the problem of the middle of the drama, which Samuel Johnson thought notably lacking. In attempting to refute Johnson, many critics have emphasized the process of regeneration, operative in Samson's successive encounters with his Philistine visitors.[14] Other critics have challenged this line of argument; for some, Samson is far from regenerate, and for several scholars—far from following divine guidance—Samson is self-deluded, and the comments of Manoa and the Chorus after the catastrophe are also erroneous.[15] In some critics—in both Samuel and Wittreich, for example— one encounters a tendency to stress the tragic outcomes of the drama, a tragedy both for Samson and for his victims, at the cost of minimizing or dismissing altogether the motif of Samson's regeneration. Actually there is little reason to underplay either the hero's regeneration or the tragic effect of the catastrophe. They may indeed be causally related.[16]

Let us consider first the problem of tragic effect.[17] This is not confined to the catastrophe, but is indeed operative throughout the drama—a fact that is not surprising if one reflects that the play partakes both of the nature of the tragedy of suffering and the nature of the complex plot. From the beginning of the drama—through the visits of the Chorus, of Manoa, and of the three Philistines—there are both pity and fear for Samson;[18] and in the dialogue immediately preceding the Messenger's appearance, Manoa voices his fears for his son's safety (1515–16). At the end of the drama, after the Messenger's report, Manoa and the Chorus feel grief for Samson, but even this tragic affect is mitigated by the reflection that Samson has "heroicly . . . finish'd a life Heroic" (1710–11) and by the realization ("which is best and happiest") that God was "not parted from him, as was fear'd, / But favoring and assisting to the end" (1718–20). Notably absent, on the other hand, are any expressions of pity or fear or grief for the fate of the Philistines. One may assume that the catastrophe may arouse a healthy fear of Israel's "living Dread" (1673), especially among idolaters and such as "band them to resist" God's "uncontrollable intent" (1753–54); but there is no indication of any specific sympathy with the slain aristocracy of the Philistine cities.[19] Indeed the visits of Dalila and Harapha have forestalled any sympathies that the audience might feel for the worshippers of Dagon.

The one tragic affect explicitly associated with the slaughtered Philistines is that of horror. This can be taken as an equivalent of Aristotle's *phobos*, though Milton in his preface to *Samson Agonistes* prefers to render this term as "fear, or terror."[20] Manoa exclaims over the "hideous noise" of the debacle, "horribly loud" (1509–10), and the Chorus identifies it as a

> universal groan
> As if the whole inhabitation perish'd[.]
> Blood, death, and deathful deeds are in that noise,
> Ruin, destruction at the utmost point.   (1511–14)

The Messenger flees from "the place of horror" (1550) and "The sight of this so horrid spectacle / Which erst my eyes beheld and yet behold[.] / For dire imagination still pursues me" (1542–44). He subsequently relates how Samson had shaken "those two massy Pillars / With horrible convulsion to and fro" (1648–1649).

This is the "scene of suffering" (or pathos) which Aristotle regards as the third part of the tragic plot (along with peripeteia and anagnorisis), and it appropriately arouses horror (or *phobos*) in the beholder.[21] Significantly, moreover, the term pathos may refer both to the tragic affects (pity and horror or fear) and to the events which arouse them. One may, accordingly, find pathos not only in the Messenger's speech and in the grief experienced by Manoa and the Chorus, but also in the sufferings Samson has experienced throughout the drama.

From the tragic affects aroused by the catastrophe, let us turn to the relationship between the earlier sections of the drama and Samson's final exploit. As Krouse and others have noticed, Milton prepares for Samson's ultimate victory over the Philistines by a series of moral victories over his

Philistine visitors. These involve minor peripeteias, inasmuch as Samson defeats the expectation of each of his enemies, but they also prepare for the final peripeteia of the drama. Not only does Samson bring unexpected death to the Philistine aristocracy—"Lords, Ladies, Captains, Counsellors, or Priests, / Thir choice nobility and flower" (1653–1654)—at the end of the drama, he also frustrates Dalila's expectations of a glorious name "among the famousest / Of women" (982–83); and besides reducing the Philistine giant to a "baffl'd coward" (1237), he refutes the giant's taunt that God will never "accept thee to defend his cause" (1179).

Milton has also prepared for the catastrophe through dramatic irony, especially the kind which Anthony Low describes as "the irony of alternatives," a kind "possibly unique to *Samson Agonistes* in its extensiveness and explicitness." According to Low, this kind of irony is "characterized by a hypothetical choice, posited by one of the characters: either this is true or that, or more usually, either this will happen or that; but in the working out, both eventuate, even though they were thought to be mutually exclusive."[22] Again, Samson's prediction (which Manoa regards as prophetic) that God "will arise and his great name assert" (467), covering Dagon's worshipers with confusion, foreshadows the catastrophe, even though Samson does not yet realize that he himself will serve as God's champion in this divine victory.

In this context we may recall the fact that this contest is indeed a *theomachia*, that (like the Dagon of *Paradise Lost* and the *Ode on the Morning of Christ's Nativity*) the Dagon of *Samson Agonistes* is a false god and a rival of the true. One must regard the Philistine idol—as Samson regards him, and as Milton regards him elsewhere—as a notorious adversary of the God of the Hebrews:

> all the contest is now
> ' Twixt God and *Dagon; Dagon* hath presum'd,
> Mee overthrown, to enter lists with God,
> His Deity comparing and preferring
> Before the God of *Abraham*. He, be sure,
> Will not connive, or linger, thus provok'd,
> But will arise and his great name assert:
> *Dagon* must stoop, and shall ere long receive
> Such a discomfit, as shall quite despoil him
> Of all these boasted Trophies won on me,
> And with confusion blank his Worshippers.   (461–71)

The motif of the *theomachia*, which reaches its culmination in the catastrophe, already has been articulated explicitly earlier in the drama.

In comparison with the catastrophe, the most notable feature of Samon's prediction is that he does not foresee his own role in the catastrophe as God's champion and as the agent of divine will. Samson prophetically points to the outcome of the *theomachia* but still assumes that he is excluded from being God's instrument.

As in his projected dramas on "Gideon Idoloclastes" and "Salomon Gynaecocratumenus or Idolomargus aut Thysiazusae,"[23] Milton gives central emphasis in *Samson Agonistes* to the conflict between worship of the true God and idolatry. Not only is this motif dominant in the final victory over the Philistines at the Dagonalia, it also underlies the hero's moral victories over Dalila, Harapha, and the Philistine Officer. In attempting to extenuate her betrayal of Samson, Dalila adduces the pressures placed upon her by the magistrates and princes of her country in the name of both patriotism and religion:

> how just it was,
> How honorable, how glorious to entrap
> A common enemy, who had destroy'd
> Such numbers of our Nation: and the Priest
> Was not behind, but ever at my ear,
> Preaching how meritorious with the gods
> It would be to ensnare an irreligious
> Dishonorer of *Dagon*.   (854–61)

In the confrontation with Harapha, Samson challenges *"Dagon* to the test / Offering to combat thee his Champion bold / With th' utmost of his Godhead seconded" (1151–53). The Philistine Officer, in turn, orders Samson to take part in the festival in honor of Dagon, thereby violating the Hebrew Law that forbids his presence at the "Religious Rites" of the heathen. In all three of these episodes the action centers in part on the *theomachia* between God and Dagon, a contest which will culminate in the catastrophe of the drama and the triumph of Israel's God over his Philistine rival.

If we take the view that the central episodes of the drama display an increasingly regenerated will, then the middle of the play, which represents this process through its effects—repentance and faith—may also be a theological precondition for Samson's major act. According to Milton's *De Doctrina Christiana*, the "form of good works" is "conformity not with the written but with the unwritten law, that is, with the law of the Spirit which the Father has given us to lead us into truth. For the works of the faithful are the works of the Holy Spirit itself."[24] Even if the middle of the play—the drama of Samson's recovery—does not actually hasten or delay the catastrophe, it nevertheless makes Samson's role in the catastrophe appear more probable—as is evident in the challenge to Harapha and in the choral ode following this episode. This ode foreshadows the catastrophe and Samson's victory over the Philistines, even though the Chorus themselves believe that Samson's more probable "lot" is one of patient endurance rather than heroic action:

> Oh how comely it is and how reviving
> To the Spirits of just men long opprest!
> When God into the hands of thir deliverer
> Puts invincible might
> To quell the mighty of the Earth, th' oppressor
> . . . .
> Hee all thir Ammunition
> And feats of War defeats
> With plain Heroic magnitude of mind
> And celestial vigor arm'd,
> Thir Armories and Magazines contemns,
> Renders them useless, while
> With winged expedition
> Swift as the lightning glance he executes
> His errand on the wicked, who surpris'd
> Lose thir defense, distracted and amaz'd. (1268–86)

The imagery of this passage recurs in the Messenger's narrative and the following choral ode. We are told that Samson offers his spectators a demonstration of strength that "with amaze shall strike all who behold" (1645). Samson draws down "The whole roof . . . with burst of thunder" (1651)—and this image is subsequently elaborated by the Chorus: "as an Eagle / His cloudless thunder bolted on thir heads" (1695–96).

In contrast to the earlier Samson, who had been tortured by a "sense of Heav'n's desertion" (632) and who had felt that God "hath cast me off as never known" (641), the Samson who defies the Philistine Officer experiences "favor renew'd" (1357), and this motif of divine favor is recapitulated by Manoa in his final speech. There is an equally striking contrast between the fallen Samson whose "virtue" seems irretrievably lost and the Samson who rouses "His fiery virtue . . . / From under ashes into sudden flame" (1690–91).

Another motif developed in the middle of the drama and finally resolved at the end is the theme of the hero's desire for death. He himself predicts that the "light of life" will not "continue long" (592), and his prayers for death (575, 650) are answered by the catastrophe. At first sight they might seem to point to a traditional view of Samson as a suicide,[25] but Milton undercuts this tradition through the comments of the Messenger and the Chorus, as well as through his Argument to the poem, which affirms that Samson perished by accident. While the middle of the drama depicts Samson's development in magnanimity and inner liberty, then, it also represents the trial of his faith and patience; and this trial, in turn, centers in part on the unfulfilled promise concerning his destiny and on his sense of the absence of God. The demonstration of Samson's moral recovery and growth in inner freedom extends through his encounters with Dalila and Harapha and his first encounter with the Philistine Officer. It is only at this point—the "highest epitasis" of the play—that he experiences the "rousing motions"[26] which prompt him to accompany the Officer to the scene of the catastrophe and thus hasten his own death.

In countering Samuel Johnson's criticism of the structure of Milton's drama, Sir R. C. Jebb raised the question, "Is it true that . . . after the point at which Manoah informs Samson of the feast to Dagon . . . no incident which advances the plot occurs until the catastrophe?" In reply, Jebb observed that the "catastrophe . . . consists in Samson deliberately pulling down the temple of Dagon on his own head and those of the spectators. Samson's will is the agent of the catastrophe. Everything, therefore, which helps to determine Samson's will and to define his purpose leads to the catastrophe." Emphasizing Samson's "resolution to die," Jebb argued, erroneously, I think, that "the force which is to produce the catastrophe is the inward force of Samson's own despair." Nevertheless Jebb recognized the fact that this force was "not an external necessity pressing upon" Samson; and he was, I believe, on firm ground in stressing the crucial role of Samson's will in bringing about the catastrophe.[27] The middle episodes of the drama center, as we have seen, on a succession of moral victories over the Philistines, in which Samson effectively exercises his free will. This process of moral development culminates in his defiance of the summons of the Philistine lords—"Commands are no constraints. If I obey them, / I do it freely" (1372–73)—and only the "rousing motions" (1382) induce him to accompany the Officer. Subsequently it is, in his own words, "of my own accord" that he shows the spectators "such other trial . . . of my strength" as will strike them "with amaze" (1643–45).[28] It is, however, a complex of causes— Samson's own free will, divine guidance, and the madness of the Philistines themselves—that will bring about the catastrophe; and in this outcome, as the Chorus correctly recognize, the controlling role is that of divine providence, "th' unsearchable dispose / Of highest wisdom" (1746–47).

In his discussion of efficient causality in *The Art of Logic* Milton defines the efficient cause as "the cause by which a thing is or is brought about," observing that it "works either by itself or along with other efficient causes, and [that] of all these often one will be the principal cause, while another is less principal, or an assisting and helping cause." "A cause," he continues, "which is less principal [*Causa minus principalis*] is either an impelling cause [*impulsiva*], one which impels or moves the principal one, or it is an instrumental cause." Of the "two types of impelling cause," the first (or proegumenic) cause "moves the principal cause from within," and the second (or procatarctic) cause moves the principal cause from without. If the procatarctic cause is "real it is called an *occasion*, but if feigned a *pretext*." Subsequently, Milton adds that impelling causes, "whether proegumenic or procatarctic . . . are not so much causes associated with or ministering to the principal cause, as they are modes of efficient cause by which someone, impelled by some emotion or because the occasion is offered, under the guidance of deliberation does this or that." In the same treatise Milton also distinguishes between "primary" and "secondary" causes and between "remote" and "proximate" causes. A cause is called primary "either absolutely (as with God) or in its genus (as with the sun or anything else of this sort)."[29]

Milton alludes to efficient causality with almost technical precision in the blessing uttered by the Chorus as Samson departs with the Officer for the Philistine theatre:

> Go, and the Holy One
> Of *Israel* be thy guide
> To what may serve his glory best, and spread his name
> Great among the Heathen round:
>   . . . .
>   that Spirit that first rusht on thee
> In the camp of *Dan*
> Be efficacious in thee now at need.   (1427–37)

Of the proegumenic or internal causes which lead to the catastrophe, the most important is the divine impulse which induced Samson ("persuaded inwardly that this was from God") to accompany the Officer: the "rousing motions in me which dispose / To something extraordinary my thoughts" (1382–83). Milton has already introduced the motifs of "divine impulsion" and occasion in the passage where Samson attempts to vindicate his marriage to the woman of Timna:

>   they knew not
> That what I motion'd was of God: I knew
> From intimate impulse, and therefore urg'd
> The Marriage on; that by occasion hence
> I might begin *Israel's* Deliverance,
> The work to which I was divinely call'd.   (221–26)

Another aspect of the proegumenic cause in bringing on the catastrophe is Samson's desire for revenge on the Philistines. His desire for death is not so significant a motive in the catastrophe as Jebb believed, inasmuch as the final section of the play explicitly rules out the motive of suicide.[30] Like the proegumenic cause, the procatarctic or external cause plays an important role in bringing on the catastrophe; in this instance the Philistines themselves are in large part responsible for their own downfall. The occasion is the "popular Feast" in honor of Dagon, "their God who hath deliver'd / Thee, *Samson*, bound and blind into thir hands, / Them out of thine, who slew'st them many a slain" (437–39). This state holiday, the Dagonalia, is also the occasion for Samson's release from his "task of servile toil" and for the succession of visitors, both Danite and Philistine. Finally, in commanding Samson's presence at the feast, the Philistine lords hasten their own destruction; and Samson seizes the occasion for their ruin.[31]

According to Milton's theological treatise, the immediate (or proximate) causes of good works are virtues (YP VI, p. 647). Samson's moral victories over his enemies and over himself, the exercise of his inner strength and virtue in the central episodes of the drama, would appear therefore to be causally related to his final victory in the Philistine theatre. Manoa sees God as "favoring and assisting" Samson "to the end," and it is possible to interpret this passage in the light of Milton's account of "helping causes" (*causis adjuvantibus*) in *The Art of Logic*. This interpretation would be consistent with the strong emphasis Milton places on his protagonist's free will throughout the drama. Samson must execute his final labor under divine guidance and with divinely given strength, but he must do so of his own unfettered volition. Though acting in obedience to God's will, he remains a free agent, not a puppet. Yet for a fuller understanding of the causal structure underlying the catastrophe one must recognize the importance of the divine efficiency which brings it about. Not only is the deity the "primary efficient cause" of good works (YP VI, p. 647); he is also responsible for deluding the Philistines, quickening Samson's virtue, and restoring his miraculous strength.

As efficient cause, God's strategy underlies both Samson's miraculous exploit and the madness which possesses the Philistines. In his chapter on "God's providence, or his universal government of things," Milton discusses both good and evil temptations, the theory of permissive evil, and God's "extraordinary providence" in the production of miracles. "Good temptations," he writes, "are those which God uses to tempt even righteous men, in order to prove them." In an evil temptation, on the other hand, God "either withdraws his grace from a man, or throws opportunities for sin in his path or hardens his heart or blinds him." "Even in sin," he goes on, "we see God's providence at work, not only in permitting it or withdrawing his grace, but often in inciting sinners to commit sin, hardening their hearts and blinding them" (YP VI, pp. 331, 338). In contrast to the series of moral crises which Samson successively meets during the middle of the drama (a "good" temptation) and the "rousing motions" he experiences near the end, God exercises his providence in deliberately deluding the Philistines, blinding their understandings and hardening their hearts:[32]

> Among them hee a spirit of frenzy sent,
> Who hurt thir minds,
> And urg'd them on with mad desire
> To call in haste for thir destroyer.   (1675–78)

This passage combines Milton's theological views on God's production of evil with the Greek concept of *atē*, a "*bewilderment, infatuation*, caused by *blindness* or *delusion* sent by the gods, mostly as the punishment of guilty rashness."[33]

The catastrophe of the drama is a joint victory for Samson and for his God; and the final miracle is one in which both share the responsibility. The hero's strength and regenerate will cooperate with God's "extraordinary" providence to destroy their mutual enemies. Before his fall Samson was "The miracle of men" (364); and even now, in his captivity, his father can recognize "this strength / Miraculous yet remaining in these locks" (586–87). The Chorus too acknowledges that "never was from Heaven imparted / Measure of strength so great to mortal seed, / As in thy wond'rous actions hath been seen" (1438–40). This miraculous strength is counterpointed by the vain hope, expressed by Manoa and the Chorus, for a divine miracle that will restore Samson's eyesight, and by Harapha's charge that Samson's strength (which the Hebrew champion avows "to be the power of *Israel's* God," [1150]) is merely the effect of magic spells. According to the seventeenth-century theologian Bartholomew Keckermann, Samson's exploits, like those of David, were "mixed miracles"— miracles in which God controls the "second causes." Samson's strength was "miraculous," inasmuch as God enhanced his natural strength (*vires illas naturales*), so that he performed exploits which would have been impossible by nature alone.[34] In Milton's view, moreover, "God alone is the primary author of miracles," and their "purpose . . . is to demonstrate divine power and strengthen our faith" (YP VI, p. 341).

Against the background of the numerous and often contradictory readings of Milton's tragedy, the most advantageous perspective for interpreting the events of the drama remains "the close"—the vantage point of the denouement. Here the Danites' gropings for understanding through the multiple ambiguities, ironies, and paradoxes of the dramatic action are ultimately resolved. Here the gradual, though irregular, progression of the Chorus from blindness and uncertainty toward comprehension concludes with a recognition of supernal design. Accomplished through a combination of divinely sent delusion, divine guidance, and divine miracle, the act of divine wrath that constitutes the catastrophe of Milton's drama is, in the final analysis, a demonstration of the extraordinary providence of Israel's God.

Huntington Library

NOTES

1. Stanley Fish, "Question and Answer in *Samson Agonistes*," *Critical Quarterly* 11 (1969), 237–64, especially 255, 259. See also John N. Wall, Jr., "The Contrarious Hand of God: *Samson Agonistes* and the Biblical Lament," in *Milton Studies* XII, ed. James D. Simmonds (Pittsburgh, 1978), p. 120. For responses to Johnson's claims, see note 15.

2. Irene Samuel, "Samson Agonistes as Tragedy," in *Calm of Mind: Tercentenary Essays on "Paradise Regained" and "Samson Agonistes," in Honor of John S. Diekhoff*, ed. Joseph Anthony Wittreich, Jr. (Cleveland, 1971), pp. 235–57. For a critique of Samuel's essay, see Wendy Furman, "*Samson Agonistes* as Christian Tragedy: A Corrective View," *PQ* 60 (1981), 169–81.

3. Lawrence W. Hyman, "The Unwilling Martyrdom in *Samson Agonistes*," *Tennessee Studies in Literature* 13 (1968), 91–98; Joseph Wittreich, *Interpreting "Samson Agonistes"* (Princeton, 1986), p. 80. For a critique of this position, see Wendy Furman's article (cited in note 2) and her review of *Interpreting "Samson Agonistes"* in *PQ* 67 (1988), 389–93.

4. William Riley Parker, *Milton's Debt to Greek Tragedy in "Samson Agonistes"* (Baltimore, 1937); Joseph H. Summers, "The Movements of the Drama," in *The Lyric and Dramatic Milton*, ed. Summers (New York, 1965); Anthony Low, *The Blaze of Noon: A Reading of "Samson Agonistes"* (New York, 1974). See also John C. Ulreich, Jr., " 'Beyond the Fifth Act': *Samson Agonistes* as Prophecy," in *Milton Studies* XVII, ed. Richard S. Ide and Joseph Wittreich (Pittsburgh, 1983).

5. Alan Rudrum observes that in *Apology for Smectymnuus*, Milton "insisted that 'the author is ever distinguished from the person he introduces' " and that, according to the *Defensio Prima*, " 'One must not regard the poet's words as his own, but consider what person in the play speaks.' " Alan Rudrum, *A Critical Commentary on Milton's "Samson Agonistes"* (New York, 1969), p. 49.

6. Aristotle includes *Dianoia* (Thought) among the formative elements of tragedy. This is "the power of saying whatever can be said, or what is appropriate to the occasion . . .
One must not confuse it with Character. Character in a play is that which reveals the moral purpose of the agents, i.e. the sort of thing they seek or avoid." *Aristotle on the Art of Poetry*, ed. and trans. Ingram Bywater (Oxford, 1909), p. 21.

7. See note 1, and John Huntley, "A Revaluation of the Chorus' Role in Milton's *Samson Agonistes*," *MP* 64 (1966), 132; Joan S. Bennett, "Liberty Under the Law: The Chorus and the Meaning of *Samson Agonistes*," in *Milton Studies* XII, ed. James D. Simmonds (Pittsburgh, 1978), pp. 141–46, 162; Mary Ann Radzinowicz, *Toward "Samson Agonistes": The Growth of Milton's Mind* (Princeton, 1978), pp. 62–64.

8. See, for example, Joyce Colony, "An Argument for Milton's Dalila," *Yale Review* 66 (1977), 562–75.

9. All quotations from *Samson Agonistes* are taken from *John Milton: Complete Poems and Major Prose*, ed. Merritt Y. Hughes (Indianapolis, 1957).

10. Milton not only omits the revenge motive from the Messenger's account of Samson's prayer, but even leaves it ambiguous whether Samson is really praying at all (1637–38).

11. Samson's "one prayer" for "speedy death, / The close of all my miseries, and the balm" (649–51) occurs significantly in the passage that gives utterance to his most intense psychological anguish and at the lowest point of his morale—*before* his moral recovery.

12. For Aristotle's views on peripeteia, change of state or fortune, and the complex plot, see Bywater, *Aristotle on the Art of Poetry*, pp. 30–33, 52–53. For Aristotle's views on the "simple" plot and on the tragedy of suffering, see pp. 30–31, 52–53.

13. According to Aristotle, "The perfect Plot . . . must have a single, and not . . . a double issue" (Bywater, *Aristotle on the Art of Poetry*, 34–35). For discussions of the question of single and double issues, see Samuel, "*Samson Agonistes* as Tragedy," p. 240; Radzinowicz, *Toward "Samson Agonistes*," p. 251; and Furman, "*Samson Agonistes* as Christian Tragedy," 175.

14. For discussion of the "regeneration theory" and its proponents, see Thomas Kranidas, "*Samson Agonistes*," in *A Milton Encyclopedia*, ed. William B. Hunter, Jr. (Lewisburg, Pa., 1979), vol. 7, pp. 157–59, and French Fogle, "The Action of *Samson Agonistes*," in *Essays in American and English Literature Presented to Bruce Robert Mc-Elderry, Jr.*, ed. Max F. Schultz et al. (Athens, Ohio, 1967), pp. 178–88. See also Edward W. Tayler, "Milton's *Samson*: The Form of Christian Tragedy," *ELR* 3 (1973), 306; Arnold Stein, *Heroic Knowledge: An Interpretation of "Paradise Regained" and "Samson Agonistes"* (Minneapolis, 1957), p. 141; Lynn Veach Sadler, "Regeneration and Typology: *Samson Agonistes* and its Relation to *De Doctrina Christiana, Paradise Lost*, and *Paradise Regained*," *SEL* 12 (1972), 155; Georgia Christopher, "Homeopathic Physic and Natural Renovation in *Samson Agonistes*, *ELH* 37 (1970), 362, 364; Phillip J. Gallagher, "The Role of Raphael in *Samson Agonistes*," in *Milton Studies* XVIII, ed. James D. Simmonds (Pittsburgh, 1983), pp. 256, 284.

15. See notes 1–3, and John Carey, *Milton* (London, 1969), pp. 139, 144–45; Helen Damico, "Duality in Dramatic Vision: A Structural Analysis of *Samson Agonistes*," in *Milton Studies* XII, ed. James D. Simmonds (Pittsburgh, 1978), pp. 105–107; and Virginia R. Mollenkott, "Relativism in *Samson Agonistes*," *SP* 67 (1970), 89–91.

16. See Christopher Grose, *Milton and the Sense of Tradition* (New Haven, 1988), p. 160; Hugh MacCallum, "*Samson Agonistes*: The Deliverer as Judge," in *Milton Studies* XXIII, ed. James D. Simmonds (Pittsburgh, 1987), p. 259.

17. Among significant studies of tragic effect in Milton's drama see A.S.P. Woodhouse, "Tragic Effect in *Samson Agonistes*," *UTQ* 28 (1959), 205–222; Martin E. Mueller, "*Pathos* and *Katharsis* in *Samson Agonistes*," *ELH* 31 (1964), 156–74; and John T. Shawcross, "Irony as Tragic Effect: *Samson Agonistes* and the Tragedy of Hope," in *Calm of Mind*, pp. 289–306.

18. See Mary Ann Radzinowicz, "The Distinctive Tragedy of *Samson Agonistes*," in *Milton Studies* XVII, ed. Richard S. Ide and Joseph Wittreich (Pittsburgh, 1983), pp. 249–50.

19. For discussion of the play's treatment of the common people, see Christopher Hill, *The Experience of Defeat: Milton and Some Contemporaries* (New York, 1984), p. 314; and the responses of Wittreich, *Interpreting "Samson Agonistes,"* pp. 78–79; and Furman, "*Samson Agonistes* as Christian Tragedy."

20. On "incidents arousing pity and fear" (*eleou kai phobou*) in Aristotle's definition of tragedy, see Bywater, *Aristotle on the Art of Poetry*, pp. 16–17. Frequently Renaissance writers render *phobos* as *terror, spavento, timor,* or *metus;* see Bywater, pp. 361–365.

21. For Aristotle's view of pathos as a part of the tragic plot, see Bywater, *Aristotle on the Art of Poetry*, pp. 32–33: "A third part is Suffering; which we may define as an action of a destructive or painful nature, such as murders on the stage, tortures, woundings, and the like." To the tragic passions of pity and fear (or *horror*) one should add the affect of admiration or wonder. See John Arthos, "Milton and the Passions: A Study of *Samson Agonistes*," *MP* 69 (1972), 210.

22. Low, *The Blaze of Noon*, pp. 77, 79; see also Summers, *The Lyric and Dramatic Milton*, pp. 157–58.

23. See Appendix A, "Milton's Outlines for Tragedies," in *Complete Prose Works of John Milton* 8 vols., ed. Don M. Wolfe et al. (New Haven, 1953–82), p. 556. References to this edition will appear as YP followed by volume and page.

24. *Of Christian Doctrine,* in YP VI, p. 640.

25. For the tradition of Samson as a suicide, see F. Michael Krouse, *Milton's Samson and the Christian Tradition* (Princeton, 1949), pp. 74–75.

26. See Grose, *Milton and the Sense of Tradition*, pp. 146–47, 167–68, for discussion of the experience of "rousing motions" in *Samson Agonistes*.

27. Jebb's article is "*Samson Agonistes* and the Hellenic Drama," in *Proceedings of the British Academy* 3 (1907–08), 341–48. For a similar emphasis on Samson's "death wish," see Samuel, "*Samson Agonistes* as Tragedy," pp. 245, 247.

28. In this passage, of course, Samson is deceiving the Philistines; and it is quite possible that he disguises a divine command to inflict slaughter as though he were acting on his own initiative. The most satisfactory interpretation, however, that he is simultaneously acting voluntarily and of his own free will in obedience to a divine command. See the discussions of Wittreich, *Interpreting "Samson Agonistes,"* pp. 74–75; and Grose, *Milton and the Sense of Tradition*, p. 169.

29. *A Fuller Course in the Art of Logic Conformed to the Method of Peter Ramus,* in YP VIII, pp. 223–226; see also the Latin text and English translation of this work in *The Works of John Milton*, ed. and trans. Allan H. Gilbert (New York, 1935), vol. 11, pp. 34–35.

30. For further discussion of suicide in the final section of the play, see Grose, *Milton and the Sense of Tradition*, p. 194.

31. Manoa emphasizes the opportunity for his fellow Danites to "Find courage to lay hold on this occasion" for winning their freedom (1716).

32. In his notes on lines 1675–1683 of *Samson Agonistes*, Merritt Y. Hughes observes that "The thought parallels the discussion of reprobation in *CD* I, iv . . . as the self-punishment of hard-hearted men"; *Complete Poems and Major Prose*, 591n.

33. See Henry George Liddell and Robert Scott, *A Greek-English Lexicon*, A New Edition (Oxford, 1925), *s.v. atē.*

34. *Systema SS. Theologiae . . . per Bartholomaeum Keckermannum* (Hanoviae, 1602), p. 467; see John M. Steadman, *Milton's Epic Characters: Image and Idol* (Chapel Hill, 1968), 193n.